THE CHARITY GAME

WALTER STEWART

THE CHARITY GAME

GREED, WASTE **AND** FRAUD
IN CANADA'S $86-BILLION-A-YEAR COMPASSION INDUSTRY

Douglas & McIntyre
Vancouver/Toronto

Canadian Cataloguing in Publication Data
Stewart, Walter, 1931–
The charity game

Includes bibliographical references.
ISBN 1-55054-512-4

1. Fund-raising—Canada.   2. Charities—Canada.   3. Canada—Social policy.   1. Title
HV41.9.C3873   1996   361.7'068'1   C96-910408-1

Editing by Saeko Usukawa
Front cover design by Tom Brown
Book design by Val Speidel
Printed and bound in Canada by Friesens
Printed on acid-free paper

The publisher gratefully acknowledges the assistance of the Canada Council and of the British Columbia Ministry of Tourism, Small Business and Culture.

*This book is for Betty and David Milner of
Calgary, Alberta, and Sturgeon Point, Ontario,
good friends and charitable souls. They will
agree with some of it and will in charity,
I hope, forgive the rest.*

Contents

Do-Gooders and Others

Whilst we have been building our churches and solacing ourselves with our religion and dreaming that the millennium was coming, the poor have been growing poorer and the wretched more miserable and the immoral more corrupt. The gulf has been daily widening which separates the lowest classes of the community from our churches and chapels, and from all decency and civilization.

——FROM A PENNY PAMPHLET,
LONDON, 1883

1. The Kindness of Strangers

I have known people to stop and buy an apple on the corner and then walk away as if they had solved the whole unemployment problem.

—HEYWOOD BROUN, 1935

The night is brutally cold, with a wind whipping out of the north, driving little needles of snow and sleet into my face. I am wearing boots over shoes, but I stamp my feet against the encroaching chill as I stand by the alleged shelter of a tree and watch the forlorn file of figures plodding across the crunching lawn. I am bundled into a parka, with a sweater underneath and long johns under that, but I think I have just frozen something vital, down deep inside. The weather woman on television was explaining, as I left my warm hotel room on reluctant feet to come down here, that in these temperatures, exposed skin begins to freeze in one minute and thirty-three seconds. I wonder if they know that, the bent, huddled figures in castoff clothes who come shuffling out of the dark, headed for the open, lighted door of a Toronto church? God knows they have exposed skin: one man has no socks; his bare ankles are exposed, along with part of one foot as his shoe flops open along a deceased line of stitching. He is shivering and shaking. "Jesus, she's cold," he mutters, "colder than a witch's tit. I hope they've got soup."

Of course they have soup, inside, within the embrace of the church, where the lights burn and the radiators steam and a clutch of saints await with cheery smiles and open hearts and food and shelter.

This one charity, underfunded, overworked, but never discouraged, keeps twenty-four churches open at night throughout Toronto. Not all at once, you understand; it depends on the volunteers available, and the degree of cold, and whether or not there is enough in the kitty to buy the food. Most nights, three or four churches across the city are open. They take the overflow from hostels that can no longer accommodate all the homeless (and where few of the homeless want to go, anyway; some of the hostels are riddled with thievery); they give them supper and breakfast, and a cot to sleep on, and a hope of better things to come. The charity is called Out of the Cold, and it is staffed entirely by volunteers who give up a night every week or so, sometimes more, to take their turns helping their neighbours.

Why do they do it? "It isn't much," one elderly volunteer says, adding, "It could be me, in that sort of fix." Not likely; he's a real estate lawyer, earning hundreds of thousands of dollars a year. Maybe he feels guilty. Maybe he's a religious person, a real one; maybe he, and the half-dozen others on duty this shivering night, are just nice people.

What they do is laudable. But it is not—and this is the dilemma the entire charitable sector faces today—it is not an answer to homelessness in Toronto or anywhere else. Providing beds for a few score derelict men and women in a city where there are hundreds, sometimes thousands, can't solve the problem of poverty, can't begin to come to grips with the fact that we are creating paupers faster than we can put up shelters. We are living a lie if we think that charity is a substitute for social policy; and when governments walk by on the far side of the road, abandoning their stricken citizens to the mercies of Good Samaritanism, they are deluding both themselves and us.

For one thing, charity has a price. Government funding provides charities with five dollars for every dollar of private donations.[1] And, since most of the donations are written off against taxes, there is another cost to the

public there, too. For another, charities cannot cope. When Ontario
Premier Mike Harris slashed welfare payments by 21.6 per cent across the
board[2] and then asked charities—the voluntary sector—to "pick up the
slack,"[3] no one with the brains God gave a graham wafer thought those
organizations could work that miracle. On the heels of his announcement,
day-care centres began plans to shut down, food banks went into a tailspin,
single parents on welfare cut down on their own food so their children
would suffer as little as possible. Then the government payments that
support the voluntary sector were cut, too. Two days after slashing social
welfare payments, the provincial government hacked $4 million off the
$16.8-million annual budget of Ontario's largest charitable organization,
the Trillium Foundation.[4] That'll learn 'em.

Ontario's savagery was only marginally more heavy-handed than the
cuts at the federal level and in other provinces, as services were directly and
abruptly withdrawn from the young and the old, the mentally and physi-
cally challenged. The voters loved it.

If, as it seems, we are determined as a society to thrust our maimed and
wanting citizens onto the kindness of strangers, we ought to know more
than we do about the charitable sector. It is far larger, far more complex, far
more expensive, and far less effective than most of us think.

CHARITY: A MANY-HEADED BEAST

Not every nonprofit organization in Canada is a charity—there are thousands of amateur athletic associations, co-operatives, agents of municipal
governments, nonregistered charities (you could set up a charity of your
own to feed budgies in the park, if you liked, and try to touch the public
for help with the seed money), and other organizations which make no
profits, thus escaping taxes. Usually, once a group has managed to duck out
of income taxes at the federal level, it will also escape provincial and
municipal taxes, and many of the nonprofit organizations follow the charities in this. But these groups cannot climb up onto the taxpayer's lap and
dip into his pockets, and they cannot issue "official donation receipts" to let
donors off the tax hook. Only registered charities can do that.

To help us along the way, Revenue Canada brings out a little booklet
called *Registering Your Charity for Income Tax Purposes*, which follows a
question-and-answer format. It begins with the biggie: "What are the
advantages of being a registered charity?" to which it replies:

- Registration allows your organization to issue official donation receipts for gifts received. This reduces the individual donor's income tax payable, and reduces the taxable income of a corporate donor.
- Once your organization is registered, it is exempt from paying income tax.[5]

And, to be registered and get a number to use on tax-deductible receipts, all a charity has to do is fill out a two-page form which contains twenty questions, most of them having to do with names and addresses, and bung it off to Revenue Canada. The organization does have to qualify, in that it must "be established and operated for charitable purposes, and it must devote its resources to charitable activities."[6] These activities, often called the "four heads of charity," are the categories that govern charities in common law, which we inherited from England. They are:

—the relief of poverty, including sickness and distress;
—the advancement of religion;
—the advancement of education;
—purposes beneficial to the community.[7]

I find it intriguing that the elimination or reduction of poverty is not charitable—presumably, that would spoil the whole racket—only its relief. It is the last category, "purposes beneficial to the community," that would open the way to my establishing the Walter Stewart Benevolent Society, if only I could work out something I do that benefits somebody, get myself a charitable number, and begin to rake in the cash.

"Charitable activities" is a broad area that has resulted in an odd mixture of what might be called semi-charities—scientific, medical, religious, and other bodies of varying degrees of worth. The kid who shows up on your doorstep flogging chocolate bars to finance his school's hockey team on a junket to Germany is a charity. So is Amnesty International. And so is the Babbar Khalsa Society of Kamloops, British Columbia, one of whose founders, Talwinder Singh Parmar, was named by the RCMP as a suspect in the Air India bombing of 1985 that killed 329 passengers off the Irish coast.[8] He was shot and killed by Punjabi police while trying to enter India, apparently to promote the breakup of that country and the establishment of a separate Sikh nation. Revenue Canada gave the Babbar

Khalsa Society a charitable number because it showed, on its application form, that it was established solely to promote the Punjabi language and Sikh religion. You may ask why the Canadian taxpayer should contribute to either of these causes, but that is no business of Revenue Canada; they just give out the number that allows the charity to take in money and give out tax receipts. The Canadian Security and Intelligence Service protested the charitable status, but in vain.

While a registered charity "must devote its resources to charitable activities," there is very little chance that anyone will ever check into this with much vigour or that it will matter if they do. The general rule is that a charity is expected to spend, in any given year, eighty cents out of every dollar for which it issued a charitable receipt during the previous year.[9] But who's to know if it does? In 1994, more than 17,000 charities, about one in every five of these registered, didn't bother to file returns on time to Revenue Canada, and those that did frequently presented inaccurate or incomplete information. It doesn't matter; fewer than one out of a hundred charities is ever likely to be audited, and the "revocation rate"—the rate at which the charitable registered numbers necessary to validate donations are withdrawn by Revenue Canada—is astoundingly low. Of the 17,000 late or nonfilers, only three had their charity numbers lifted for cause;[10] another 237 withdrew from the field, usually because the founders had become bored and gone away.

Obviously, a charity could operate for quite a while without telling us much about what it is up to, and it might not matter much even if it did get caught. Canada's auditor general turned up a number of cases where charities were found to be at fault, and they were defrocked, officially stripped of their charitable numbers, but still went on issuing tax-deductible receipts.[11] When a charity loses its registered status and number, it has a year to straighten up its accounts. The normal practice is for it to donate whatever money it has left to another charity; otherwise, it is subject to a 100 per cent tax, so it is never the case that a charity that cheats and is caught has to return the money to the donors, which would probably be an impossible task, anyway.

I asked Ron Davis, head of the Charities Division of Revenue Canada, "What happens if a charity isn't doing what it was set up to do?" He replied, "Nothing, unless someone gets in touch with us. We try to do the best we can, but we rely a lot on people writing to us, and every time we get a third-party reference we investigate. If we feel it justifies an audit, we will do one."[12]

Davis thinks his department has come in for a lot of unfair criticism— "People think we're a bunch of dolts"—because of the stories that appear with monotonous regularity about the defalcations of various charities. He points out, "We cannot act on rumour or hearsay. If you go into court you must have real information, not just gossip." If a check suggests that the charity is cheating and hasn't simply made a mistake in its numbers, the case is turned over to the Special Investigations section, which may lead to criminal charges, in the end.

It struck me that there ought to be some system short of throwing people into the slammer to ensure not so much that charities obey the law but that they do what they say they are going to do, and with a reasonable amount of efficiency. Still, when I wanted to know how the donating public could be assured that their dollars were going to bona fide charities performing necessary work without wasting too much money, Davis replied, "The onus should be on the giver." It is up to us, as individuals, to dig out the information about the charities that the department doesn't or can't or won't get.

In short, the charitable sector is one of those self-regulating operations we hear about, bearing in mind that "self-regulating" is a fourteen-letter word for "watch out for your wallet."

Within this broad and spacious sector, there is, to begin with, a major difference between registered charitable organizations and charitable foundations (which are looked at separately, in Chapter Seven). Then, there is the split between what you and I think of as charities, and institutional charities. Institutional charities include hospitals and educational institutions, both of which I regard as pseudo-charities; they have the appearance of and enjoy the tax benefits of charities, but they are really government bodies, mainly funded directly out of taxes. We know quite a lot about them, and they are only incidental to the thesis of this book as they receive only about 6 per cent of their funding from individual donations and are subject to rigorous, often raucous, public debate. That leaves us with what most of us would recognize as the real charitable sector: outfits like the Salvation Army, the United Way, the World Wildlife Fund, CARE, and Foster Parents Plan, the ones who ring our phones and our hearts, knock on our doors, and recruit us as volunteers.

A CHARITY FOR EVERY 397 CANADIANS

We have 73,000 charitable outfits in Canada, and the total is going up by 200 a month.[13] The figure includes 5,519 charitable foundations,[14] some of them wonderful and some of them rackets. They all write off their expenses and they all give out tax-deductible receipts. Not a single one of them pays income taxes, although they represent an industry larger than the entire Canadian construction industry, and many of them compete directly with taxpaying concerns that resent it like hell but hate to say so out loud.

There is a charitable organization in this country for every 397 Canadians. (Divide the population of 29 million by 73,000, and see for yourself.) What we have here is a new collective noun, to go with a flock of sheep, a murder of crows, or an exaltation of larks—a charity of Canadians, meaning about half a battalion.

AN $86-BILLION INDUSTRY

In 1993, more than $86 billion flowed through Canada's registered charities, between 12 and 13 per cent of the nation's gross domestic product. This is an amount approximately equal to the entire output of our third-largest province, British Columbia.[15] Charities paid $40 billion in salaries and benefits to 1.32 million employees, 9 per cent of the Canadian labour force.[16]

However, full- and part-time employees of charities represent the smallest part of their work force. The army of volunteers who do the bulk of the work includes 5.3 million Canadians, one in every six. Every year, they put in more than one billion hours of work—the equivalent of 617,000 full-time jobs, representing $12 billion at the average service-sector wage.[17]

There is a trick to these, as to all statistics. Revenue Canada treats teaching institutions and hospitals in exactly the same way as it does Mothers Against Drunk Driving, the Church of Christ Ascendant, the C. D. Howe Institute, Nancy's Very Own Foundation, or the Alzheimer Society, so more than half the money represented here goes towards educational institutions and hospitals. Even with these giants taken out, however, charities represent a huge sector of the economy. In 1993, this smaller group raised $36.4 billion, spent $33.9 billion, and collected $15 billion from government coffers (besides all the tax write-offs).[18] This slimmed-down version of charities employs 319,000 people full-time and 519,000 part-time, a work force only slightly smaller than the entire payroll of all three levels of government put together.[19]

RAISING FUNDS: STUNTS, ARM-TWISTING, AND DONOR FATIGUE

Charities raised $8.2 billion from individuals in 1994, about 2 per cent of all personal spending.[20] Canadians gave more to charities than their combined retail spending on men's and women's clothing and shoes.

Corporate charity is big but not nearly as big as private donations; about $1.2 billion was contributed by corporations in Canada in the last year for which figures have been compiled.[21] Alarmingly, corporate donations are falling off and have been doing so for years. The Conference Board of Canada reported recently that donations fell by $25 million in 1994, after a $55-million drop in 1993.[22] Part of this decline is because the modern corporation is lean and mean in more ways than one, part of it because the people who make the decisions are incensed by the increasing incidence of fraud, waste, and overspending.

The big money comes from government grants and fees, which represent 56.5 per cent of all charitable funding. Without the influx of public funds, these outfits would shrivel; most would disappear. The only sector of the charitable front that raises more on its own than it sucks from the taxpayer is places of worship—churches, mosques, synagogues, and the like—which took a meagre $84 million from governments in 1993 while pulling in $3.1 billion in donations.[23]

In other words, 14 per cent of all government spending, a figure that has held fairly steady for a decade, goes to charitable institutions.

Or, to put it another way, you are an involuntary donor to every outfit with a charitable number, from the Red Cross to the AIDS Society for Children, which, so far as I can discover, has yet to spend a dime on services to kids with AIDS. You give to all these outfits whether you want to or not, whether you support their goals or not, whether you share their religious views or not, whether they are scam artists—as a tiny minority are—or not. You make your donation in three ways. First, in direct grants to the charitable sector from federal, provincial, and municipal governments. Second, in tax breaks to the charitable groups, including real-estate exemptions at the local level, sales-tax breaks in most provinces, and income-tax breaks everywhere. Third, in income-tax deductions to those who support the charities with their gifts.

The *Financial Post*, as part of a series of articles designed to boost the charitable sector, ran a headline proclaiming that "More than 65% of donations go to intended cause,"[24] which certainly gave me pause; overall, 35 per cent of the money you put up to feed the poor or to help out the dear old Fraser Institute seems to go up in smoke. It costs the federal government about one cent out of every dollar raised to raise it, because the federal government has means of persuasion that are considerably more forceful than the picture of a beguiling kid and a begging letter. Pay up or see the judge, says Revenue Canada, and while we curse the hellhounds who prevail upon us, we have to admit the process is efficient.

If you look at the $86 billion spent by charities and write off 35 per cent of that to overhead, fund raising, and administration, you are talking about a sum of $30 billion. I guess if the *Financial Post* headline had read "Charities blow $30 billion," a somewhat different meaning might have been conveyed than that intended by the warm-hearted editors.

I do not argue that all this money was wasted; I do argue that if we are looking for efficient ways to collect money and deliver social services, we will not find them in charities. If we start with $30 billion, we find that it comes to almost three times the national defence budget, or as much as is spent annually by the departments of External Affairs, Agriculture, Communications, Consumer Affairs, Employment and Immigration, Fisheries, Forestry, Indian Affairs, Industry, Justice, National Revenue, Transport, Veterans Affairs, and Public Works, all rolled into one.[25] It is about two-thirds of the budget of National Health and Welfare. And remember, we are only talking about the *overhead* costs of charity here.

Whatever may be said of waste and folly in the public sector (quite a lot), it often pales by comparison with the inefficiency of charity stunts staged to raise money. At the 1993 Canadian National Exhibition, forty charities provided twenty-four volunteers each to work at the gambling casino, in return for a cut of the profits. The casino raked in $2.9 million, but that was before the operators, Casino Amusements Canada, deducted their costs. Among them: $1,446,354 in salaries, $347,465 in rent, $360,000 for renovations, $119,000 for advertising, $47,331 for "operating expenses,"

$75,000 for management, and $52,680 for administration (as opposed to management). By the time the CNE got around to adding $150,000 for "recovery costs," the venture was in the red. Not good for public relations, so the CNE board "donated" $5,000 as a gesture of goodwill to each of the bodies that supplied volunteers. For many of the charities, staff time and incidental expenses wiped out the $5,000 entirely, and the goodwill had gone long since.[26]

One way companies cash in on charity is through "cause-related marketing," as when a Toronto brew pub promoted its in-house beer on the back of the Special Olympics for Children.[27] Quaff a draft and boost a kid. Some of these efforts, like the Ronald McDonald houses, seem worthwhile, but others are dodgy indeed. Nobody cares.

The big new development in the charity game is high-tech arm-twisting. The charity hires a professional, who gets paid up to 40 per cent of the take, and uses databases, automatic telephone systems, and other technical marvels to milk the market. One disgruntled fund-raiser told me: "Government cutbacks are a wonderful boon to the United Way. They turned it into a marketing opportunity with all those ads telling us we had to dig deeper. Frankly, I found it disgusting."

There's another problem in that money raised for charity is dependent, has to be dependent, on the selling power of the Good Cause. Kids and dogs have appeal, old folks not so much. This drawback was described in agonizing terms in a letter to the editor that appeared in the *Toronto Star*, written by Cathy Lazorov of Sudbury, who is dying of breast cancer. She wrote, in part:

> I have breast cancer that has spread to my bones. Yes, this will kill me painfully and, hopefully, quickly.
>
> The number of women in the United States and Canada who die of breast cancer, compared with the number of people who die each year of AIDS, is staggeringly high, yet funding for research is very low.
>
> AIDS has Liz Taylor. What famous fundraiser works for us? Elton John and Michael Jackson sing no songs for us. No big stars attend our funerals or honour our memories.
>
> We are so impressed with the AIDS quilts that can cover football fields. If people cared enough to make quilts for us, our quilts would cover a country.[28]

Does the popular appeal of a star determine, in part, which worthy cause gets the bucks? Oh, my, yes. The amount of cash that goes to try to solve any of hundreds of problems now being turned over to charity depends directly on the saleability of the disease, disability, or whatever.

Frankly, I don't think that's a very good way to go about sorting out priorities. The heavy-handed government way has its drawbacks—and that is why charities will always be crucial to a pluralistic society, to take up the undone tasks—but as a method of sorting out the competing claims of society, government funding is a long way ahead of charitable balls or the Jerry Lewis Telethon as a cornucopia for care.

Not long ago, governments put people in jail for running the numbers racket; now they are in the business themselves, through lotteries, and justify it by pointing to the portion of money that seeps through to charities, sports facilities, and public works. Next came casinos. Casinos, folks: gambling hells, sucker-stripping machines, greenhouses for the forced growth of organized crime. But it's all okay, because some cash trickles through to charity. Now, charities that raise money through casino gambling are going to lose a lot of it to video gambling, which is already legal in every province but British Columbia, but whose take goes to the operators and the provincial governments that authorized them. Our governments are so busy skinning the citizens with gambling games that they are literally looting the tills of the charities.

As if the pressures on the voluntary sector were not sufficient already, our governments also are starting to horn in on the charities' fundraising front by competing for the same dollars. Health Canada, in partnership with eighty corporations, has been raising money to promote programs like breast-feeding, antismoking, health, and nutrition, all of which already have both public and charitable organizations at work for them. Our universities are seducing away the wealthy by setting up crown foundations, where the donor can get a bigger bang for his or her buck than any other charity can provide (see Chapter Eight), besides getting the family name stuck on the front of a building by contributing a tiny portion of the capital required.

We are beginning to tire of it all. We are sick of the hands and hats thrust under our averted eyes as we walk down the street—"Got any change?" We are sick of the smile-and-dial phone calls that pull us from the television to ask us if we would like to support wheelchair basketball—

"Well, no." We are bored with the flood of letters from a score of charities every month, each with its own special whine. Faced with yet another television portrait of a bloated African child with flies swarming across his or her tear-streaked face, we are as likely to reach for the channel changer as the chequebook. In Alberta, the teachers' association passed a resolution to end the raising of charitable funds in schools, because there were so many campaigns that they interfered with work and drained energy that was supposed to go to education.[29] We are surfeited with the constant pleas and the drain on our pocketbooks, to say nothing of the fact that it all makes us feel crummy.

The official name for this state is "donor fatigue," and it is a virus running through Canada and every western nation. Perhaps, then, this is not the best time for our political masters to tell us to dig deeper and try harder, because otherwise the unthinkable may happen, and they may have to start taxing some of the obscene profits of our giant corporations, who will all then move to Mexico, leaving us bereft.

TAX WRITE-OFFS: GIVING AS AN ACT OF GREED

Every year, more than five million Canadians declare charitable donations on their individual income-tax forms. In 1994, the last year for which this statistic has been reckoned, Canadians wrote off $3.39 billion this way, a direct loss in tax revenues of somewhere over a billion dollars.[30] The charities issued $6.6 billion in receipts (which many people forget or don't bother to file) and collected another $1.6 billion for which no receipts were issued.[31]

One of the reasons there is such a boom in charities is that clever accountants and slick operators have been able to work the system so well. Newspapers and magazines are chock-a-block with articles telling us how to "Get the Biggest Bang for Your Charity Buck" or "Give Art, Get Back Taxes." We are turning charity into another tax break, giving in to an act of greed.

Corporations, like individuals, are learning to play the tax rules, donating outdated equipment to charity and taking a tax write-off. The Canadian branch of Hewlett-Packard wrote off $1.25 million it contributed to charitable groups, 90 per cent of which was in equipment. In total, during 1993, charities in Canada received $540 million worth of donations "in kind."[32]

As in so many things, we can see our own future across the border in the United States. For example, under American tax law, you can give your old computer to a school or your worn clothes to Goodwill and get back a nice tax write-off; donate a few hours of volunteer work and write it off at the minimum wage for your state. We are moving that way. For Canadian corporations, the racket is even richer; companies get a tax write-off equal to twice the actual cost of gifts in kind. Or, as an individual, you can donate a work of art, having first made sure that it is "properly" appraised, and receive a tax deduction. Thousands of people among the nonsuffering sector of the population will get a nice tax write-off this year while cleaning out the basement. They call it creative giving. The charitable impulse, the desire to share with others less fortunate in society, is surely a noble thing. Obtaining a tax write-off by palming off junk is not quite so noble. This would not matter except that the tax write-offs not only cost all of us lost revenue but deprive the government of funds that support—or don't—the dwindling social safety net. The Americans have also worked out sophisticated accounting procedures under which money spent on, say, a glorious dinner for the charity's top officials becomes an "educational" expense and appears as a donation, not an administrative cost, in the annual report.

"Fraud by connoisseur" is a new heading on Revenue Canada's books, covering taxpayers who buy low and donate high to museums and art galleries, getting tax deductions worth several times what they paid. In a typical case, a financial adviser bought a Turkish rug for $4,800 and gave it to a charity after having it appraised for $29,000, the amount he deducted from his taxes. Thus the phrase "lie like a rug." He might have got away with it, except that he and his wife claimed the $4,800 the next year and got caught.[33]

PRIVATIZING THE SOCIAL SAFETY NET
The amount of money that governments give to charities is starting to lessen, as governments discover the pleasures and votes to be garnered from Social Darwinism, with its assurance that the high cost of the fraying social safety net is rooted in the frauds and deceit of welfare recipients, and its conviction that anybody who really wants to can get a job. There is no sentiment easier to tap than the notion that someone out there is screwing us, and if the enemy can be identified as the poor, weak, young, old, or helpless, well, that's great, because then we can cut the buggers off without

a dime and without remorse. But here's a funny thing: the law hasn't yet caught up to this liberating philosophy, so governments are still required to provide shelter and food and a modicum of services to those who can prove a need that our bureaucrats cannot red-pencil into oblivion.

Accordingly, governments are increasingly hiring charities to take over social services and run them. The Canadian Mental Health Association handled government housing contracts worth $16 million last year[34]—fee-for-service work that still costs the government the same, or even more (since there are administration costs and a level of profit to be taken off) than government housing, but which is somehow considered more acceptable. In the United Kingdom, the fees and charges that charities collect from the government now represent close to half their incomes,[35] and we are heading down the same road. Perhaps it is an efficient way to go, but shouldn't we discuss the ramifications before we make the move? The effect is that instead of a faceless bureaucrat deciding how much and to whom, based on political decisions publicly arrived at in our legislatures, the money is doled out as a favour through the charities, with no public accountability.

The Toronto Humane Society has a contract with the city that pays it $726,000 for sheltering services but will not make public any of the details. When the province's privacy commission ordered it to release the contract, the charity went to court to block the order, in a case that will probably drag on for years. We are shovelling ever-larger wads of public money through organizations that have no obligation to tell us what they do with it. Is this what we want?

As governments retreat from providing welfare and social services, as they shift more and more of the burden to charity, leaving private individuals to bind the wounds of the socially stricken on a voluntary basis, we are not merely reversing much of the progress in social stability created since the Second World War, we are fashioning a social and economic disaster.

CUTTING OFF THE POOR TO SPITE OURSELVES

The federal government, in the 1994 budget, cut 5 per cent from all non-statutory grants (i.e., all those not mandated by legislation), including those to most charities. The Canadian Centre for Philanthropy, which is itself a charitable foundation, has calculated that these cuts, combined with declining donations, will precipitate a financial crisis for the charities, over time, especially when additional cuts are made.[36] The people who run charities already know about that, as, everywhere across the country, food banks scramble for supplies, shelters for the homeless struggle to serve the growing numbers, and day-care centres raise their fees or lower their blinds.

For every one per cent cut in government grants, the Centre for Philanthropy calculates that "a 5.8 per cent increase in individual donations would be needed to keep overall funding constant."[37] There is no sign of any such increase; rather, donations are declining, in current dollars.[38] In 1994, even though personal donations went up by one per cent over 1993, the inflation rate of 1.5 per cent wiped that out and more, while governments slashed welfare by billions.[39] Charities are being forced to cut back at the very time when they are most needed.

You can see the direct consequence of government budget cuts at the food banks. These were established as a "temporary measure" (like income tax, come to think of it) to tide us over the recession, to serve the small population of unfortunates who fell through the cracks of the system. Now, they are trying, with shrinking resources, to handle a much wider segment of the population. They are being called on to serve the needs of people who used to be middle class and now no longer have enough to eat. A survey in Toronto showed that 4,400 families using the food banks had given up a house because they couldn't keep up the payments; 10,350 families had sold the car. In all, 80 per cent of food-bank clients had given up something to raise money; the other 20 per cent had nothing left to give up. In Toronto, 50,000 families collect food hampers every month, but demand has caught up with the supply, and, at many food-bank locations across the country, the shelves are empty.[40]

The Ontario Association of Food Banks released a survey of thirty-two communities in April 1996, showing that the cuts in social assistance translated into a 49 per cent rise in dependence on these frail reeds.[41] The number of children requiring assistance was up 68 per cent from 1995, and the directors of the social agencies reported "a sense of hopelessness" and "increase in stress" among clients. "They're devastated," Roxanna Felice, executive director of Project Share in Niagara Falls, told the *Toronto Star*.[42]

You can also measure the consequences in the fact that, during the winter of 1995–96, three homeless men froze to death on the streets of Toronto.[43]

Our cruellest blows are aimed at our children, which seems odd until you reflect that kids can't vote, can they? Child poverty has increased 35 per cent in Canada since 1989.[44] We now have enough poor children—1.5 million—to form a province that would have the fourth-largest population in the nation. Six of ten children in single-parent families in this country live in poverty. Among young families, child poverty has increased by 39 per cent since 1989 and almost doubled in the past decade. It does not take a trained social worker to reckon what this will mean to us in social terms.

Children from poor families are more likely to use drugs, have problems with alcohol, or come into conflict with the law than those in what we used to call the middle and upper classes (now they are "median income" and "higher income" groups—we don't have classes, darling). The death rate due to fires, drowning, accidents, suicides, and homicides is up to ten times higher for poor children than the general population. How do you expect these children to behave when they reach maturity? Will they not feel a certain resentment, a certain sense that perhaps they have not been fairly dealt with, a certain distance from the bumper stickers that tell them to shun drugs, work hard, and trust Jesus to sort things out?

Bluntly put, we are creating the population that will swell our jails, courts, and mental institutions; we are doing this to save money, and, at the same time, we are signalling our willingness to spend tax funds for the jails, alarm systems, and police we need to protect ourselves from this growing crime base, rather than on social programs to prevent the problem. We do not count the higher costs to come.

A MONUMENTAL WASTE OF MONEY

The kindness of strangers absorbs more work hours than the federal government, spends more money than any private industry, costs more to the public treasury than federal budgets for social security and unemployment insurance rolled together, and operates almost entirely without public scrutiny. This would not be so important except that the charity system is under unbearable strain. It has been handed a task it can never fulfil, entrusted with a mandate it never sought, lumbered with a responsibility shoved off on it by retreating governments. The irony of the situation is that we are doing this to save taxpayers' dollars by substituting private compassion for fading public responsibility, but the net result is a monumental waste of money, public and private, on a system that cannot cope.

And that is presuming that the money goes where we intended it to go in the first place, which is not always the case with charities. The Salvation Army probably makes better use of my $25 than the minister of finance, but what about the Canadian Missing Children Association, Canadian Parents Against Drugs, Persons United for Self-Help, or the Canadian National Institute for Mobility Difficulties? These are all fine-sounding charities that have raised money which is largely gone now, without ever getting through to the intended recipients. Or, take the case of a charity set up to provide "food, shelter and clothing" to the poor of a Canadian city. The charity took in just over $1 million. Of this, a little over $2,000 trickled through to a food bank and $800 was doled out to the Variety Club. But you mustn't think that the other $997,000 went to waste; not at all. After changing its mandate to "providing quality entertainment," the charity bought an old movie theatre, refurbished it, and put on a musical comedy. The record does not disclose how many of the poor and homeless got to enjoy the show; not many is my guess. Possibly, they were not in the mood for musicals, anyway. I asked Ron Davis, director of the Charities Division of Revenue Canada, whether this was okay by him, and he said, after some hesitation, that it was really none of his business. "If the new purpose fell under one of the four heads of charity, we would have no position one way or the other," he said. If I had given the charity $20 to provide food for the poor and thought I had been hard done by, I could sue, he suggested, to get my money back.

Charity is charity, in law, taxes, and public policy. You can fritter away your money a buck at a time giving it to some homeless bum on a street corner or give a worthy whack to the Canadian Television Series Development Foundation. The difference is that the foundation will provide a nice tax receipt so you can write it off, and the bum will not.

The problem is that while most charities are run by people who have nothing but the best intentions, they are also run, in the main, by amateurs. The recipients are supposed to be grateful, even if most of the money headed in their direction disappears in administrative costs, salaries, advertising, mileage, and all the other oddments of public endeavour. A government department that took in $86 billion and expended nearly $30 billion of this just staying alive would draw the attention, anger, and outrage of the auditors, the Members of Parliament, and the general public, in the order named. There would be Royal Commissions and Task Forces and enquiries without end; editorialists would thunder denunciations and economists would issue forecasts of doom. "We can't go on this way" would be the general tenor of the remarks. "The economy cannot stand it." However, in the case of charities, we extend an astonishing forgiveness in the matter of waste, not because we are such a forgiving people but because we really haven't the foggiest idea what is going on. If the Minister of Foreign Affairs rose in the House of Commons to announce that the government had spent several million dollars every year "to promote the religion of Jehovah's Witnesses," there would be questions. But it has spent money in tax breaks for the same purpose, and there are no questions, because nobody knows.

Charities—to put the point plainly—are, to a large extent, run by the elite for the elite, on the assumption that the lads and lasses who fork out $200 for a black-tie dinner, and a swell book of pictures of starving Ethiopians, are better judges of how to spend money on good works than public policy makers. "Look at the ribs sticking out on that kid. Say, Harry, do you think the bartender heard us order another round?" Instead of buying a kid a school lunch, we give a tax break to the Fraser Institute, a charitable organization, so it can hold a dinner where a gaggle of academics will bring forth papers to prove that poverty is essentially the fault of the poor and richness is God's reward for superior worth. How many Canadian voters do you suppose would rather the Fraser Institute had the money than the kid? How many of us even know the question is on the table?

Lady Bountiful with a tax-receipt book cannot close the poverty gap created by government withdrawal; we cannot succour the homeless, the poor, the economic victims of the market, by attending dinners and balls. One of the most alarming aspects of this problem is that, as in so many areas of our society, Canadians appear to be substituting American judgments, American approaches, and American politics for our own. And here is a really neat twist: you can donate money to an American university and write it off on your Canadian taxes; just part of the melding of our lands, whether we like it or not.

I do not say that we should shut down charities, but I do say that if they are going to spend billions of our dollars, they ought to be accountable and answerable. The whole strength of the charity sector lies in its diversity, its capacity to serve all kinds of people in all kinds of ways, to fill in the interstices that government cannot possibly hope to cover. Nobody pretends it is efficient; if small economic units were efficient, we wouldn't have Wal-Mart, just the neighbourhood pharmacy. However, trying to bend the sector into a major provider of social services will not save money in the long run; it will cost us more, but we will pay it through other pockets, that's all.

Our social policy in the past was based on the notion that we had collective rights and duties which took precedence, from time to time, over individual choices, for what used to be known as the public weal. In this scheme of things, voluntary charities played an important, but limited, role.

Now we believe, with the Americans, that governments are boobs, collective action is immoral, and welfare, if we must have such an odious thing, is something to be administered with a gun and a whip. Whatever humanity remains in the system is to be entrusted to what the nineteenth-century poet John Boyle O'Reilly called "The organized charity, scrimped and iced, in the name of a cautious, statistical Christ."[45] We are in danger of making that cautious, statistical Christ the arbiter of social policy in this country, because, after all, he seems to be in charge in the good old U.S. of A.

There is no mystery about what will happen as we follow the Americans all the way down the free-market road and deliver our responsibilities increasingly over to Mothers Against Drunk Driving, the YMCA, and Lotto/649. When people become more desperate, hope fades, crime escalates, violence multiplies, and the social fabric frays. It's a hell of an expensive way to try to save money, and it doesn't even work. Ask the folks in Detroit, Watts, or any other major urban centre across the line.

It is the argument of this book that we are already going down the wrong road, but I am not naive enough to suppose that we are likely to change direction soon. However, it seems to me that we ought to know a good deal more than we do about the charitable sector to which we are handing over so much responsibility, and that we ought to consider ways of making that sector, since we are doomed to depend upon it, work better. We do not even have, in this country, any clear and easy way to discover which charities are efficient and which are so inefficient that, if we send them our money, we might just as well pour it out of the top of a boot. At the back of this volume, you will find my attempt to begin this process, a series of tables that look at some of the largest charities in the land on the basis of the information available on their (sometimes misleading) income-tax returns.

If you come to the end of this volume convinced that the kindness of strangers is, in fact, a proper response to the pressures of our age, I will be surprised, but satisfied; I am not trying to push you into agreement, merely into considering the issues. But if you put down this book convinced that Canadians know all we need to know about our charities and how they operate, I will be bloody well astounded. The reforms suggested in Chapter Eleven are no more than an attempt to open the door to a debate we have never even had in this country, about whether or not the charitable sector is the appropriate place to dump our social welfare problems.

2. God's Ladder

Thousands give Money to Beggars from the same motive as they pay their Corn-Cutter, to rest easy. Pride and vanity have built more hospitals than all the virtues together.

—BERNARD MANDEVILLE,
An Essay on Charity and Schools, 1723

Charity has always had an element of *quid pro quo* about it, the notion that shelling out to the less fortunate provides what Ben Whitaker, a British commentator, called "a fire escape to heaven for the rich."[1] The trouble with this image is that you escape *downward* on a fire escape, and unless my sense of geography has gone wrong, that is not the way to heaven; more correct, I think, to see charity as a ladder to God, a way in which good works, which are seldom uplifting enough in themselves for most of us, offer a positive payoff. It is best to wrap this sentiment in vague piety, because it is so hard to prove—we are assured by St. Matthew that a camel can pass through the eye of a needle more easily than a rich man can enter heaven, but no one has come back with positive evidence that the trick cannot be worked, and quite a few of the well-heeled are counting on buying their way past St. Peter. Not up there, but down here, in advance. Pay now, fly later.

This may not seem the soundest basis for social policy, but for centuries, it was what we had, and, as we seem to want to go back along this road, we should know something of the topography.

SHELLING OUT IN ANCIENT TIMES

Hammurabi, the Babylonian ruler who stuck his great Code of Laws on a seven-foot column about 2000 B.C., included, besides the famous "eye for an eye" crack, a line to his fellow citizens to see that "justice be done to widows, orphans and the poor."[2] Or else, he said.

It is my belief that charity is based in large part on the innate decency and/or guilt of many people, but I can't prove it. What I can show, however, is that these feelings, if they exist, have always needed the underpinning of two other reasons for charitable support: the hope of rewards and recognition in return, either here or beyond; and the need to keep the underclasses from becoming so desperate that they take to the streets. Piety, prestige, and property values are the spurs, at least as much as kindness and guilt.

Every religion has worked this combination. Harkhuf, an Egyptian, had his gifts to the poor recorded on his tomb with the note that he "desired that it might be well with me in the great god's presence."[3] The *Khuddaka Patha*, the scripture of Theravada Buddhism, explained that "By charity, man and woman alike can store up well-hidden treasure," and Mohammed appended the timely warning that "A man giving in alms one piece of silver in his lifetime is better for him than giving one hundred when about to die."[4] If you wait until the Grim Reaper is actually banging on the door, the authorities are likely to get the wrong idea—or, worse, the right idea—about why you decided to shell out.

The Hindus hit on the notion, now taken up by many modern charities, of having the donor give repeatedly, over time, instead of getting the thing done in one go. Because a single lifetime was not enough in which to gain purity and knowledge, the spirit came back for another try, on either a higher or lower plane, depending on behaviour in the current life. If you were wealthy, you were expected to do your share for the poor, because if you didn't, you might come back as a cockroach. Those who could afford it were expected to set aside a portion of their incomes, usually 4 per cent, for donations to the poor, and the village was collectively responsible for feeding any strangers who arrived unannounced, or there would be, you should excuse the expression, hell to pay.

In that same vein, the Greeks believed that if you spurned the afflicted, they might call down the wrath of the Furies on you. These were a trio of goddesses of vengeance, the Andrews sisters of angst, and it didn't pay to have them after you, because they would hound you to death. Born of the blood of Uranus, they had bat's wings, dog's heads, and snakes for hair.[5] Not a pretty sight. The Greeks also believed that you could gain credit on the other side of the River Styx by performing acts of benefit to the general community, as Xenophon did when he laid on an annual feast at Scillus. He anticipated the charity ball by about twenty-four centuries, with food and favours now, and glory in the afterlife. The Greeks had a term for it, as always—*philanthropia*, a combination of their words for "love" and "human"—although it seems just as likely that other motives were involved, including vanity. There was a vigorous competition among wealthier Greeks to see who could put on the finest spread. The well-to-do also were expected to make contributions to public works and to finance the theatre; they not only paid for the actors but for the chorus, during training.

There was no organized social welfare in the modern sense. While education was given great importance, it was left entirely in private hands, except that the sons of citizens who had been killed in battle were supported in school by the community. The family was expected to take care of the old and helpless, but there was a sort of two-tiered medical system, in which the community chose and paid for physicians to treat citizens who could not afford to pay. The shrines at Epidaurus, which were devoted to Asclepius (he was the son of Apollo and Coronis, and so skillful in healing that he could raise the dead, which ticked off Zeus, who killed him), provided massages and baths to the poor, as well as spas run by private physicians who soaked the rich in baths and bills alike.

The Romans were preoccupied with what Juvenal called the "Two things only the people anxiously desire—bread and circuses,"[6] but the spectacles were not put on in the hopes of improving the lower classes. The idea was to take their minds off their troubles. Chucking a Christian or two to the lions had a marvellously soothing effect on the unruly mob, though possibly not on the Christians, and made the masses forget that they didn't have enough to eat, while their overlords ate so much they made themselves throw up, so they could start in again.

LOVE THY NEIGHBOUR: CHRISTIAN CHARITY

Christianity emphasized the notion of love for one's neighbour as a spur to charity, but there is a familiar note in the Sermon on the Mount, where Matthew has Jesus saying, "If thou wilt be perfect, go and sell that thou hast, and give to the poor, and thou shalt have treasure in heaven."[7]

As Christianity spread through the Roman Empire, its churches took on the role of providing for the poor, especially after the Emporor Constantine cleared the way to finance the affair. In A.D. 312, he permitted citizens to will money or property to the church, opening a cornucopia of giving quite unlike the occasional splurges of the past. Much of the money went to build massive edifices to the glory of God, with well-marked nameplates for the donors, just to avoid confusion up yonder. Still, there was money left over to help the poor, aged, and infirm by setting up orphanages and almshouses, which were buildings where alms—food, clothing, or money—were dispensed.

There was still no organized, regular source of funds, since so much depended on the right people dying at the right time, a problem that the early Jews had met by tithing. The Mosaic Code held that giving was not charity but a duty, and the Hebrew word for charity, *tsedaka*, means "righteousness" or "justice." There were degrees of this righteousness, set down by the theologian Maimonides, beginning with this one:

> To take hold of a Jew who has been crushed and to give him a gift or a loan, or to enter into partnership with him, or to find work for him, and thus to put him on his feet so that he will not be dependent on his fellowmen.[8]

The last and lowest degree of justice, incidentally, was "When one gives grudgingly." We call it income tax.

In France, the Council of Tours, in A.D. 567, urged Christians to follow the Jewish practice of tithing and, later, tried to make it mandatory by threatening excommunication to the slow givers. The Emperor Charlemagne put the weight of the state behind this idea in the late ninth century, when tithing became a legally enforceable civic duty. Obligatory tithing gradually spread throughout Europe, and Lord, how the money rolled in!

By the twelfth century, in England, the Church held close to half of the nation's entire public wealth.[9] Monasteries and churches ran the alms-houses that distributed some, but far from all, of the money left to them by men and women trying to buy their way into heaven. Jakob Fugger the Rich, a Bavarian merchant, left a fortune to a foundation that hired monks to pray for his soul every day. The foundation still exists and the prayers still go on, making Fugger's soul one of the best-tended on record. There were also jousting tournaments, with the proceeds going to charity, just as today part of the take from those lavish golf tournaments is shuffled off to aid the stricken. There was also "church ale," made from donated grain and sold to provide alms.[10]

To care for the old, infirm, insane, and diseased, the monks set up hos-pitals, which were adapted from the hostels they had formerly kept for travellers. Churches were kept open for days at a time at Christmas, Easter, and Whitsuntide, when gifts of food were passed out. On Maundy Sunday, small red and white purses containing money were given to old people; these were called "doles," from the Middle English word for shar-ing. Doles were also often given as part of the funerary service, and a rich man might order that a thousand loaves of bread be distributed in his name or that pennies be passed out in return for prayers for his immortal soul, at his funeral or on the anniversary of his death. In 1322, as the mob scrambled for the doles given on behalf of the soul of Henry Fingue, a for-mer fishmonger and Lord Mayor of London, fifty-five people were killed in the crush.[11]

In what was to become the most-repeated note of the charitable sector, the Royal Council of England, in 1349, passed an ordinance to ensure that the recipients of charity deserved it. This was on the heels of the Black Death, when labour, for a change, was in short supply, and the working stiffs were getting above themselves:

A great part of the People, and especially of Workers and Servants, late died of the pestilence, and many will not serve unless they receive excessive wages, and some rather willing to beg in idleness than by Labour to get their Living.[12]

The Royal Council therefore passed a series of rules, beginning with one requiring "Every person Able in Body and under the Age of Sixty Years" to work when asked, "or else be committed to the Gaol," moving up through "The old Wages, and no more, shall be given to Servants," and ending with "No person shall give anything to a Beggar that is able to labour."[13]

These rules were widely disregarded, but they set the theme for social assistance to this day—that it must on no account interfere with the possibility of screwing down wages, and no one should get anything without working for it.

Throughout this period, there were complaints that the money set aside for the poor out of the huge amounts brought in by tithing was minuscule—they received less than 3 per cent of the income of the monasteries[14]—and that the almshouses and hospitals were becoming dumping grounds for the discarded servants of the wealthy, while the real poor were shut out.

One of the great ecclesiastical money-making rackets was to sell indulgences to wealthy sinners; you could pay on Sunday for what you had done on Saturday and hoped to do on Monday. After confessing a sin—harbouring lewd thoughts, drowning your nephews in a vat of Malmsey, whatever—you were assigned a penance to perform, such as switching yourself with a hazel bough in the public square next Tuesday, repeating prayers, making a pilgrimage, joining a crusade against the infidels, or building a bridge. Before starting in on the penance, you had a little chat with the priest, money changed hands, and, voila! The penance vanished. This was no small matter, because, while the indulgence was meant to be temporal only, the church had tucked in a neat little argument to the effect that few people could rely on dying with all due penances performed, so they would have to pay for the balance by years of suffering in purgatory, God's waiting room. Thus, by paying off the penance, you could immeasurably improve your chances of serving only a short stint in purgatory, and at the same time buy the bishop that nice new clock for the church.

The racket was improved when *questiarii*, or "pardoners," were allowed to retain a percentage of the indulgence, a practice which caused the Chancellor of Oxford University to complain that:

> These indulgence-mongers wander over the country, and give a letter
> of pardon, sometimes for two pence, sometimes for a draught of wine
> or beer, or even for the hiring of a harlot.[15]

Selling indulgences became such a lucrative scam that indulgence missions were mounted for particular projects, such as building a whole church on the cash from requited sins. When Johann Tetzel arrived in Saxony in 1517 to proclaim an indulgence aimed at rebuilding St. Peter's in Rome for Pope Leo X, a dour local professor of theology named Martin Luther objected and posted his arguments on the door of the castle church. In ninety-five theses entitled "Disputation for Clarification of the Power of Indulgences," Luther argued that salvation was the free gift of God and could not be purchased, and he raised a question that could not be answered:

> Why does not the Pope empty Purgatory for the sake of holy love and the dire need of the souls that are there, if he redeems a number of souls for the sake of miserable money with which to build a church?[16]

The Pope demanded an instant recantation. When Luther refused, the Reformation was under way.

HENRY VIII DEALT HIMSELF INTO THE RACKETS

In England, the Reformation was not prompted by theological niceties; it was a straightforward power struggle between the Church and the state, in the corpulent person of King Henry VIII. In Henry's time, the income of the monasteries surpassed that of the crown itself,[17] and the church didn't have to fight any wars, while the king did. Henry was orthodox to his fingertips; he was not knocking the hierarchical structure which signalled that he was God's anointed, but he did object to the fact that the local priests kicked up a fuss every time he wanted to get married again. He dealt himself into the rackets, extorting £119,000 from the clerics in 1531, a vast fortune in those days, as the price of his newly invented role of "Supreme Headship" of the Roman Catholic Church in England.[18]

Two years later, when the Pope declared that Henry's marriage to Anne Boleyn, who had already given birth to Elizabeth, was invalid, Parliament passed the series of laws that set up the Church of England. The Act of Supremacy which made Henry the head of that Church was not aimed at charities in any way, but it had a profound effect upon them nonetheless by doing away with the monasteries and leaving nothing but private offerings and the crown to pass out alms.

The monasteries had become, in the words of S. T. Bindoff, a British historian:

> Convenient dumping-grounds for unwanted men and surplus women, profitable posts for needy younger sons of the nobility and gentry, pensions and perquisites for innumerable hangers-on, and board and lodgings for travellers who, like the kings who so often availed themselves of it, took for nothing what they should have paid for.[19]

Still and all, it was the monasteries that provided what little support there was for the downtrodden, and Henry promised Parliament that, when he quashed them, he would take over this role and perform it far better than the churches had done. Then Henry and his Tudor successors, in a move we recognize instantly today, passed down the regal responsibility to the next level of government, the parish, which was quite incapable of coping with it.

The economic transformation that overtook a society moving out of feudalism into capitalism, combined with a rapid population growth, led to an increase in poverty far beyond anything the parishes could handle, as the roads teemed with vagrants, beggars, and "Sturdy Rogues" looking for food, work, or just a place to sleep. Instead of providing these, the parishes tried to ship the bums along. The local poor were issued badges and licences to beg within the home parish; if any strangers showed up without a badge, they were driven out, sometimes after a whipping. Thievery and robbery with violence were the inevitable results of depriving thousands of artisans and farmers of any way to earn a living. To add to the problem, the breakup of the monasteries tossed thousands of former church servants and tenants out of jobs and homes, and many of them joined the roving mobs of vagrants.

Henry's England lived in terror of the tramp, and the notion of the worthiness of poverty soon vanished under the onslaught. Paupers were divided into two classes: the deserving, who kept their place and were thankful for crumbs, and the undeserving, who could have worked had they wanted to, really. The Protestant Church agreed with this notion, preaching the stern ideology of the "work ethic." Martin Luther had been against begging, which he regarded as a form of blackmail; he wanted it outlawed, and alms given only to the old, weak, and those who had "honourably laboured at their craft or in agriculture" but who could no longer find the means to support themselves.[20] The others should be put back to work; like our modern political leaders, he didn't say precisely where, just back to work.

John Calvin, the French Protestant theologian, took this idea a step further, arguing that idleness was usually the product of immorality or inborn laziness. Either that or fate. While the Catholic contended that any man might be saved by his faith and conduct (with perhaps a helping hand from the primed priest), and the Lutheran that he could be saved by faith alone, the Calvinist knew that God had predestined every person to heaven or hell, and there wasn't much you could do about it.[21] It was a theory welcomed by the emerging capitalists: the poor were not the victims of circumstance but of their own "idle, irregular and wicked courses"[22] or God's will, and helping them was not merely a waste of time, it was positively harmful. Richard Tawney, the brilliant analyst of this period, wrote:

> Such doctrines turned severity from a sin into a duty, and froze the impulse of natural pity with the assurance that, if indulged, it would perpetuate the suffering which it sought to alleviate.[23]

THE ELIZABETHAN POOR LAW

Charity was considered to be an act that was of benefit mainly to the giver, since it proved his noble character. "It is not giving but lending, and that to the Lord, who in his good time will return the gift with increase."[24] This attitude became enshrined in a series of laws that were codified in 1601 in the Statute of Charitable Uses, still referred to in court cases concerning charity as the Elizabethan Poor Law. Its purpose was political, not religious or humanitarian: to prevent civil disorder in an increasingly unruly society.

Special taxes (or rates) were levied in each parish for the relief of the poor, who were strictly a local responsibility. Each parish appointed charity commissioners who were responsible for setting the poor rates and collecting them (on pain of imprisonment, if they couldn't get the job done). To prevent paupers from roaming, which also, incidentally, prevented the poor labourers who were sincerely seeking work from finding it, there were houses of correction for vagrants, who were punished and then sent home.

Begging was illegal except for those deemed incapable of self-support; the punishment was public whipping and/or imprisonment. The giving of doles was prohibited. Work programs were provided for the able-bodied poor, and workhouses were set up to shelter them in conditions so deliberately unattractive that no one would go there unless he or she had to.

While the statute seems crude and cruel to modern eyes, it had two great advantages over what had gone before and what was available elsewhere in Europe. In the first place, it defined charitable purposes in its preamble, in words that are still quoted today:

> For the relief of aged, impotent and poor people, some for the maintenance of sick and maimed soldiers and mariners, schools of learning, free schools and scholars in universities, some for repair of bridges, ports, havens, causeways, churches, sea-banks and highways, some for education and preferment of orphans, some for or towards relief, stock or maintenance for houses of correction, some for marriages of poor maids, some for supportation, aid and help of young tradesmen, handicraftsmen and persons decayed; and others for relief and redemption of prisoners and captives, and for aid or ease of any poor inhabitant concerning payment of fifteens, setting out of soldiers and other taxes.[25]

With the possible exceptions of "marriages of poor maids," who are on their own these days, and "setting out of soldiers," these are all still recognized as charitable purposes.

The other great advance in the Poor Law was that it made the provision of public help and the raising of funds to that end a matter of law, not conscience. If you fell within the definition of a "meritable" pauper, you were entitled to relief. Of course, it was not to be fun; what it often meant was that your family was broken up, your children sent to orphanages (if they were too young to be bound out as apprentices), and your own life turned into an unending hell of drudgery for a wage that was always kept below the pitiable minimum paid outside, so that no one would be tempted to join a workhouse and wallow in the luxury of a flea-infested cot and a bowl of mouldy bread. It was better than starvation, but only by a little, and was meant to be that way.

Besides paying the obligatory poor rates, many Elizabethans gave to educational charities, or almshouses, or both. The reasons for establishing charities often were (and remain) quixotic. Dame Alice Owen built a church, ten almshouses, and a school near the spot in Islington where she had nearly been killed by an arrow as a child; the missile was miraculously stopped by her cap. Joan Smales of Shoreditch set up a fund that would pay ten shillings to a preacher to salute her virtues on her death —and twice as much to those who had to listen to him.[26] The Earl of Huntingdon gave much of his vast fortune to universities at Oxford and Cambridge, inspiring a popular ballad that noted:

> He built up no palace nor purchased no towne,
> But gave it to scholars to get him renowne.[27]

The Puritans shared the Calvinist view of charity, which held that the poor were to blame for their predicament, and there was very little change in this attitude for another three centuries. However, when a calamity occurred that could obviously not be the fault of the poor, like the Great Fire of London in 1666, gifts of goods and money, and offers of help, poured in from all over the country, with the result that the city was rebuilt within four years of the blaze. It became the custom to raise funds through "Charity Briefs," which were licences from the king or Parliament to raise money to relieve this kind of suffering.

The charitable trust was another way of soliciting funds; money was donated by one or a few benefactors and controlled by trustees who were responsible for seeing that it was properly invested and used. This was a form of giving available only to the very rich, but the joint-stock companies springing up everywhere suggested another way of accumulating cash—subscription lists, which were very like the lists of shareholders in commercial concerns, and to which those of lesser means could contribute. Charitable societies became the most common form of giving in the late seventeenth century.[28]

THE RISE OF CHARITY SCHOOLS AND HOSPITALS

One of the favourite beneficiaries of these charitable societies were schools, founded by independent charities such as the Anglican Society for Promoting Christian Knowledge, founded in 1698 by Thomas Bray to teach religion and "the habits of industry" to the children of the poor. By the mid-eighteenth century, there were 25,000 such schools in England, training boys for apprenticeship and girls to be domestics.

Britain's class system ensured that the kids were not encouraged to be uppity. Hannah More opened a school in an impoverished mining area and was met with the complaint that "the poor were intended to be servants and slaves: it was pre-ordained that they should be ignorant." She replied, primly, "My plan for instruction is very limited and strict. They learn of weekdays such coarse works as may fit them for servants. I allow no writing."[29]

Daniel Defoe, the author of *Robinson Crusoe*, turned out a pamphlet in 1704 whose title said it all—*Giving Alms no Charity*. His point was that idleness was the most common cause of poverty, and was only made worse by charity. Not everyone was convinced, however, and the new mode of raising funds by subscription led to an expansion of the charitable sector, especially in the construction and operation of hospitals. In many of these, an annual subscription of five guineas earned the donor the right to recommend patients to the hospital.

Thomas Coram, a retired sea captain, launched one of the most valuable of the subscription hospitals. He lived outside London and was dismayed, on his trips to the capital, to see the bodies of abandoned, newly born infants dumped on the roadside by unmarried mothers who could not afford to look after them. He sought to obtain the necessary royal charter to raise a subscription for a foundling hospital, but for years he was refused on the grounds that such an institution would only persuade more women to have illegitimate children. After seventeen years of petitioning, he got his charter, and the hospital opened in Bloomsbury. On the first day, 117 children were left at the hospital gates, and before long, the foundling hospital was overwhelmed by a flood of 4,000 infants. There was some government funding as long as the institution agreed to admit all the children that were brought, but when this became impossible, the funding was withdrawn. Mothers had to draw a coloured ball out of a hat to determine whether their children would be admitted; those who drew a white ball were the winners.[30] The hospital became a fashionable meeting place for London's smart set and attracted such eminent donors as William Hogarth, Joshua Reynolds, Thomas Gainsborough, and George Frederick Handel, who left a copy of the score to the *Messiah* to the institution.

As the eighteenth century drew to a close, the state of the poor in

England was, if anything, worse than it had been two centuries before, when the Elizabethan Poor Law had been put in place. The Industrial Revolution, enclosures (the process by which common pasture lands were "enclosed" or privatized, destroying the living of the peasants who grazed their animals on them), and the decline of the rural areas were caught perfectly in two lines of Oliver Goldsmith's *The Deserted Village*:

> Ill fares the land, to hast'ning ills a prey,
> Where wealth accumulates, and men decay.[31]

However, there was just enough assistance available to keep the indigent from open revolt, which was more than you could say about the rabble over in France. John Stuart Mill, the liberal philosopher, made the point this way:

> The hatred of the poor for the rich is an evil that is almost inevitable where the law does not guarantee the poor against the extremity of want. The poor man in France, notwithstanding the charitable relief that he may get, has always before his eyes the possibility of death by starvation; whereas in England he knows that, in the last resort, he has a claim against private property up to the point of bare existence; that not even the lowest proletariat is absolutely disinherited from his place in the sun.[32]

Louise Michelle, a French visitor to England, reported that she was "more struck by English poor relief than any other English institution . . . A like system in France would have prevented the French Revolution."[33] Actually, it was the failure of the first French Republic that kept the citizens of France from a state of social welfare far in advance of anything then proposed in Britain. The National Assembly passed legislation that would have, among other things:

—sold all hospitals, foundations, and endowments for the poor, and turned poor relief into "a national debt"
—provided free medical care by a licensed physician serving in each canton
—provided jobs or financial support, to anyone who needed them, at "the place of their residence," rather than in a workhouse

—paid a subsidy to parents unable to support their children on their own income.[34]

Regrettably, the French became occupied with other matters, such as chopping off the heads of aristocrats and trying to conquer the world, so very little came of these bold ideas.

Moreover, the fact that the British underclass refrained from revolting, like those vulgar French, only made their own lives worse, since the wars against Revolutionary France ruined trade and pushed up the price of wheat. To meet the threat of famine, soup kitchens were set up, including one at Spitalfields established by the Quakers, who were immediately attacked because their kindness would act as a magnet for paupers. Thomas Malthus, the Anglican cleric, had already made the point in his widely read *Essay on Population* that charity only increased poverty and misery, prolonged the miserable lives of the sufferers, and was "against the laws of nature."[35]

THE NEW POOR LAW

As England grew more prosperous, it was clear to the right-thinking element that anyone who wanted to work could find a job. What was not made clear was that the wages were so low that even those in full-time work often could not survive. The "working poor" have long been with us. The system had the advantage of providing an ever-ready pool of cheap, tractable labour. Besides the workhouses, the parishes put their charges to work on outdoor relief projects, either on the roads, bridges, and quays of the community, or as agricultural help.

However, property owners found the poor rates an increasing burden, and the growing industrial class objected that the law confining relief to the home parish interfered with labour mobility. After a series of hearings and commissions, the law was finally amended in 1834 to bring it up to date.

The underlying principle of the New Poor Law was the same: poverty was the result of "fraud, indolence and idleness";[36] all that was required was some adjustment in the way the law was administered. The main changes were the provision of a modicum of central administration, supplanting the parish as the administrative unit, and the abolition of outdoor relief projects. The first change ensured that workers could move from parish to parish, so the owner who fired his factory workers would not then be stuck with providing for them through local poor-relief taxes. The second change meant that the unemployed worker had no alternative to the workhouse, and workhouse life was made as bleak and degrading as possible so that a job, any job, at any wage, would be preferable. To enter the sour sanctity of such a place, paupers had to prove that they were indeed destitute; they could have no possessions. Finally, there were to be no exceptions for unemployables, as there had been in the past, because they had no one but themselves to blame for whatever disability made them unfit to work.[37] As historian A. V. Dicey put it, with a sniff:

> The object of the statute was in reality to save the property of hard-working men from destruction by putting an end to the monstrous system under which laggards who would not toil for their own support lived at the expense of their industrious neighbours, and enjoyed sometimes as much comfort as or even more comfort than fell to the lot of hardworking labourers.[38]

Private charity still carried the main burden of providing assistance, and it had the twin advantages that it made the donor feel better and that it could be withdrawn at any time, ensuring the poor would be less likely to abuse it. The value of charity as a social poultice had already been recognized, for when William Pitt introduced the first Income Tax Act in 1799, charitable organizations were exempted. The result was the multiplication of thousands of charities, vying for funds and the patronage of the royals and nobility. By 1837, a royal commission counted 28,840 charitable organizations in the United Kingdom, with scores more being added every year.[39] William Ewart Gladstone, then Chancellor of the Exchequer, tried, in 1863, to challenge the tax-exempt status of the charities, as "a subsidy of uncertain proportions given by the state to institutions of questionable value," but he was defeated. He put this down to "the skilful manner in which the charitable army, so to call it, has been marshalled."[40]

Charity was still not for the poor; they were merely the means for the spiritual uplift of the well-to-do. Charitable visiting, which required no training, was one of the few occupations regarded as suitable for ladies in the nineteenth century, and squadrons of Lady Bountifuls fanned out over the countryside, with bowls of soup for the poor. They were often shocked by the conditions they discovered in the hovels, and even more shocked by the resentment they often stirred up, when they expected a proper deference and gratitude.

THE RAGGED SCHOOLS

The advance of the Industrial Revolution produced, besides the outpouring of wealth built on Britain's new trade, an outpouring of poverty, as artisans, tradespeople, and farmers were driven from their homes by the vagaries of the new economy. In every one of the sprawling new urban centres, the destitute children of vagrants, tramps, convicts, and beggars roamed the streets, slept under bridges or in the open, and survived by begging and thievery. Gradually, a network of charitably financed "ragged schools" grew up to provide them with a bit of education and, sometimes, shelter.

By 1861, there were 176 ragged schools throughout England. Although they offered little education outside of Bible study, they did provide a minimum of social welfare through clothing clubs, penny banks, and holiday funds.

Thomas John Barnado wanted to be a medical missionary in China. In preparation, he decided to study medicine in a hospital in the east end of London, and that was as far east as he ever got. In the streets and alleys around him, he saw children starving, skulking, and thieving when they should have been learning, so he established a ragged school, the East End Juvenile Mission, in 1867, in what had been a donkey stable. One of his students, a ten-year-old boy named Jim Jarvis, took him, one day, to see where he and other children slept at night, on a nearby open rooftop, and Barnado resolved to make the care of London's waifs his life's work.

Barnado received help and advice from Lord Shaftesbury, who was a social reformer active in a number of charities. Shaftesbury believed the government should play a leading role in the relief of the inequities and displacements associated with the Industrial Revolution, a role that went far beyond what charity could accomplish. He sponsored legislation that prohibited the employment of women and children in mines, provided care for the insane, and limited factory workers to a ten-hour day. Or, to put it another way, he was a dangerous radical. Shaftesbury helped the new young doctor to establish a cottage-style home for destitute boys. Over the door of that first home—and hundreds of others since—was the slogan "The Ever Open Door—no destitute child refused admission."[41]

THE SOCIAL CONTRACT

The idea of a "social contract" was mooted by the English philosophers Thomas Hobbes and John Locke in the seventeenth century. Hobbes said that "in a state of nature," each individual was responsible only to himself, and there was no coercive state to make him (or her, though Hobbes never mentioned her) mind either his manners or another's welfare. Hobbes pointed out that this state of anarchy was not pleasant:

> No arts, no letters, no society and, which is worst of all, continual fear and danger of violent death, and the life of man solitary, poor, nasty, brutish and short.[42]

To enjoy the safety and pleasures of an organized state, Hobbes said, man agreed to give up some individual liberties. If you want to live in safety, your neighbour has to be curbed from killing you; he and you, and the rest of us, accept the imposition of outside order to this end. That's the social contract.

Locke took the argument a step further with the notion that, because there was a social contract, the monarch or government had to reflect the general will of the people; otherwise, the contract would be broken. Jean Jacques Rousseau, in *Le Contrat Social*, made such a contract the means of establishing the reciprocal rights and duties of rulers and ruled, which formed the basis of any organized state. The rulers of France said *"Mon dieu, quelle blague!"* and passed the cake, but these dangerous doctrines were used as justification for both the French and American revolutions. Thomas Jefferson argued that the social contract established certain "inalienable rights" that made the consent of the governed fundamental to any exercise of governmental power, and stuck the phrase into the American Declaration of Independence.

Modern political scientists dismiss the social contract, since there is no evidence that there ever was such a thing, implicit or explicit. Well, nuts to them. I think most of us accept the notion that we give up individual liberties and take on collective responsibilities in exactly the way that Hobbes and Locke described. Many of our political arguments have to do with the degree to which we think we ought to do this and the balance we ought to seek between individual rights and collective duties.

For historical reasons, Canadians, by and large, believe in a stronger sense of community and a weaker set of individual rights than do Americans, but this is a difference in degree, not kind. The majority of the inhabitants of every modern democracy are well aware that they have traded a certain amount of liberty for a certain amount of safety and that they all have joint responsibilities within the surrounding community.

It is not hard to see, as part of that contract, the idea that a minimum of food, shelter, housing, and support are responsibilities of the state—collective, not individual, responsibilities. This basic support is a right, not a favour. You don't have to earn it, although it is far better for everyone if you can and do work: it is part of what we owe each other—the fail-safe, the safety net.

If the state is to have any role in this business, there are really only two ways to go. One, proposed by the English philosopher and political theorist Jeremy Bentham in the eighteenth century, is the National Charity Company, a prison established and run by the state as humanely as possible, where the poor would labour for their suppers, but in a much more organized and efficient way than in the Elizabethan workhouses.[43] The other is the social contract. However, what happened was the simple abandonment of responsibility.

By the late nineteenth century, the role of the state had been effectively rescinded by the new doctrines that accompanied the rise and triumph of industrial capitalism. The poor were poor because they damn well wouldn't work; it was better to let them die than to help them, although we might grudgingly allow our womenfolk, clergy, Quakers, and other weird critters to cater to them, because it gave the dear oddballs something to do and stored up frequent-flyer points in heaven. Conspicuous charity, where you got your name stuck onto a hospital by ponying up the last of the funds needed to build it, was also acceptable, but social services were entirely voluntary, and the suggestion that they should be a duty on the state was nothing but dangerous socialist claptrap. It was only prudent to provide just enough help to keep the unwashed masses from taking to the streets the way they had in that regrettable affair in France, but anything beyond that might interfere with the working of the market, through which God in his infinite wisdom decreed that there would always be a sufficient supply of hungry workers to undercut those foreign blighters when it came to world trade.

The modification of this robust philosophy came about through timid, indirect, and stealthy steps, which always accepted the principle that poverty was a sin and should be relieved only enough to keep the neighbourhood safe. When Mary Carpenter launched her campaign to establish reformatory schools in the mid-eighteenth century, she called her book *Reformatory Schools for Children of the Perishing and Dangerous Classes and for Juvenile Delinquents*. Not a grabber, but it got the point across. At that time, children could be sent to prison for theft from the age of seven; Carpenter doubted that this would really reform them. If the propertied classes wanted to rest easy, they should think about providing schools that would be supported not only by voluntary subscriptions but by state funds, to get the little buggers off the streets. The Young Offenders Act of 1854 was the result, and it provided Treasury moneys to support institutions where the courts could send straying juveniles.

THE SALLY ANN MARCHES ON STAGE

Still, most charity remained private, personal, and dependent on the energies of characters like William Booth, the Nottingham pawnbroker who became a revivalist preacher. In 1865, with his wife, Catherine, he launched the "Christian Mission to the Heathen of our own country," soon to be renamed the Salvation Army. With military-style uniforms and a brass band, General Booth marched out to sweep the gutters and clean up the streetwalkers and drunks and, in general, "Storm the forts of darkness." Booth's street-corner meetings featured "saved" sinners who gave powerful testimony, including "A Milkman who has not watered his milk since he was saved" and "Fiery Elijah, the Saved Sweep from Rugby."[44]

One of the strong points of the Salvation Army, then as now, was that it was never judgmental about individuals, only wickedness. Its members served midnight suppers to feed prostitutes and vagrants, and founded homes for unmarried mothers and their children. In a Victorian England where many churches slammed their doors on such sinners, Booth and his followers welcomed them in, fed them, and kept them warm. And they still do.

CHARITY BECOMES FASHIONABLE

As the ranks of the impoverished grew and reformers, journalists, and busybodies began to write about their miseries, society responded by making pets of the poor. Charity became fashionable, and hundreds of institutions sprang up to absorb the energies and spare change of the propertied classes.

Queen Victoria became a patron of a number of charitable organizations, and Prince Albert became the president of the splendidly named Metropolitan Association for Improving the Dwellings of the Industrial Classes. Charitable balls and splendiferous suppers, where the wealthy could get stuffed and saved for one inclusive ticket, were all the rage.

Really, it was one's duty to share with the less fortunate not so much one's money—which would only be vulgar—but one's company on select occasions. Thus, an aristocratic lady who had been at the bedside of a dying pauper was able to reflect, "These little incidents made 'slumming' a real pleasure. One gave so much happiness with so little trouble."[45]

Social pressure to pile into the business of ladling out soup and manners to the poor came from the top. Prime Minister William Gladstone's wife, Catherine, was an enthusiastic soup-ladler, and Gladstone himself, during his fifty-two years in political life, constantly got himself into trouble by attempting the charitable rescue of prostitutes, whom he accosted on the streets, prayed at, and aided with gifts of money.[46]

Once the queen and the prime minister had shown the way, the upper crust treated charity as a social pursuit, with the result that, by 1885, the income of London charities alone exceeded the national revenues of Sweden, Denmark, or Portugal.[47] And yet, the poor kept on getting poorer. Charles Booth, a Liverpool shipowner, spent eighteen years documenting the lives of London's underclasses and produced a study, *Life and Labour of the People in London*, which pioneered new approaches to social research. Using the census returns of 1881–91, a team of his workers did a house-to-house survey that showed one million Londoners were living below the mark he established as the poverty line—one pound of income per week. The survey examined the hours of work, the pay, the size and state of dwellings, and the extent of joblessness among the teeming hordes. Booth concluded that the root causes of poverty were not indolence and fraud but low wages, unemployment, old age, and illness. Moreover, the outpourings of Victorian charity had done nothing to relieve the situation: "The poor are no less poor."[48]

He argued for much more generous treatment of the underprivileged and a state pension scheme to provide a modest pittance to be paid to those past working age, who could never, under current wages, save enough to put anything by. The proposal was dismissed as absurd, expensive, and unnecessary, but it was becoming clear that something had to be done. On the continent, two revolutions, in 1848 and 1870, which redrew the map of Europe, were largely driven by social unrest among populations that felt they had little to lose by taking to the streets.

THE IRON CHANCELLOR'S LIBERAL REFORMS

When Germany emerged as an imperial power under William I, his Iron Chancellor and man of all work, Otto von Bismarck, shoved through a bewildered Reichstag a series of astonishingly liberal reforms in the 1880s. Among them were compulsory old-age insurance, to which the employee, employer, and government all contributed, and compulsory sickness insurance, funded by the employee and employer. Bismarck was not moved by concern for the lot of the poor so much as by the need to outflank the Socialists, who were threatening to become a real power after the scribblings of that troublesome madman, Karl Marx, became widely circulated.[49]

Whatever his motives, Bismarck's activities were soon copied elsewhere. France passed a National Law for Free Medical Assistance in 1893, under which those who could not afford to pay for medicine or hospital treatment were accommodated at no cost. Both France and New Zealand had their own versions of contributory old-age pensions before the end of the nineteenth century, and the radical ferment soon invaded England.

THE POOR GET POORER

In 1905, a royal commission established to examine the operation of the New Poor Law found that it was not working very well. There were more poor than ever, who remained in poverty despite the best endeavours of the workhouses to drive them out to work by making life miserable within the institutions, and the private charities were, at best, indiscriminate, and at worst, bereft of reason. The commissioners described a woman who was so moved by a Sunday sermon on the perils of the poor that she took to the streets to distribute champagne and grapes to London's helpless hordes.[50]

The majority report of the commissioners abandoned the cosy notion that most of society's ills were caused by sinful sloth, and suggested that instead of deterring the poor from applying for assistance by making its availability as harsh and spare as possible, the government should recognize that at least some poverty was a direct result of the way the industrial system operated. There ought to be an old-age pension, free hospital treatment for those in need, and more residential homes for orphans and foundlings. These would be provided in the main by the existing charities on a voluntary basis, but, where it was required—and especially in the matter of old-age pensions—the necessary funding would come from government.[51]

A minority report, written by Beatrice and Sidney Webb, early members of the Fabian Society and supporters of the Labour Party, went much further. (Beatrice, the daughter of a wealthy industrialist, had worked with Booth on his study of poverty before she married Sidney James Webb, a senior civil servant and economist; together they helped to launch the London School of Economics in 1895 and the *New Statesman* in 1913.) The Webbs proposed scrapping the New Poor Law entirely and bolstering private charity with state social services to protect everyone, not merely the poor, against illness and misfortune. There would be a "framework of prevention" in place of the vicar's daughter, and a state-supported pension in place of the almshouses of the church.

Indeed, the Webbs argued in a series of books and tracts, private charity was doing more harm than good, since it relieved some of the symptoms of poverty without attacking the base cause, which was an industrial system founded on the exploitation of one class by another. Voluntary agencies would always be needed to supplement the state, but the main burden ought to be borne by government. The Webbs foreshadowed the welfare state, with its underlying principles of universality and government funding of the major elements of social care. Their minority report was a direct attack on the private charity system then in place and was swiftly relegated to a footnote of history, although its arguments continued to percolate through academic and political circles.

THE BEGINNING OF THE WELFARE STATE

Between 1906 and 1914, successive Liberal governments gradually transferred the major responsibility for the welfare of the underprivileged from private charity to the state. The centrepiece of this advance was the budget of 1909, drawn up by Lloyd George as Chancellor of the Exchequer.

"Four spectres haunt the poor," Lloyd George told Parliament, "old age, accident, sickness and unemployment. We are going to exorcise them."[52]

His budget proposed just that; it provided for a system of social insurance, including noncontributory old-age pensions, labour exchanges, and a fledgling program to provide at least some unemployment and sickness insurance. This system would be financed in part by contributions from earnings, but also from land and income taxes. The House of Lords rose as one man to veto the budget, and Prime Minister Herbert Asquith asked King Edward VII, who hated the idea, to create enough new Liberal peers to overwhelm the old Tories so as to get the budget through. Edward dithered and did nothing, so Asquith called a general election, which he won handily in January 1910, on the basis of the 1909 budget, now beefed up to include a National Health Scheme, which would be financed by workers contributing four pence, employers three pence, and the state two pence per week. The payout would be ten shillings per week to those who needed it to help pay medical bills.

The social insurance scheme was now enacted, along with legislation to provide labour exchanges, school health services and meals, remand homes, and juvenile courts for youngsters in trouble with the law. However, private charities continued to provide most of the funding for social needs, since no one could actually live for long on the ten shillings per week that was the top payout under the insurance scheme. Moreover, there was no such thing as universality; a means test, under various names, remained the only entry to assistance.

In the years between the two world wars, the pressure on private charities became insupportable as the vagaries of the economy dumped more and more of the growing population on the trash heap of unemployment. With the onset of the Great Depression, a bad situation became much worse. In the blighted regions of northern England, Scotland, and Wales, government agents contributed most of the money for the voluntary organizations that provided food and shelter for those unable to fend for themselves, and a number of politicians on both sides of the House began to wonder if, since the state was picking up the bills anyway, it mightn't be more efficient to take over the whole shooting match. Harold Laski, the socialist guru, wrote that social problems could be dealt with better "without the intervention of gracious ladies, or benevolent busybodies, or stockbrokers to whom a hospital is a hobby."[53]

THE WELFARE STATE ELBOWS OUT LADY BOUNTIFUL

The wartime coalition government turned for a plan to Sir William Beveridge, an economist and the master of University College, Oxford, to ensure that, after the war, the same deplorable conditions would not recur. The result was the Beveridge Report, officially a White Paper entitled *Social Insurance and Allied Services,* which was handed to the government in 1942. It proposed a social security system that would cover every British citizen "from the cradle to the grave." It would be funded, in the main, from taxes, and would provide a "social minimum" of income, health, housing, and education for all.[54]

The Swedes had already adopted a similar scheme, under a Social Democratic government, which threw in motherhood benefits, marital loans, and subsidies for school lunches. There was even a tax on state construction expenditures to finance the acquisition of art for Swedish public buildings, leaving charities there with very little of importance to do.[55]

The Beveridge Report did not go as far as the Swedes: the voluntary sector was still important, and was in fact encouraged. The report also led to the passage of the Education Act in 1944, providing free secondary education; the National Insurance Act in 1946, providing contributory retirement pensions, widows' pensions, maternity grants, and workmen's compensation; and the National Health Service Act in 1948, introducing comprehensive free medical care on a universal basis.

Beveridge is often called the father of the welfare state, although he was more properly its uncle, since, like most effective reformers, he borrowed most of his ideas. The implementation of his main recommendations finished the notion that social assistance was something that could be left to the charity schools, voluntary hospitals, free clinics, and church almshouses. Welfare was a right; if you qualified, you got it, by law.

There were more charities than ever, and they controlled billions of pounds of assets, but whether or not an unemployed labourer, a pregnant single mother, an ailing oldster, or an abused child received aid was no longer dependent on whether a small band of gallant volunteers had the funds, the time, the inclination, and the attention span to address the problem. The Nathan Committee, appointed in 1950 to consider the role of the voluntary sector in the welfare state, described private social services as "One of the most magnificent failures of our history."

Henceforth, the state would look after things, and the volunteers would

rally around to fill in the gaps, where required, such as the Battersea Dogs'
Home, the Benevolent Association for the Relief of Decayed Tradesmen,
or the St. Barnabas Trust for Distressed Gentlefolk, all of which have been
rolling along since early in the nineteenth century. Two of my favourites in
the still-at-the-old-hitching-post category are a trust originally set up to
combat white slavery, which now helps *au pair* girls, and another, founded
to determine whether there is an afterlife. It provides funds to hire
observers to stand by the beds of the expiring and make note of their
expressions as they pass beyond the vale. The idea is that if they smile,
there is a heaven, but the returns are not yet all in.

It is now half a century since the main elements of the welfare state
were put in place and Lady Bountiful was elbowed aside by a government
employee. They are still in place, but they are under attack in a way that
seems to me to harken back, if not to the Elizabethan Poor Law, at least to
its sour successor, the New Poor Law of 1834. We believed, for one brief,
shining moment, that poverty was not a condition that many people had
brought upon themselves but an inefficiency in the system of distributing
the profits of the economy. Today, we again believe that unemployment,
and even hunger, are the result of personal failure and that when we cut
social welfare, we are merely weeding out the bums.

That is why, in 1994, the New Democratic Party government in
Ontario, which was on the verge of bankruptcy, came up with $20 million
to hire snoopers to crack down on welfare cheats, although the only hard
evidence pointed to a loss of about $1.5 million annually to fraud. The $20
million was an investment in ideology, a downpayment on the purchase of
the philosophy that the rich are rich and the poor are poor because God
intended it that way.

The NDP in Ontario were joined at the butcher block by their successors, a Conservative regime with even longer, sharper knives and harsher
ideologies, and a federal Liberal regime that instituted the most concerted
attack on the social contract since the House of Lords got overturned back
in 1910.

Before we look at this counterrevolution, we ought to have some
account of what was going on in Canada during these centuries, so we are
in a position to examine what is going on today.

3. Maple Leaf Rags:
The Good Old Days

*Pauperism only exists because of charity and
would soon pass away if almsgiving ceased.*

—J. J. KELSO,
Poorhouses and Charity, 1905

The Elizabethan Poor Law set the tone for British North America,
although the set of laws embodied in it were imported holus-bolus by only
a few of the new colonies. As in Britain, the town or parish was responsible for levying the taxes to provide relief for the poor, and the vagrant who
turned up without visible means of support was apt to be marched out to
the town line and bid farewell. In North Carolina, there was even an ordinance, passed in 1775, to provide for whipping the wanderers before sending them off.[1] Institutionalizing the indigent was another imported
notion, and workhouses worthy of the worst of England became part of
the colonial landscape. Poverty was considered either sinful or criminal, or

both, and its cure lay in work. Cotton Mather, the savage-minded Puritan divine and cheerleader of the Salem witch hunts, wrote that it was "Not lawful for a Christian to live ordinarily without some Calling." He did allow that charity had its uses, though, in maintaining public order.

In New France, a different tradition prevailed. From the beginning, the colony was ruled with a strong, paternalistic hand from the court of France, and this included provision for the poor. In 1685, when public begging had become a problem in the developing towns, the colonial authorities established a Bureau of the Poor, whose tasks were to see that no one starved, that those capable of work were given it, and that the beggars were kept under control.[2] The parish priest was the key operative in each locality, but the main source of funding came from an annual crown grant of 6,000 *livres*. Fines levied by the local courts were often allocated to the Bureau of the Poor, and two women were appointed in each town to go door to door, seeking alms.

Almshouses were established by the end of the seventeenth century, and the old, orphaned, and infirm were moved into these. Foundlings were the responsibility of the state, and Samuel Martin, author of one of the few books on Canadian charity, relates the 1736 case of a local crown prosecutor being given the duty of obtaining a wet nurse for abandoned children and, later, finding homes to adopt them.[3] The schools, which were established and run by the clergy, also were subsidized by the crown, on condition that they should be free, a condition that did not last long.

However, the hospitals, such as they were, were entirely private charities. The first was set up in Quebec City in 1639, a gift of the Duchess D'Aigullon. It was staffed by doctors imported from France on a fee-for-service basis; the poor went without professional medical treatment, which, considering the standards of the time, was probably just as well.

The General Hospital in Montreal was taken over by the Grey Sisters, an order founded by Marguerite d'Youville in 1755, only four years before the battle of the Plains of Abraham. The order was set up under the Suplicans to serve the poor, but the townspeople, unable to think why a bunch of women would want to live by themselves and associate with the riffraff, assumed that the outfit was established to sell brandy, made in the seminary, to the Indians.[4] They invented the name Soeurs Grises as an insult; the nuns later embraced the term and now wear the colour, but when they took over the hospital as something practical to do with their time, they wore brown uniforms. Mme d'Youville designed these with a loose sleeve turned back over the wrist, for convenience in the hard, dirty work that engaged the nuns, but Bishop Briand was unhappy with the vision of women showing their bare-naked wrists to the world, so the sisters devised a washable undersleeve to keep the men from forearm-ogling, and the bishop approved the new outfit.[5]

After the British took over the colony, there was of course no more funding from the French crown, and the only extensive group of active social workers in the province were these communities of nuns. To finance their charitable activities, they turned their cells into workshops, where they produced purses, workboxes, artificial flowers, slippers, maple sugar, jam, peppermint, and biscuits, which they sold to the British merchants.

The hard-working nuns could only begin to cope with the poverty, disease, filth, and unemployment that marked the life of the underclasses in Montreal, Quebec, and Trois-Rivières. In the winter, when jobs were scarce, crowds of beggars roamed the streets, carrying bags and hoping for handouts from their neighbours.[6]

The Catholic Church was the bulwark of the French-Canadian language and culture, and defending them necessitated the rejection of state interference in the social life of the colony, for that was bound to mean domination by the Anglophone, Protestant, merchant minority. As late as 1938, a leading Catholic sociologist wrote:

> The Church lays on the faithful the personal duty of charity even unto the gift of one's self . . . It is the bounden duty of each individual to provide, according to his means, for assistance to the destitute and unfortunate, and the state should intervene only when private initiative finds it impossible to supply existing needs.[7]

As a matter of fact, private initiative found it impossible to supply existing needs through most of the province's history, but, since the shortfall was borne by the lower classes, their survival was deemed less important than the need to protect the Church against the state.

The dominance of Church charity remained a characteristic of Quebec society right up to the Quiet Revolution of Jean LeSage's government in 1960, which was, as much as anything, a revolution against the Church. Still, things did not work out much better for the poor in the rest of Canada.

THE HOUSES OF INDUSTRY

In Upper Canada, municipalities were allowed, but not required, to provide outdoor relief projects and to build "Houses of Industry," supported mainly out of local taxes, where the misfits could be tucked away out of sight as punishment for being born into the wrong class.

One of the prevailing myths of our history is that in a pioneer society, where there was always work to do, neighbour helped neighbour, and unemployment was unknown. Neighbour did help neighbour, sometimes; at other times, neighbour left neighbour to starve, to freeze, or to perish untreated, unshriven, and unsung from one of the many diseases that swept across the country from sea to shining sea.

As for employment, it varied from place to place and time to time, and included a good deal of indentured labour imported from England or orphans sold into bondage. A Kingston newspaper announced on May 7, 1836, the impending arrival of "70 boys and 30 girls" who had been "trained to habits of industry and instructed in moral and religious duties" and who could be hired for "Ten dollars per annum, Seven of which to be invested in the Savings Bank, for the future benefit of the child."[8] A kid who survived ten years of indentured labour would have a whole seventy bucks to launch him or her on the rest of life.

Those who couldn't compete in a society where a year of child labour could be bought for ten dollars might wind up in one of the Houses of Industry—"Suitable buildings for the reception of the Poor and Indigent, and of the Idle and Dissolute, where they shall be kept diligently employed in labour."[9] Providing, that is, that the town, township, or county had bothered to erect such an institution; some did, some didn't. If yours hadn't, you could move on—that was the great safety valve we had in North America, although it was available mainly to strong, young males— or survive as best you could. Domestic service, which was as near slavery as made no mind, was another alternative, but not much favoured.

The Atlantic colonies were more progressive, in theory, than either of the Canadas. Municipal assessments were mandated by law to provide funding for outdoor relief projects and a modicum of support, rather than leaving it to chance, as in the Canadas. The attitude remained the same, though, and when the flood of Loyalists came pouring into the area after the American Revolution, they were left pretty much to their own devices, except for a "Royal Bounty" of food and provisions. This was regarded as "a Relief to Indigence and a Spur to Industry" and was never to be given to "those in a position to support themselves by trade or profession, nor to the dissolute and indolent."[10] The Bounty was cut off as soon as the Loyalists were able to support themselves, and many never did get the standard food ration of a pound of flour, half a pound of salted meat, and a dab of butter per person per day.

For the blacks, escaped slaves, conditions were much worse; they received almost none of the Royal Bounty, and at Shelburne, where 3,000 of them were dumped, "Some killed and ate their dogs and cats; and poverty and distress prevailed on every side." If they were found to be "stubborn or idle," they could be shackled or whipped, and if they protested, they could be sold back into slavery.[11]

By and large, the Atlantic colonists were in no position to help the incoming horde of Loyalists; they were poor and struggling themselves. Still, it is astonishing how little was done; government was supposed to look after things, and when government declined, about all that happened was that local councils passed resolutions blaming the newcomers for almost everything. The crop failure of 1789 in Nova Scotia, which brought a famine that winter, led the town of Shelburne to take concerted action at last. The council passed a law "forbidding Negro dances and Negro Frolicks in this Town," and any blacks who danced or frolicked were charged with "riotous behaviour."[12] To the surprise of all, this did not end the famine.

PROMISCUOUS ALMSGIVING IS FATAL

Still, there were always those kind and zealous folks who did their best to help out, through outfits like the Halifax Poor Man's Friend Society, which provided wood and potatoes to that city's stricken during the winter months. The great thing about it was that "Each subscriber shall at any time be at liberty to withdraw his name,"[13] so if the whole thing became too much of a bore, you just hopped out and let the shiftless shift for themselves, or die. They were still too inculcated with the doctrines of their ancestors to shake off the conviction that wickedness and poverty went together, and that extending a helping hand was likely to do more harm than good. Or, as one nineteenth-century newspaper editorial put it:

> Promiscuous almsgiving is fatal . . . A poor law is a legislative machine
> for the manufacture of pauperism. It is true mercy to say that it would

be better that a few individuals should die of starvation than that a pauper class should be raised up with thousands devoted to crime and the victims of misery.[14]

What was really wanted was for someone else to take on the burden, and when the Salvation Army arrived in North America in the late nineteenth century, the Maritime authorities heaved a sigh of relief. After all, members of the army probably knew what they were doing, which was more than you could usually say for the kindhearted but untrained church volunteers; an editorial in the *St. John Daily Sun* made the point:

> If it sometimes happens, as we in St. John know it does, that kindly institutions unhappily are needed in our cities, they are managed more successfully by the Army than by the churches. This is due mainly to the fact that the Salvation Army has in its service a body of trained nurses, and other capable officers, who seek no reward beyond a mere subsistence, and who have no other care or interest than their religious and benevolent work. In this respect, the Army most resembles the Roman Catholic Church with its core of ministering sisterhoods.[15]

SCHOOLS AND HOSPITALS

The difficulty was that as society grew more complex, the shortcomings of private charity, even Sally Ann charity, became more obvious, especially in the area of schools and hospitals.

Egerton Ryerson, the superintendent of education in Canada West (now Ontario) from 1844 to 1876, studied a number of foreign educational methods before designing a new system for his own province. He discovered that it was quite normal to provide a minimum of schooling out of government coffers and, in 1846, proposed a property tax to finance free elementary education for all. The right-thinking element in the province were opposed on the grounds that they didn't want to have to pay for the schooling of the bratlings of the poor, and it took twenty-five years to get the tax in place. However, free education had become commonplace elsewhere by this time, and in 1871, government funding of schools became the norm.[16]

In Lower Canada (now Quebec), two state-aided school systems were established by the School Act of 1846, and, although both remained firmly under the thumbs of Catholic and Protestant religions, their financing was removed from the charitable sector to the public sector and supported by property taxes. Before the end of the century, the largest private charity, education, had become state-supported, to a lesser or greater degree, everywhere in Canada.

In the same way, the large capital costs of hospitals required the infusion of government funds to supplement what could be raised by and through wealthy individuals. The first provincial operating grant for a hospital in Upper Canada was allotted in 1830, to York General, and grants-in-aid, operating grants, building grants, and all the plethora of state funding gradually assumed the major role in building and operating these institutions, long before there was such a thing as Medicare.

There were charities by the hundreds, by the thousands, in nineteenth-century Canada, and they all competed and quarrelled. There were meetings at the provincial and national level to try to ease some of the bickering, but they never did much good. Samuel Martin writes:

> Every church and every ethnic and interest group had its own charitable society or charitable foundation, fragmenting, even balkanizing, volunteer effort. Charitable organizations in the Atlantic colonies, as well as in the Canadas, divided along religious and ethnic lines with each catering exclusively to members of its own group. This continued to occur despite attempts throughout the period by the most public-spirited citizens to promote comprehensive, non-partisan relief.[17]

Bickering and wasteful duplication are built into the charitable system; the whole point of being part of a voluntary organization is that you can quit it if you don't like what the chairman said, or don't approve of the way the money was spent, or get cheesed off because your hours of work for the annual bunfight got you only a crummy letter of thanks while Mavis Bighead, the shameless hussy, got a huge big plaque. So you start your own outfit instead. This kind of waste doesn't matter much, until we try to make charity into the major delivery system for social assistance.

Confederation in 1867 made very little difference; education and health, the two largest charitable targets, then as now, were given to the provinces, but these were not major expenditures at the time. For the next sixty years, nothing much changed, except that, as we grew more prosperous, charity became a social activity, just as it had in England: something to keep the little woman busy and out of trouble. As immigrants flooded into the West, benevolent societies sprang up to serve them, such as the Hebrew Benevolent Society in Winnipeg, which was founded in 1887 to provide relief, railway fares, and job placement for Jewish immigrants.[18]

Voluntary service became de rigueur for politicians, provided that they remembered, as one Ontario MLA put it, that "It was well known that establishments supported by voluntary contribution were invariably more efficient than those assisted by Government grants."[19] Since it was well-known, there was no need to prove this truism, and nobody ever has.

J. S. Woodsworth, a Methodist preacher who became a social worker and, much later, one of the founders of the Co-operative Commonwealth Federation, visited the homes of the poor in North Winnipeg just after the turn of the twentieth century and made notes of the appalling conditions in which many of them lived, untouched by any form of public or private assistance. There was the Yakoff family, Russian immigrants, who had four children:

> He has only one leg and acts as a caretaker in a hall for which he receives $12 a month. They live in three rented rooms for which they pay $8 a month. They keep some roomers. Pieter, the eldest boy, eight years old, has to go out along the streets and lanes where he can find sticks of wood, empty bottles, etc., for which he gets a few cents to help keep the family. Of course he does not go to school.[20]

Conducting the burial services of children who died of minor illnesses that might have been cured became a regular duty for Rev. Woodsworth. He refused to use the prescribed words "The Lord giveth and the Lord taketh away" in such ceremonies, because it appeared to him "blasphemy of the worst kind, an attempt to fasten on the Lord the responsibility for the criminal negligence of the citizens of Winnipeg."[21]

It was the failure of private charity that made Woodsworth into a politician, but he had almost no impact whatever until the Great Depression began to persuade a few Canadians at last that something more than a soup ladle and a collection plate were required to meet the exigencies of economic breakdown.

A NATION ON THE DOLE

A kind of nostalgia now washes over those days of the Great Depression, leaving us with images of neighbour aiding neighbour and everyone getting along on less, but there was nothing romantic about huddling in a shack, lining up for meagre sustenance at a soup kitchen, or freezing to death in the street—a condition the nation returned to in the winter of 1995–96. The federal government maintained throughout the Depression that social assistance was primarily a matter for the provinces, which said it was primarily a matter for the municipalities, which passed the buck to private charities, until it became evident to the meanest intelligence that hundreds of thousands of people were living in privation and despair through no fault of their own. Even then, not much happened, because the wisest of our political elders kept assuring the voters that the economy was about to correct itself and that to interfere with the right of the poor to suffer was willful disobedience to the will of God, or worse, the Market.

Almost the only government assistance in place was a $20-a-month pension, payable to those over seventy years of age who could prove they were destitute. This had been forced on the minority Mackenzie King government by J. S. Woodsworth and his small band of western MPs; it was the only program of social legislation passed at the federal level during the 1930s.[22] Ottawa agreed, under the Old Age Pension Act of 1927, to share the cost of providing this pittance with the provinces; by 1930, the four western provinces and Ontario had taken it up, but there was nothing east of the Ottawa River except municipal relief and private charity.[23]

As unemployment soared, people began to lose their homes, livelihood, health, and families—thousands of which were broken up because the men took off, either to rid themselves of the burden or because it was the only way their families would be eligible for relief. The federal and provincial governments spent most of their time trying to shuffle the burden off onto the other level, and the private charities were simply overwhelmed.

In Toronto, hundreds of tramps roamed from door to door, begging for food, or work, or money; they slept in the parks, in the brickyards, and on the floors and benches of restrooms (we've fixed this: public restrooms are now mostly locked at night). They lined up for hours to receive "wrapped lunches" from charitable ladies in community halls. They shuffled hopelessly through the streets or took off and rode the rails, leaving their wives and children to the mercy of handouts in tin cups on street corners. And when the system broke down entirely under the strain, the private agencies were forced to direct their clients to the House of Industry at 87 Elm Street, where, every morning, 4,000 people lined up to receive a bag of groceries. It contained about $2.50 worth of food, which was said to be, but was not, enough to feed a family of five for a week.[24]

Ontario, the richest province, had decided to let the municipalities carry the load the province would not take on, at whatever level they chose. In 1938, when a "Standard of Relief" was finally established, it set the maximum, not the minimum, the local authority would provide, at $5.00 worth of food per week for a family of five, $8.25 for a family of ten. There was no nutritional rationale for this allotment; it came from the brain of H. L. McNally, sales manager of National Grocers, and sounded about right to him. The ceiling for housing allowances was set at the same time at $15 per month.[25]

ALONG WITH THE HELP, HUMILIATION

The Canadian Red Cross and churches collected and distributed food and clothing. The Saskatchewan Voluntary Relief Committee—and other such committees in every province—distributed gifts and donations, and developed a voucher system to help the poor buy needed articles. The humiliation, for most of those who needed this help, was unbearable; they knew, because they were constantly told, that their presence on the dole was a mark of personal failure, and that, as W. K. Baldwin, the Liberal MP for Baldwin's Mills, Quebec, insisted, "there is work in Canada for anyone who wants it."[26] (Baldwin wanted anyone who wouldn't work deported and cited the example set by that fine fellow Benito Mussolini: "In Italy, the chief ruler makes the people stay on the land.") So, they lined up, or they begged, or they stole, because the ramshackle system of voluntary aid was swamped.

When the burden of relief was shifted to governments with the collapse of private charity, these bodies were determined to ensure that nobody got away with anything; the emphasis was on "works relief," where the "Sturdy Beggars" could hack and hew for their supper. However, this system soon broke down as well, because it was not possible to organize and finance public works on the scale necessary to begin to meet the problem. In one Ontario project, relief applicants were put to work levelling a hill and filling in a hollow.[27] (The modern counterpart of this sort of idiocy occurs in cities where low-income families are forced out of rental housing by cuts in government support, then are placed in motel rooms by the city welfare department, at a cost far higher than the withdrawn support.)

As municipalities were plunged into bankruptcy because their tax bases had vanished with the jobs, their relief duties were inherited by the provinces, and soon they, too, were threatened with bankruptcy. It became clear that the Dominion government could either step in or stand by and see the provinces slide into insolvency, which would make it difficult for the government to borrow anywhere, because the bond market would dry up. So, Ottawa moved on reluctant feet and took over much of the financing of relief through the Dominion Unemployment Relief Act, which, while disclaiming any federal constitutional responsibility, did appropriate $20 million to aid the junior governments. By 1937, Ottawa was spending more than twice this on direct relief, but the problem only grew worse.[28]

In Saskatchewan, the pitiful medical services then being provided to the impoverished were curtailed when many of the doctors themselves went on relief.[29] A Red Cross worker travelling the province found a family of nine children near Shaunavon dressed in gunnysacks. One child had died, and another wanted to commit suicide. At Bone Creek, a family of eleven lived in a one-room shack so flimsy that drinking water froze in the pail.[30] There was very little the Red Cross worker could do, except report the pitiable facts.

The jobless were not, it turned out, just goofing off; nor were they the old, ill, and handicapped. In 1936, the *Historical Statistics of Canada* showed, two out of three of those on relief were "employables."[31] However, there was still to be no free lunch; all these hearty slackers were to put their shoulders to the wheel. Through the Department of Defence, the federal government took over the operation of the provincial relief camps across the country. (Today, we call it workfare.) The camps would get some of the tramps off the trains and out of the cities by having them cut brush and improve railway overpasses, rake leaves, or do whatever else the local overseers could come up with, for twenty cents a day per man.[32] Of course, the men had to be separated from their families to live high on the hog like this, in tents or huts.

The system was an unmitigated disaster, as the layabouts in the camps, instead of showing proper gratitude for the generosity of their betters, began to agitate for social and economic reform. There were marches and protests and placard-waving, and agitators who said rude things about their overlords. The protests culminated in the "On to Ottawa" trek of relief-camp workers from British Columbia in June 1935. More than 1,000 protestors decided to ride the rails east to lay their complaints before Prime Minister R. B. Bennett. They were stopped by the RCMP in Regina, after a riot in which one detective was killed. Many of the leaders were arrested without warrant and deported without trial.[33]

The trek had been derailed, but a growing sense of unease, reflected in the emergence of two new political parties in the West, the Canadian Commonwealth Federation and Social Credit, and the Union Nationale in Quebec, suggested that not everyone accepted the inevitability of depression as a necessary trade-off for our wonderful economic system. By 1936, eight out of the nine provincial governments had been replaced by the voters, opening up the possibility that politicians might have to listen to the voices of discontent after all. As T. C. Haliburton wrote, "Nothin' improves a man's manners like an election."[34]

As the costs of relief spending grew, they were accompanied by the belief, still with us, which holds that most of the money goes to ne'er-do-wells, welfare cheats, and foreigners. The Ontario government of George Henry sent relief inspectors out to track down the rascals; one of them reported that in Hamilton, the supervisor of relief, one Sam Lawrence, was "a labour man . . . even a Red." He was committing the unpardonable sin of distributing relief "according to individual circumstances," rather than following the minimum guidelines. Being a Red, Sam had "foreign friends," who were "well stocked with all they asked for." While none of these things could be proven, who needed proof when everybody knew that foreigners living in Hamilton were getting allowances for family members "probably living in Central Europe"?[35] As in our own modern demonology, these unsubstantiated anecdotes were enough to convince many of the taxpaying populace that government support simply was being thrown away, so there was very little sustained pressure for its expansion, except by the larger and larger army of victims. This was the view of Prime Minister R. B. Bennett, a rich corporate lawyer who knew where the real problem lay:

> The people are not bearing their share of the load. Half a century ago people would work their way out of their difficulties rather than

look to a government to take care of them. The fibre of some of our people has grown softer and they are not willing to turn in and save themselves.[36]

When Bennett was finally moved to take some action, by the certainty that he would be defeated next time out if he did nothing, he borrowed elements of the New Deal of U.S. President Franklin D. Roosevelt. Bennett actually introduced sweeping legislation, including a Prices Commission, the Bank of Canada Act, the Wheat Board Act, the Companies Act, and an Employment and Social Insurance Act. Unemployment insurance was backed by a number of major banks for the same reason the Tudors had backed almshouses—to keep the rabble in line. Sir Charles Gordon, president of both the Bank of Montreal and Dominion Textiles, wrote a letter to Bennett in early 1934 deploring the "waste" of municipal spending on relief and worrying that these costs might lead to bankruptcies. To restore stability to the system and "for our own general self-preservation," he recommended a scheme of unemployment insurance, which would not only steady the working classes but would remove some of the strain before the whole system collapsed.[37]

Bennett was impressed. He believed, as did many business leaders of the time, that workers, unlike corporations, did not have the sense to save against a rainy day, so a contributory scheme that was, in effect, a forced savings plan would save everybody money in the long run.[38] Alas, the legislation, along with many other reforms, was declared *ultra vires* by the Judicial Committee of the Privy Council in England, and Bennett was defeated in October 1935, by Mackenzie King, on a promise of—does this have a familiar ring?—"fiscal restraint" and a balanced budget "within a reasonable time."[39]

Except for closing the relief camps and adding more cash to direct relief programs, the King government did very little until public agitation reached the point where King's own political survival hung in the balance.

WAR, NOT CHARITY, MET THE PROBLEMS OF THE POOR

It was the arrival of the Second World War that provided jobs, and if there was one lesson to come out of the Great Depression, it was that, despite what were often magnificent individual efforts, charities and their army of volunteers could not contend with the results of widespread economic displacement. The lesson went almost entirely unheeded. When another depression struck in the late 1940s, we were hardly better equipped to deal with it.

A 1947 study for the Department of Health and Welfare reported that most of Canada had not advanced beyond the local poor-relief stage of public aid for needy persons: "The provisions for general assistance are limited, mean and inadequate . . . They are literally disgraceful and unworthy of a nation of Canada's status."[40] Until 1949, there was no provision whatever to pay relief to the "employable unemployed," because, as we all knew, it was their own fault. In Nova Scotia and New Brunswick, "Overseers of the Poor" would refuse relief to paupers in their own homes "if accommodation in the local almshouse was available."[41]

However, the world was now beginning to be swept with the radical notions that had come out of Europe, via England. A copy of the Beveridge Report was brought over from England in 1943, and Dr. Leonard Marsh, a social sciences professor at McGill University, was commissioned to prepare a document on "Social Security for Canada," which he did, recommending many of the same reforms.[42] The only one that survived was the Family Allowance, introduced in 1944.

King kept the rest of the goodies on hand for the next election and had the Cockfield Brown advertising agency produce a series of pamphlets offering "womb-to-tomb" security—old-age pensions, health insurance, unemployment aid, and housing subsidies—which helped him to win the 1945 election handily.[43] Then he put the entire program away and forgot about it.

However, in Saskatchewan, the CCF under Tommy Douglas had lunged into power and introduced hospital insurance in 1947. The Ottawa Liberals, and even some Conservatives, began to shift positions to forestall the left-wingers, advancing just enough to convince mainstream voters that capitalism could accommodate change; we didn't need socialism.

Still, when the government passed the first Unemployment Insurance Act in 1949, it was not because Ottawa had embraced the welfare state but was inspired mainly by a federal strategy to bully the provinces into giving up, permanently, the tax powers they had surrendered during wartime. In return for provincial support for a constitutional amendment that made unemployment a federal responsibility, Ottawa agreed to provide a minimum, limited payment to workers who had been laid off through no fault of their own and could prove it. They and their employers paid into an insurance fund; for the first time, Canadians did not have to be entirely destitute—only out of work—to receive relief.

THE RIGHT TO WELFARE

The winter of 1949 brought the highest level of unemployment since the Depression, and that led to a series of conferences between federal and provincial officials to see what could and should be done. Very little, it turned out. The bureaucrats and politicians could not agree on a common policy, but then, thank God, along came another war, this time in Korea, and the problem was solved again, temporarily, as the workless went back to the factories to build bombs.

The notion that any time economic malaise becomes too much for the charitable system, there should be another war, did not recommend itself to the more thoughtful of our political observers. Thus, when another "recession"—we were beginning to change the language to distinguish the normal periodic downturns, in which only a few hundred thousands lost their jobs, from real economic malaise—struck in early 1954, the apostles of discontent began to find a ready audience within the mainstream parties. At the same time, government bureaucrats, allied with the Canadian Welfare Council, began to press for comprehensive welfare "rights," including a legal right to health and welfare assistance anywhere in the country.

The guardians of conventional wisdom were appalled. A legal right to relief, notes Canadian historian James Struthers, constituted "a doctrinaire formula forming part of the Marxist canon," which could only come about "in a socialist state."[44] Nothing was done.

By March 1954, a record 570,000 Canadians were out of work, and "people were actually suffering hunger because of unemployment."[45] At this time, the unemployment insurance fund had accumulated almost one billion dollars surplus to any estimated need, by restricting access to the funds. (The same patterns are being repeated today; by early 1996, what is now "employment insurance" was substantially in the black, with more than a million Canadians out of work.) The government of Louis St. Laurent, who had replaced King, responded that "unemployment was mostly seasonal" and that helping the victims was "not beyond the capacity of local communities."[46] But the local communities would only pay relief "to those who are starving,"[47] soup kitchens were reopening, vagrants were being shipped out of town by train, and families were again being broken up by the desertion of husbands and fathers so the rest of the family could collect relief. In Vancouver, British Columbia Premier W. A. C. Bennett told St. Laurent that the charitable organizations "had exhausted their funds," and the same was true in most major cities.[48]

The Liberals refused to call a federal-provincial conference even to discuss the situation. Finance Minister Walter Harris explained that "If the federal government took such an initiative the other governments would immediately expect it to bear a share of the cost of any solution." In response, the Canadian Welfare Council, made up of social workers, academics, and other troublemakers, launched a publicity campaign, with pamphlets outlining the suffering in the cities and the inability of private charities to meet the emergency. Then it called the conference Ottawa refused to call. That was going to be embarrassing, so St. Laurent finally agreed to a series of meetings that resulted in the Unemployment Assistance Act of 1956, which, as Struthers notes, "marked the first permanent federal commitment to social assistance for employables on welfare and provided a crucial bridgehead into the wider welfare reforms of the 1960s."[49]

Government assistance was not a matter for shame; it was part of the package of civilization, and this concept led, as all the right thinkers had said all along that it would, to an astonishing extension of government programs at every level, which marginalized the work of all those thousands of charities out there. The charities kept on working, and indeed multiplying and performing many worthwhile tasks; but they were no longer key elements of the welfare system, if indeed they ever had been.

In an astonishingly short time—between 1956 and 1975—Canada became a modern welfare state. We had the Unemployment Assistance Act in 1956; federal hospital insurance in 1957; Saskatchewan's Medical Care Insurance Act in 1962; the Canada Pension Plan in 1965; the Canada Assistance Plan in 1966 and the Guaranteed Income Supplement a year later; federal aid to education in 1967; federal Medicare in 1968; major changes to unemployment insurance in 1970; provincial supplements to the elderly, beginning in British Columbia in 1972; major changes to family allowances and the CPP and Quebec Pension Plan in 1973; and Spouses' Allowances in 1975.

THE CANADA ASSISTANCE PLAN

The Canada Assistance Plan was perhaps the key to shucking off the claims of Lady Bountiful; it came into effect on April 1, 1966,[50] and was intended to bring together a patchwork of federal and provincial programs into a general plan to assist anyone who needed help. The provinces would administer the funds, with the federal government sharing the cost. Coverage would be by way of a "needs test" rather than a "means test." The distinction is that, with a means test, your eligibility is determined by how much you have in assets and income from other sources. If you have other money, your public support is either reduced or eliminated according to an exact scale.[51] With a needs test, the issue is whether or not you must have the money in order to maintain a decent standard of living, and the preamble to the act said that the assistance must be "adequate." That's a lovely, vague term, but it clearly meant that how you got to be poor was not anyone's concern; if you needed help, you were to get it, and on a scale that was related to your needs, whether you were a pensioner, disabled, or simply out of work.

When the Guaranteed Income Supplement was added, it meant that any Canadian living on a pension was assured of a minimum income, no matter what. The rest of the package ensured, and was meant to ensure, that Canadians would have a job when they could work and a benefit when they could not,[52] and, by 1975, that is roughly what we had.

By that time, the notion that poverty was a sin had received some hard—but not, it would turn out, fatal—knocks. Most Canadians were beginning to believe that it was normal and natural for the state, not charity, to take on the main burden of undoing some of the damage caused by an economic system that, whatever its other virtues, makes no pretence at fairness. We had become, and we were proud (some of us, for some time) to have become, a modern welfare state. I have only seen one definition of this vague term that struck me as satisfactory:

> A Welfare State is a state in which organized power is deliberately used, through policies and administration, in an effort to modify the play of market forces in three directions—first, by guaranteeing individuals and families a minimum income irrespective of the market value of their work or their property; second, by narrowing the extent of insecurity by enabling individuals and families to meet certain

social contingencies (for example, sickness, old age and unemployment), which would otherwise lead to individual and family crises; and third, by ensuring that all citizens, without distinction of status or class, are offered the best standards available in relation to a certain agreed range of social services.[53]

We thereafter convinced ourselves that we had always been a kinder, gentler people, that it was in our nature, and forgot almost entirely the centuries-long struggle that brought us to this point.

I set down all this history for one reason alone: we must understand that, in asking charities to take on the tasks government has fulfilled for the past few decades, we are heading back down a blind alley, one where we have already bumped our noses on the bricks. Government was burdened with the responsibility for social services precisely because we found—as had other nations—that the voluntary sector, with the best will in the world, simply cannot do the job, and its failure is counted in shattered lives, social disruption, and political turmoil. The pattern has been repeated time and again; when economic disaster strikes, the gallant troops of charity march out in serried ranks, work like hell, and retire in confusion and despair. Only after we had been through this process three times in the first fifty years of this century did we begin to put to work the lessons learned in other lands, and then, and only then, did public pressure and the fear of being outflanked by opposition parties force reluctant governments to grasp the nettle and pass laws that a few years earlier their ministers had dismissed as impossibly utopian at best, or seditiously communistic at worst. They didn't want to do it, most of the time, but they did it because the alternative was to get chucked out of office. It was called "pandering to the multitudes" or "buying voters with their own money" every time a government successfully adopted a social reform. It is also called democracy, the process by which a minority (nowadays, an interest group) of determined disciples manages to persuade enough voters to raise hell so that the government has to listen. It is the opposite of timorous charity.

There is no long-standing tradition of government support or inherent decency behind our social safety net; it was stitched together piecemeal, over the years, out of borrowed materials, by reluctant weavers, which is why, when it began to come apart, the strands parted so swiftly.

4. Goodbye Welfare:
A Very Mean Society

*We must ask ourselves what people experience on
realizing that social assistance benefits are neither
obtainable nor adequate. For them, at that point
in time, there is no public safety net. It has indeed
collapsed. They have no rights, no citizenship.*

—GRAHAM RICHES,
Feeding Canada's Poor, 1987

Lynne Toupin is the executive director of a charity, the National Anti-
Poverty Organization, centred in Ottawa but active across the country. She
is a tall, slender woman, very bright, articulate, and fired with what I can
only call a contained zeal that strikes me as somehow quintessentially
Canadian. She has a cause, something she feels very deeply about, but it
would not do to shout, wave her arms, flash her eyes, or carry on as if the
things that are so desperate, so charged with emotion, matter so much.

Sitting in her sparely furnished office, which overlooks the dubious beau-
ties of the east end of Ottawa, I ask her, "What is the charitable object of
your organization?"

She replies, in a level voice, "To eliminate poverty."

"Oh," I say, "and how's it going?"

"Not too well," she says, and gives a short, barking laugh. "As you can
see, not too well at all."

NAPO grew out of a conference of poor people in Toronto in 1971, a
conference not of social workers, academics, or others *representing* poor
people, but of poor people themselves. They hitchhiked, bummed rides,
borrowed train or plane fare, and even got a little money from the government to help put on the conference. They got, and still get, federal funding
which provides half the $600,000 annual NAPO budget, for reasons that
Toupin explains:

> This whole notion of providing support for outfits like ours derived
> through the environmental movement, because the government was
> being besieged by large companies who could put up a battalion of
> lobbyists and PR people to fight any attempt to establish decent envi-
> ronmental controls. Every time a committee met to consider a new
> measure, it was inundated with these guys, waving slick brochures.
> The MPs realized they were only hearing from one side, because only
> one side could afford the freight. So, they decided they had to even
> out the playing field, and began to give grants to organizations which
> would otherwise have no effective voice.[1]

NAPO has an effective voice; it is, as a senior bureaucrat explained to me
once I had turned my tape recorder off, "a royal pain in the ass," because it
is always getting up petitions, holding rallies, buttonholing MPs, besieging
parliamentary committees, turning out pamphlets that say in the same
measured tones that Toupin uses to me, that the feds are not, after all,
doing a good job of looking after Canada's social welfare system; they are
doing a lousy job, and it is getting worse. The organization has a legiti-
macy about it that makes it hard to attack; the twenty-two members of the
board who make the day-to-day decisions are nearly all poor, or close to it.
Currently, sixteen of them live below Canada's official poverty line. When
they hold meetings, in the cheapest halls they can find, with no banquets

and no frills, the delegates from ten provinces and two territories are nearly all poor, too, and none of them arrives in a corporate jet or an executive limousine. When they pass resolutions, they are usually based on solid research. They know what they are talking about, when it comes to poverty, in a way that none of the outside experts who have set all the standards and made all the rules for so many years can possibly match; you cannot shout them down, you cannot sneer them away, you cannot shut them up.

I think it is heartening that we have a system that makes the government pick up part of the tab for a charity whose main function is to be a pain in the ass, and which allows that pain in the ass a charitable number so that it can issue tax receipts to people who want to help it become a bigger pain in the ass. But I can see, and Lynne Toupin can see, that this benevolence may be coming to an end, because we live in a very different world from the one that spawned NAPO in the first place.

In 1971, we were a bumptious bunch, with a prime minister, Pierre Elliott Trudeau, willing to instruct the entire world in how matters ought to be conducted, with a social safety net as advanced as any in the Western world, except those in France and the Scandinavian countries, and far ahead of anything available in the big backward nation to the south of us. We certainly had plenty of poor people, despite a wonderfully wacky War on Poverty conducted by the previous government, that of Lester Pearson, in the days when people actually believed you could make war on poverty, and defeat it, too. Even if we didn't win that war, there was a growing list of remedies to aid the indigent, and they were based on the notion that such aid was a right, not a favour.

NAPO set up a headquarters in Ottawa precisely because this was where so many of the crucial decisions were made about what kind of society Canada was and would become. The federal government was taking a larger and larger role in welfare, unemployment insurance, pensions, family support, and post-secondary education. It was the ultimate guarantor of the welfare state. How could the earnest souls of NAPO know that the gods, always known for a twisted sense of humour, were about to reverse the process?

Many Canadians—not most, but enough—believed then that those who fell between the cracks of our economic system deserved support for as long as it took to get them back on their feet again, and believed that the stricken, or most of them, would get back on their feet, in time, and would contribute again to the system that helped them out. What a lark! What a zany bunch we were, to be sure. Today, most Canadians believe that we cannot possibly afford to pay for the social welfare system we constructed in those mad years, and that if we don't do it in, it will do us in.

There is a nice irony in the fact that much of the argument, on this side, comes from two other charities, the C. D. Howe Institute, centred in Toronto, and the Fraser Institute, centred in Vancouver, which have ten times the heft and represent hundreds of thousands of times the money available to NAPO, but who have almost no idea what it is like to live in poverty, only very firm opinions that it is much better for an increasing number of us to live that way than it is to try to get any more cash out of their clientele in the corporate sector. They have won this argument; it is now received wisdom, even in the charitable sector, that no more public money will be forthcoming, that, like it or not, the social safety net will be shredded because we can no longer afford it.

THE RISE OF CORPORATE WELFARE BUMS

Gordon Floyd, Director of Public Affairs for the Canadian Centre for Philanthropy—another charity, and the repository of most of the nation's reliable information about charities—says the notion that we cannot afford to maintain the social safety net because it would mean higher taxes "strikes me at first glance as a lot of self-serving baloney." But, he adds, "I don't think any of us can simply dismiss the rules of a global marketplace and the need to be competitive in fiscal policy."[2]

Or, to put in another way, if baloney is all that is being served, it is what the Canadian electorate is going to eat, at least for the foreseeable future. Toupin told me:

> If three years ago someone had told me that we would see what we are seeing today in terms of poor-bashing, I would have said, "You're dreaming." But it has happened with a rapidity that alarms me, and one of the things we have to deal with is the idea that the people who are poor are somehow to blame. It has become a very mean society."[3]

Because the social safety net is an economic issue, we tend to assume that these are matters of incredible complexity best left to the experts, though the dismal science of economics is as vague and nutty as numerology. However, it seems to me that what has happened to dry up the funds that were once available to government, the process that dumped the despairing into the laps of charity, is quite simple. I can even put a date to it: June 18, 1971, when Finance Minister Edgar Benson brought in his "tax reform" budget.

The background to that budget was a sharp battle over the "fairness" of the tax system, initiated by an accountant, Kenneth Carter, whose Royal Commission Report[4] on taxation opted for an approach that would put all income on the same basis—"A buck is a buck."

In other words, you would pay the same rate of tax on all income, whether it came by way of salary, expenses, interest, dividends, or capital gains. This was about as well received in the nation's boardrooms as a tag day for Karl Marx; it ran directly counter to the argument of futurist Herman Khan that the nation state was at an end, that multinational corporations were to be the new engines of progress, and that, therefore, a tax regime must be structured for the benefit of these giants.

This notion had been part of the American Dream since the William Paley Commission of 1950 argued that American economic growth—and, by extension, "Nothing less than the survival of the human spirit against the threat of Communist world domination"—demanded a tax system that would allow multinational corporations (for which read U.S. corporations) to take over the resources of other nations. In the 1954 U.S. budget, companies were permitted, for the first time, to write off against U.S. taxes the costs, including the interest costs, of acquiring the shares of other corporations abroad. This allowed American firms, which paid tax at a rate of 50 per cent, to buy the corporations of other nations, such as Canada, for half price. The other half came from the American public purse. This change led to the mushrooming of American companies around the globe; mergers, takeovers, plant closings, and the centralization of decision-making became characteristic of multinational corporations in the new global economy.

For this system to work efficiently, nation states must not interfere with the free movement of goods, capital, or intellectual capital, else the economy would collapse. It followed that there must be rough parity between the fiscal (tax) regimes of industrial nations, or any company that felt that it was paying too much in one country would simply up stakes and move to another. And, though it was never spelled out, it also followed that all nations would have to have roughly parallel social welfare systems, because any nation that offered more than another in the way of help would impose higher taxes on its corporate sector to pay for them, and they would up stakes, etc. QED.

This theory was put in its bluntest terms by George W. Ball, former undersecretary of state in the Carter administration and later chairman of Lehman Brothers International:

> In order to survive, man must use the world's resources in the most effective manner. This can be achieved only when all the factors for the production and use of goods—capital, labour, raw materials, plant facilities and distribution—are freely mobilized and deployed according to the most effective pattern. And this in turn will be possible only when national boundaries no longer play a critical role in defining economic horizons.[5]

Canada rejected this argument; we had a different economy, a different approach to the social responsibilities of the state and the community, and we did not want to become part of the American corporate empire. By 1971, however, we had changed our minds. Not coincidentally, by 1971, more than 60 per cent of our manufacturing sector was owned abroad (three-quarters of it by Americans), along with 99.7 per cent of petroleum and coal products, 82.3 per cent of mineral fuels, 81.3 per cent of chemicals, and 62.8 per cent of mining.[6] The heights of the Canadian economy all belonged to outsiders. Many of the takeovers had been funded in the first place by the American taxpayer; the rest came from the earnings of the captured companies.

When the Canadian government consulted our business sector on what to do, it was, in fact, consulting *their* business sector, and their business sector told the government to do what the Americans had already done, or lose out in the global economic race. So it did. The 1971 budget allowed Canadian corporations to write off the costs, including interest costs, of purchasing the shares of other corporations against earnings, on the grounds that only in this way would they be able to compete effectively— "on an even footing with foreign corporations" is the way Benson put it.[7]

Of course, that wouldn't do much good if the Canadian firms were still at a huge disadvantage in the area of taxes, so the same budget set up a complex system of write-offs that transferred, deferred, or delayed corporate taxes through rules that, for example, gave a huge tax break to any company that invested in plant and equipment, and substituted capital for labour. A company could write off more than 100 per cent of the cost of equipment, then depreciate the equipment at more than it cost, so that the tax was never due. It paid to fire people, so companies did, while chanting the other part of the economic mantra: This is the way to prosperity. Economist Eric Kierans was a member of the Trudeau cabinet which approved the Benson budget, and his disapproval of it drove him to resign.

He explained the reasons for his resignation to me, in characteristically blunt fashion, on the road to Montreal, the day he quit. I was covering Parliament for *Maclean's* magazine at the time; when I found out about his decision, I telephoned his Ottawa office and offered him a lift back to his home, then in Westmount, where he was to talk things over with his riding association. What I actually meant was that my wife, Joan, would drive, while I sat in the back seat of our car and interviewed him on a tape recorder. "As long as you're not driving," is all he said. We picked him up outside the Centre Block, and I asked the crucial question about why he quit just about the time we hit Wellington Street, or, to put it another way, one hundred yards from the start of the trip. He responded with a long, acute analysis of the Trudeau government and ended up with the Benson budget:

> It was a bribe to build factories in a hell of a hurry, but the effect was to discriminate against labour and in favour of capital. If you're going to build a factory for $2 million that employs fifty people and this thing comes along, you figure that maybe you can build a factory with more machinery in it that employs only thirty-eight people. It may not be the best way in the long run to manage the plant, but it gets you a tax gift of $450,000, so you do it that way.[8]

Kierans had been an enthusiastic proponent of the liberal—and Liberal—policies that built the welfare state in Canada. Tom Kent, as a senior policy adviser to Lester Pearson and later deputy minster to Jean Marchand, had been one of the main architects of those policies. He quit, too: "I left Ottawa in 1971 because I could not live with a government whose economic policies were inducing unemployment."[9]

Kierans later calculated that, by 1984, the provisions of the 1971 budget amounted to a "gift from the taxpayer to the large companies" of $27.6 billion per annum and rising.[10] The federal government was pushing two absolutely contradictory policies at the same time: one to reaffirm and consolidate an expansive social policy, the other to ape an American approach heading quite the other way. Before long, the cash drain imposed on behalf of what NDP leader David Lewis called the nation's "corporate welfare bums" settled the issue. It remained only to rewrite history to show that it was the excessive cost of the social programs that caused their demise, and it is that fable that has been swallowed whole.

In short, one place the money really went was to corporations, most of them owned outside of Canada. When the accelerated depreciation gimmick was played out, a dozen dubious replacements were hustled into place to guard our corporate giants from the pain of taxes. We may disagree as to whether this was a good or bad thing, or simply inevitable, but it takes no economic training to see what the effect was on national public income of the decision to hand over the keys to the treasury to the corporate sector.

The 1995 issue of *The Canadian Global Almanac* shows that, in 1970, the year before the "tax reform," Ottawa collected $35,480.8 million from Canadians in income taxes. Of this, individuals paid $24,739.7 million, or 69.7 per cent (in 1950, individuals paid 47.8 per cent); corporations paid $9,945.1 million, or 28.0 per cent.[11] (The figures do not quite add to 100 per cent, because some tax was withheld on payments to persons outside the country; these are not broken down by individuals or corporations.)

In 1993, the latest year for which tax returns have been analysed, individuals paid $83,989.6 million and corporations $6,537.5 million. Our share had gone up to 91.8 per cent; theirs had gone down to 7.1 per cent. We, the people, had had a tax hike of 339 per cent; they, the companies, had had a tax cut of 35 per cent. If the corporations had paid taxes at the same level in 1993 as in 1970—that is, if their income tax had risen by 339 per cent over twenty-three years, as ours did, they would have paid $83,867.6 billion in 1993. There would have been a considerable surplus, rather than a deficit, in every year in between, as well, because interest payments on the national debt would have been wiped out. And before you say how unreasonable that is, can you buy anything today for 35 per cent less than you paid in 1970?

The provincial governments followed suit, so that, today, in the entire tax regime, individuals pay more than 90 per cent and corporations less than 10 per cent.[12] We could restore the national books to a credit position simply by increasing corporate taxes and shifting some of the burden back to them.

Well, of course, that's just dreaming, because we have been told, and do in part believe, that we cannot raise taxes on the corporations or they will leave. Globalization is now an accomplished fact, and we are already its victims. In 1980, three-quarters of the manufactured products sold in this country were made here; today, the figure is less than 40 per cent.[13] Any lip from government, and the gang will simply ship more of the work down to the *maquiladoras* along the Mexican border, where the workers are paid two dollars a day. Thus, the ever-rising costs of the social safety net have been transferred to individuals, until we can't raise taxes on them any more, or they will scream—and worse, vote.

TEMPTING WITH HONEY, DRIVING WITH WHIPS

We are stuck with the proposition that more and more of the national income has to be shovelled into the pockets of fewer and fewer people. Curious, really. Apparently, Canadian society is made up of two distinct species, some of whom work at their best when tempted with honey, and the rest when driven with whips. Those in the first, much smaller, group, have to be given more money to encourage them to save and invest, and so they can work at their greatest productive efficiency. We do this through the tax system. Those in the other, much larger, group have to make do with less to encourage them to save and invest, and so they can work at their greatest productive efficiency. We do this through the employment system. Thus, it is wrong for a factory hand, or a farmer, or a welfare recipient, or a government employee, or a social worker, to ask for more money. That makes us less competitive in the global economy. However, it is right to pay a baseball player $6 million, or the head of a corporation who has just bounced a few thousand employees out onto the street a bonus of $2 million. That makes us more competitive. In the same way, money spent on education, training nurses, building hospitals, or raising the salaries of social workers is wasted, or worse, inflationary; whereas money paid as bonuses to corporate executives will make them think harder and work better, and is money well spent.

The difference between the two groups of citizens is easily detected; the first, or honey bunch, ride around in Cadillacs, and the second, or whip contingent, do not.

There is a certain crushing inevitability about the situation in which we find ourselves today. Having decided that our corporations had to be given all the goodies they would get elsewhere, we could not tax them with anything like the rigour that once we did, or they would go away mad. That left a shortfall in the national income of some $40 billion annually, which we call the deficit. That forced us to raise money, rather shadily, when you think about it, through sales taxes and fees and levies, which are not called taxes, but really are. Still, that left us short. It also left us cranky, because all these extras are regressive; they cost the middle class much more in proportion than the rich, because the tax is level, but the incomes are not.

Since we were short of funds, and cranky, and unable to set things right through the fiscal system, we were left with only one option—say it all together, now: "Cut government spending."

It is at this point that we decided that we could no longer afford the social safety net; at this point that the federal government slashed transfer payments to the provinces and the provinces dumped the deficit on the backs of the municipalities; at this point that everybody, at all levels, began to hack away at education, health, and welfare costs.

The real, hard, bottom-line justification for this is that we have neither the will nor, I guess, the power, any more, to reverse the process we began in 1971.[14]

David Crane, the *Toronto Star*'s economics editor and a sensible fellow, argues that "An increase in corporate taxes could shift more Canadian investment to the United States, affecting jobs in Canada." His solution is to give the companies more goodies: "It is only through an increase in Canada's wealth-creating capacity, which means boosting our companies that produce tradeable goods and services, that we will be able to afford our social programs."[15] Apparently, there is a saturation point, as yet undefined, when the leaders of our corporate sector will decide that they have taken enough out of the trough and allow an expansion of social programs once more. Possibly with the help of the tooth fairy. The ideology of global competition has swamped common sense, and we truly believe we have no choice but to make cuts in social welfare.

To justify the cuts, we have gone back to the old mythology, our rich inheritance from Elizabethan times: the poor are to blame. President Ronald Reagan made up a welfare widow who was, he said, collecting over $100,000 a year by milking the system. He could never produce her as she didn't exist, but she has joined the mythical legions of bums and crooks whose defalcations justify cracking down on welfare recipients and turning them over to the tender, but strained, mercies of charity. This is where Reagan always believed they belonged; welfare would work just as well, and cost much less, if it were voluntary:

> I just have faith in the American people that, if through some set of circumstances welfare did disappear tomorrow, no one would miss a meal. The people in this country, in every community all over, would get together, form emergency committees, and take up the slack.[16]

The reporter on whom Reagan laid this theory noted, "Just why, in a country in which thousands of people still go to bed hungry each night, despite a welfare program, such community action has not occurred, Reagan did not say."[17]

George Bush, who had denounced Reagan's "voodoo economics," then adopted them, setting his nation aglow with the "thousand points of light" that would replace state support:

> This is America: the Knights of Columbus, the Grange, Hadassah, the Disabled American Veterans, the Order of Ahepa, the Business and Professional Women of America, the union hall, the Bible study group, LULAC, Holy Name—a brilliant diversity spreading like stars, like a thousand points of light in a broad and peaceful sky.[18]

Georgie bids us shine, with a clear, pure light, and please don't expire on the sidewalk. That was during the 1988 U.S. presidential campaign, but many of Canada's political leaders are saying the same thing today, though not quite so bluntly: Don't fuss about what is happening to the disadvantaged as benefits tumble; charity will kiss the place and make it well. We can afford to give the breaks to the business sector, and we can't afford not to.

There is a nice symmetry about these things; for every cut in corporate taxes, a few thousand more Canadians get fired out the door. The layabouts who clog up the aisles of our churches on winter nights are direct beneficiaries of the lower taxes paid by companies, and would no doubt be grateful, if they knew about it. In April 1990, 87 per cent of Canada's unemployed were eligible for unemployment assistance; by April 1995, the figure was down to 50 per cent.[19] This miracle was worked by the simple process of changing the eligibility rules and dumping responsibility for the jobless onto the provinces, through the welfare system. In British Columbia, working a straight parallel to the Elizabethan Poor Law that booted out strange vagrants, welfare officers began doling out bus tickets to send the bums back home.[20] Soon, all the provinces had responded to Ottawa's new tight-fistedness by tightening up their rules in turn, flushing the flotsam and jetsam onto charity. Unfortunately, nobody thought to inquire as to whether charity could handle the job.

A Toronto newspaper ran two interesting items on separate pages of the same issue on December 19, 1995, that show how this symmetry works out. The first was a letter to the editor, praising the Harris government of Ontario for cracking down on welfare spending:

> To the special interest groups ["special interest groups" is code language for the poor, when they get up a parade], and there have been far too many getting government handouts: You must also reduce your spending. If you cannot manage your affairs with fiscal restraint, the province cannot and must not be expected to bail you out.[21]

A few pages earlier, in a column by Thomas Walkom, was evidence that the province was, by golly, making sure it got value for money. A 48-year-old woman named Stella May Williams, who lived in a basement apartment near Welland, Ontario, had been diagnosed as a "chronic depressive," so she was allowed to collect welfare of about $700 a month, in addition to working part-time in a laundromat. After the province decided to tighten up the criteria for welfare recipients, she no longer qualified as disabled, and she was cut off her monthly payment. Soon after, she committed suicide, leaving behind a note that said, "I feel I just can't take the pressures of this world any more."

Welfare paid the cost of her funeral, but decreed that there could be no headstone on the family plot, purchased years ago by her parents, until the province had been reimbursed for these charges. To this end, the bureaucracy grabbed her last, puny paycheque from the laundromat.[22]

I guess that's mean enough. I guess we are seeing the development of a system that will not stand for the reckless waste inherent in a bureaucracy which, a few years ago, probably would never have thought to grab that last cheque. Stella May was moved off the government's books and into the responsibility of charity, which, of course, had no way on earth of knowing of her existence. That is the great advantage of the system we are moving into; when it conks out, nobody knows, except the victims, of course. Gerard Kennedy, then executive director of the Daily Food Bank in Toronto, estimated that, before the 1995 round of cuts to public support, there were "18,000 children going hungry despite the fact that they are in contact with food banks."[23] Of course, he was just guessing; nobody really knows. If a couple of hundred thousand children don't get enough to eat every day—with measurable, consequential impacts on their intellectual, physical, and social development—who gets the blame? Not the charities; they are doing their damnedest, most of them. Not the government; it has bowed out. It must be the poor themselves.

The Institute for the Prevention of Child Abuse, a charity recognized around the world for its research into child abuse and for training social workers and police officers who have to deal with the problem, closed its doors in August 1995 and laid off all its eighteen staff when the Province of Ontario withdrew funding.[24] We can look at this as a darn shame, but not a measurable shame, since we will never know how many kids will get battered to death who might not otherwise have met that fate, or we can look at it as a challenge to the charitable sector to come up with something else to replace the lost institute. Maybe a bingo hall?

THE RISE OF THE FOOD BANKS

It took ten years from the time the Benson budget of 1971 opened the national cash-box to the corporate sector until the first food bank opened in Edmonton, Alberta.[25] The two events are connected by a straight line; detailed studies done in Edmonton and Regina, and confirmed by food bank managers across the country, point to "the inadequacy of social assistance benefits" as the major reason for people applying to food banks.[26] The gradual disappearance of a decent level of state support led directly to attempts by private groups to make up the difference, and food banks were their response. The first American food bank, in Phoenix, Arizona, was set up in 1966,[27] but that is because the Americans took an axe to their social system a long time before we did. The food banks became necessary because government support was either made unavailable by tightening the welfare rules or the monthly payments were trimmed back to the point where families ran out of food before the end of the month and were reduced to lining up for food in exactly the same way that our grandparents had in the 1930s.

Graham Riches is the academic who made the studies of food banks referred to above. He counted seventy-five of them, in every province but Prince Edward Island and Newfoundland, by 1985, but there are many more today. He has no doubt that food banks came about as a direct response to the withdrawal of government:

> Food banks are concrete evidence of the breakdown of the public safety net. They also act, no doubt unintentionally, as symbols of neo-conservatism. They are tangible expressions of the view that the social costs of change caused by demographic, technological, as well as deliberate government policies, should be passed back to the voluntary/charitable sector. The consequence of such policies is of course that the most vulnerable members of the community—women, children, those on social assistance, the unemployed, people of native ancestry, and low income earners—end up carrying the fullest burdens of such change. In the sense that food banks are acceptable to the public, they can be seen to act as ideological marker flags of the new right's thinking that welfare state spending has been profligate, and a major cause of economic and social decline.[28]

Forcing the people we have made victims of our economic system to line up for baskets of food is an exquisite form of punishment. It teaches them their place. It lets them know that, by God, they have failed in the race, they are living on the bounty of others, they have lost their rights—those evanescent, glimmering rights of two decades ago—and are down to favours.

If you talk to the people in the food bank lineups, which is often hard to do because they don't feel much like chatting with some stranger lugging a tape recorder, you quickly learn that some of them are damned resentful, but most of them are resigned.

"I don't know what I did wrong," a woman of about thirty told me, as she waited wearily, with one child on her hip and a toddler at her feet, at a food bank in a small city north of Toronto. "I worked all my life; then I was fired. I went on welfare, then it was cut. Then I had to come here." She looks up, and tears begin to come. "I feel so embarrassed."

This has nothing to do with rights, does it?

Another client of the same food bank was a man who felt doubly ashamed because he did have a job, but it paid so little that, by the time the rent was covered, the kids' clothes bought, the instalment on his wife's dentist bill met, along with the credit cards for gas on the car he used to get to work from his place in the country, way past the last stop on the bus line, the family money ran out by the end of the third week in the month. He could let his kids go hungry, or he could ask for a handout. "I couldn't bring myself to go on welfare," he said. "It seemed better to be coming here now and then than to admit I was whipped."

To make the dilemma more poignant, David Perry, executive director of the Canadian Tax Foundation, points out:

> The food banks are about the most inefficient way you can go about feeding people. You get the food after all the processing and distributing costs and markups have been paid, and then you make a gift. If people would just give the money, it would be much more efficient. You could buy in bulk and make deals. But then you wouldn't have the pictures on TV and in the papers, which is what brings the stuff in.[29]

THE DISAPPEARANCE OF "ADEQUATE" ASSISTANCE

For a time, going on welfare paid better than getting work at the minimum wage, and there was a lot of grumbling about that; it violated the New Poor Law requirement that it should never, ever be better not to work than to work. Why wasn't there a lot of grumbling about wages that are so low that welfare is better? Because, silly, wages are set by global competition; in return for letting them escape taxes, our multinationals have arranged to pay the peons badly enough to allow them to compete with the masses in Mexico, Puerto Rico, Indonesia, and other outlands of enlightenment. When these low rates make welfare seem too attractive, the answer is to slash welfare, thus righting the balance.

A few years ago, the existence of the food banks could have been taken as an argument that the federal government was breaking the law. As we saw in the last chapter, the Canada Assistance Plan, passed in 1966, said that people in need should receive "adequate" assistance. If the provinces that administer the funds didn't make the monthly cheques generous enough, Ottawa had the power, and the duty, to do something about it. If the funds were adequate, the food banks would not exist. However, we fixed all that in April 1996, by replacing the Canada Assistance Plan with the Canada Health and Social Transfer.[30] Under this new arrangement, Ottawa provides a single block of funding to each province for health, post-secondary education, and welfare. The block fund is, in every case, much lower than the CAP funds; the other major difference is that, while "national standards" are to be negotiated on access to government assistance,[31] there is nothing to say how much welfare the provinces are required to provide.

SLASHING THE SOCIAL SAFETY NET

There is no clearer symbol of the sea change that has overtaken us than the food banks, but they represent only a tiny corner of the charitable field. The drop in funding to provide social services and unemployment benefits has also been reflected in a huge increase in the number of Canadian women and children seeking shelter from abusive husbands and fathers. Statistics Canada found that in 1995 there was a 17 per cent jump in the number of those living in the shelters from two years earlier (when the first such survey was taken); that there were 85,000 admissions to the shelters, both public and charitable, and another 3,000 more were calling every day, asking for admission; and that 80 per cent of the women had been abused by a partner or ex-partner.[32] The greatest need, not surprisingly, was in Ontario, the largest province. The province responded by cutting the funding of emergency shelters, those where shelter is offered for up to eleven weeks, by 7.5 per cent, and cutting off funds entirely for counselling at second-stage shelters, which offer longer-term assistance. Many of these shelters were left with no staff as of January 1, 1996. And, of course, all these people were victims of the 21.6 per cent cut the same government levied across the board on all social assistance.

These cuts also thrust thousands more out into the cold, because they could no longer pay their rent. To take up the slack, charities like the Red Door Shelter in Toronto expanded—they took over a former convent and filled it with cots—and Project Warmth rounded up blankets and sleeping bags to distribute to the homeless.

But this is not the same thing as the state providing "adequate assistance." It is the state hoping to God that the private charities can provide adequate assistance, despite all the evidence that they cannot.

To see how this is likely to work out, it is time to examine the shape of the charitable sector, which is now in the process of inheriting the consequences of our collective decision to screw the poor before they can screw us.

SAINTS, SINNERS, AND SUCKERS: CHARITY IN CANADA TODAY

Perhaps the most overrated virtue in our list of shoddy virtues is that of giving. Giving builds up the ego of the giver, makes him superior and higher than the receiver. Nearly always, giving is a selfish pleasure, and in many cases is a downright destructive and evil thing. One has only to remember some of the wolfish financiers who spend two thirds of their lives clawing a fortune out of the guts of society and the latter third pushing it back.

—JOHN STEINBECK,
The Log from the Sea of Cortez, 1941

5. Taking a Charitable View

Jesus never instituted a charity ball where, amid the voluptuous swell of the dance, the rustle of silks, the sparkle of diamonds, and the stimulus of women dressed decolleté, he could dissipate his love for the lowly.

—ANONYMOUS NINETEENTH-
CENTURY CLERIC

The dinner was held at the Metro Toronto Convention Centre in early November 1995, and everybody who was anybody was there: business-people, politicians, publicans, and priests. For an hour before the lights dimmed in the glittering hall, the Cadillacs rolled up to the front doors like an invading army from General Motors, and the mink-wrapped ladies and their elegant escorts emerged, nodded to the hoi polloi, smiled at their peers, and preened for the cameras. Inside, the sleek cocoons were shed, and the fair ladies and brave men, after a suitable interlude for cocktails, murmured their way into the banquet hall, commenting on each other's splendiferous dress.

The hall itself was a thing of beauty, glistening with silver and gold and the stark white of starched linen; the sheen of opulence lay over the place like a benison. Gerald Emmett Cardinal Carter, the Roman Catholic eminence, was in his place at the head table, for this was his dinner, "The Cardinal's Dinner," as it is called, held once a year as a fund-raiser for charity, at $150 a tax-deductible pop. The 1,600 diners whose expense accounts had borne the brunt bellied up to tables that were covered in fine damask, laden with china, silver, bouquets, and bottles of wine. Everyone was about to dig into the jumbo shrimp that nestled in goblets at each setting when a young man got up, rushed to the microphone on a lectern near the head table, and did his best to ruin the evening.

He said he was a member of the Catholic Workers movement, and he thought that, instead of sitting down and stuffing themselves, the people at the dinner might do better to go outside and get to know the poor who were the putative beneficiaries of the feast. Frankly, he didn't think scoffing jumbo shrimp and filet mignon was likely to touch the root causes of poverty in the nation, and he invited those present to do something more. The crowd, stirring uneasily when the young man began to speak, were soon exchanging indignant whispers. Who was this yo-yo? What right did he have to come barging in, wrecking everything? Had he even been invited, for God's sake? Why didn't somebody do something?

Somebody did. Two security guards advanced on the podium, glowering. The interloper held up his hands in supplication and, marching between the guards, left the hall. A sturdy round of applause cheered his departure. Later, there were speeches, lots of speeches, including one from the Cardinal, who congratulated everyone there on the fine spirit that brought them out on a chilly evening to help those less fortunate than themselves, and one from Ontario Premier Mike Harris, who said, as he so often does, that, while his government was of course deeply committed to the downtrodden, it was unfortunately forced to make deep cuts in social spending, which was why the generosity of all our good friends attending here tonight would be even more essential in the future than it had been in the past. He got a swell hand.

That is modern charity in action. On behalf of people who haven't got enough to eat, 1,600 fat cats eat too much, drink at least enough, write off most of the cost from taxes, and donate the residue to whatever outfit staked the action, to the accompaniment of a drumroll of favourable publicity. The one thing you could be sure of at this splendid gathering is that, given the income brackets of the attendees, it cost the federal and provincial governments who can no longer afford the upkeep of the social safety net a hell of a lot more in forgone taxes than ever trickled through to the disadvantaged as a result of this night's browsing and sluicing.

Well, no, that's not quite fair. Modern charity in action is also an army of people who attend no banquets, make no speeches, but spend their days and nights helping other people, whether it is driving for Meals on Wheels, collecting for the Cancer Society, helping in a hospital, listening on a help line, or rounding up blankets and sleeping bags to distribute to the homeless in Canada's larger, and ever more desolate, cities. Modern charity is Amnesty International going to bat for political prisoners in foreign jails, and the National Ballet, and the C. D. Howe Institute, and the Boy Scouts, and a gang of thieves who thought up a scheme whereby folks who thought they were buying ads in a magazine to help the downtrodden ended up helping no one but the gang who dreamt up the scheme.[1]

The trouble is that charity in this country is so wide in scope, so diverse, so all-embracing, that it is almost impossible to quantify, let alone judge. This chapter, then, seeks to outline the main branches of this dense and thorny thicket, to begin the process of discovery that will allow the reader to make up his or her own mind whether the banquet scene played out in Toronto was an aberration, a typical abomination, or a necessary part of the complex business of succouring the poor in a modern society.

PEEKING BEHIND THE CHARITY CURTAIN

In other countries, detailed financial information about charities is an ordinary part of the public record, but in Canada, we are as shy as vestal virgins about what goes on behind the charitable curtain that swathes the land. So I had to chase down the facts myself. First, I approached the Canadian Centre for Philanthropy (hereafter, the ccp) through Gordon Floyd, its director of public affairs, and asked for the centre's data on the top 200 Canadian charities, by annual revenue. I knew the ccp had this information in the database from which it drew the numbers for its *Portrait of Canada's Charities*.[2] (The ccp does not produce tables with the names of the charities attached, because the accounting methods of the organizations vary so widely that the CCP, which is their lobby, thinks it unfair to compare them directly. I don't agree; if comparisons are invidious, let the charities get their numbers straight.)

In a remarkably short time, the research section of the CCP produced a computer print-out of the 200 top charities by income, which I took to Revenue Canada in Ottawa. I asked for the most recent income-tax returns of the organizations named, information that any member of the public is entitled to, by law. Revenue Canada rounded up all the forms I asked for within a few days, and when I went back to them, again and again and again during the following months, they were just as quick and efficient at providing every T3010 I requested. These formed the basis of an attempt to sort out the sector.

Each charitable organization must fill out a form, called a "T3010 Rev 90, Registered Charity Information, Public Information Return" (a copy of which appears in Appendix II), as part of its income-tax return. The form consists of four pages of relevant financial information, often with attachments spelling out the objectives of the charity. There have been a number of attempts to shoehorn more questions onto the pages of the T3010 in order to elicit more information. Liberal MP John Bryden, who is one of the nation's harshest critics of the charitable sector, believes the T3010 should show what each of the top officers of each charity is paid, in the same way that corporations are now required to supply this information to stockholders. I think he has a point, but it was relatively easy for the charity lobby to derail the private member's bill that would have brought about his goal.[3]

You cannot tell, from the T3010, what the head of a charity makes. However, you *can* tell, if the charity manages to fill out the form correctly, what it spends on administration in general, what it spends on fund raising, how much it gets from government, how much it spends in Canada and how much abroad, and—most crucially—how much of the money that it gets, from whatever sources, actually finds its way into the hands of the people who are its supposed beneficiaries. This is on page 2 of the form, line 114: "Total amount spent on charitable programs carried out by your charity." If a charity raises a million dollars but spends $600,000 raising it, then spends another $200,000 running the office, it is not going to do a heck of a lot of good with the $200,000 that remains.

This is where we come to another difficulty. In the T3010 I have used in

Appendix II, World Vision Canada spent $11,173,708 to raise money, plus $8,388,751 on salaries, and another $7,480,931 for "Management and general administration costs." Quite a whack out of its total income of $95,672,730, especially when you see, in line 108 on page 1, that it got $14,867,766 of this from "Federal, provincial or municipal grants and payments received." You might conclude that World Vision Canada was only a moderately efficient organization, if it cost $27,043,390 to collect and administer $80,804,964 (the first figure is the sum of the money-raising, salary, and administration costs; the second is total revenue minus the government money). How much of the total actually got through to the "people in suffering and need" who are the objects of its work? This is a fair question, because, after all, World Vision gave out $76,908,851 in income-tax receipts. In addition, we spent—you and I and other taxpayers—about $15 million in direct payments in the form of government grants to this charity, and as much as twice that in tax expenditures (i.e., forgone fiscal revenue) to allow it to plant trees, dole out emergency food rations, provide farm implements, and sponsor children in far-off lands, to say nothing of its work here in Canada, publishing church bulletins and "providing resources to Canadian churches for national ministry."

World Vision spent $69,105,732 outside Canada. Did it do a better job than might have been done by government agencies, the United Nations, or another charity? We could get a rough measure of this by comparing what it raised with what it spent on "Charitable programs," but in this case, World Vision chooses not to tell us. Actually, almost all the money raised in Canada is spent from the head office in California;[4] we have no way of knowing how it is spent because World Vision declines to tell Revenue Canada, or you and me, what proportion of the money collected was spent on the objects of the exercise. Instead, we get a number showing that its total disbursements and its spending on charitable programs are exactly the same. They argue that "As a charitable organization, World Vision Canada is required to devote all of its resources to its own charitable activities."

I am thinking of trying this on Revenue Canada in my next income-tax return; I am required to devote all my resources to scrabbling for a living, so my expenses equal my income, and sucks to you.

I have a feeling that I would not be as, uh, charitably received as World Vision Canada, but there it is. The charities stick a lot of relevant and interesting information on the form, but quite a lot of it is dubious and dumb. While trying to make sense out of dozens of forms with many of the questions not answered, I telephoned an official at Revenue Canada to ask what happens when a charity sends in an incomplete form.

The official replied: "If they find something missing, there is a letter that goes out, an attempt to inform them about filling out the forms correctly. And, of course, there may be information from the general public."

I said, "Ratting on them, you mean?"

"Well, information, or questions from people like you."

"Anything else?"

"No."[5]

Seems odd. What we are entitled to know by law ought to be on the form, it seems to me, as a matter of course. Most of the elisions are obviously born of carelessness or contempt, not crookedness; you shouldn't need snitches to straighten things out.

Still, a patient person can learn quite a bit from the forms, and I have used them as a way to look at the charities in a general way. At the back of this book, in Appendix 1, is a set of five tables that set down, for the first time to my knowledge, at least the basic details about the core operations of our largest charities.

THE TOP 25 CHARITIES BY REVENUE

The first table in Appendix 1 covers the top 25 charities by revenue. These include such old standbys as the Canadian Red Cross and the United Way of Greater Toronto—proper charities—along with such strangers as Triumf, which turns out to be a scientific research establishment funded almost entirely by government. It is not a teaching institution or a hospital, but it isn't anything most of us would recognize as a charity, either. It appears to have charitable status for convenience, and one of the conveniences is that it keeps itself to itself. Even within the modest demands of the tax form, Triumf is another organization that refuses to show any detail on what it spends, except that it spent more than it took in, which may or may not be a good sign.

Canadian charities are mostly registered by province and/or municipality, so there is no such thing as a file showing all the spending of every United Way in Canada, or all our YMCAs. The Foster Parents Plan of Canada is organized federally, as is the Red Cross, so there are national totals for them. However, the Salvation Army has more than 600 separate temples, all registered locally; consequently, there is no national set of numbers on the public record, and the same is true of other "Places of Worship," whether churches, mosques, synagogues, or temples. Cancer charities have both provincial research arms and a national office. What is needed is for some Ph.D. thesis-seeker to spend a year or so going through the 73,000 forms in Ottawa to provide a more accurate picture of how the charities compare on a national basis. Even so, we can see by this table that many of our largest charities receive an overwhelming share of their money from the three levels of government, while a few get little or nothing.

These are not all grants or handouts, by a long shot. In most cases, the charity submits a proposal to a government department to perform specific work in return for either a grant or a fee; in many cases, it acts as an agent of the government and oversees the dispersal of funds for a part of the take. There is no way of knowing, and hardly anyone ever asks, whether the money is well spent.

If we take a ramble down the top 25 list, we can get some idea of how some of our favourite charities operate.

THE RED CROSS
The Canadian Red Cross, with an annual income of more than $460 million, is the largest of our charities by revenue. It is the Canadian branch of the International Red Cross, which was founded in 1864 as a direct result of the publication of Swiss author J. Henry Dunant's account of the horrible and needless suffering among the wounded left on the field following the 1859 battle of Solferino, in northern Italy, between the Austrians and the French and the Sardinians. *Un Souvenir de Solferino* suggested the formation of an international voluntary aid society to intervene in such cases and to seek to impose neutral treatment for the ill and injured in all wars. A Swiss welfare agency took up the suggestion, and the result was a meeting in Switzerland, with sixteen nations attending, and the Geneva Convention of 1864 for "The Amelioration of the Condition of the Wounded and Sick of Armies in the Field."[6]

Gradually, as the Red Cross spread to more than 100 countries, its duties broadened to include relief aid of all kinds and the supervision of blood programs in many countries. The familiar symbol of the red cross on a white background—the Swiss flag with colours reversed—has become a beacon of aid and hope all over the world.

In Canada, the charity cites as its major activity "the collection and distribution of the entire blood program."[7] Most of the society's $461 million annual revenue to carry out this important work comes from governments, but there is a good deal of dispute—to put it no more strongly than that—as to its competence in this area.

A Commission of Inquiry into the Blood System of Canada, under Mr. Justice Horace Krever of the Ontario Court of Appeal, was established to discover how it was that as many as 1,000 Canadians contracted HIV through blood transfusions between 1980 and 1985. Testimony before the inquiry has shown that the agency was advised in December 1982 to screen out blood donors from AIDS-susceptible groups, and that other nations began such screening in 1983, but the Canadian Red Cross did not begin screening until November 1985.[8] The organization's response in testimony before the inquiry has been marked, in my view, by an unwillingness to accept responsibility that has sometimes been stunning.

The inquiry has shown that the charitable status of the Red Cross allowed it to remain, as I see it, unaccountable for years after serious questions were raised concerning the competence of this top-heavy, bureaucratic monopoly. As a department of government—surely the proper place for the assembly and protection of the blood supply—it would have been subject to the tender mercies of the auditor general, to say nothing of the probes of opposition MPs, when the alarm was first raised. As a public corporation, it would have had to reveal a great deal more than it has ever done about its capacity and efficiency.

You will note in Table 1 that only 41.4 per cent of the Red Cross's revenue ($461,951,000) went to "Charitable programs"; according to its income-tax return for the year ending March 31, 1994, it spent $248 million on "Other disbursements," almost all of it, apparently, on "remuneration to employees." (The official return calls on the organization to specify the disbursements, but the Red Cross does not do so; however, it does show salary figures.) Was that wage bill smart and sensible, or hopelessly overblown? Although most of the money comes from government, we're told this is none of our business. Can you imagine a government agency or department getting away with this? Or a public corporation coming to its annual meeting with a report indicating that more than half its spending was on "Other disbursements"? Mr. Justice Krever will have his own comments on the Red Cross, but I doubt whether he will raise the crucial issue: Should the blood supply of the nation be in the hands of a charity in the first place?

The Ontario Cancer Treatment and Research Foundation, Canada's second-largest charity by revenue, is one of the score or more scientific and health organizations funded by government but run as private charities (of its $158 million in revenue, only $2.9 million came from donations). It has been running since 1943 and no doubt does some wonderful work, but its activities are, like so many other organizations, safely cloaked behind the screen of charitable silence. It may work well; it may be a complete mess. We will never know.

THE NOT-QUITE CHARITIES

The International Development Research Centre, our third-largest charity, is one of the leading members of the Not-Quite Charities, bodies with all the advantages of charitable status but no compelling reason, beyond the convenience of being able to operate off-stage, for this status. It was set up by an act of Parliament in 1970 as a corporation designed to meet "The challenges of sustainable development and equitable development," and it funds studies in Canada and elsewhere into "integrating environmental, social and economic policies; technology and the environment; food systems under stress; information and communication for environment and development; health and the environment; and biodiversity."[9] The environment was all the rage back in those days, and you could get money ladled into almost anything that had a green tinge to it. I spoke to one researcher for this outfit, who said that it was "a god-awful mess, churning out reports nobody ever read and spinning money into presents for academics." Disgruntled employees are not a reliable source of information; this might be hogwash. On the other hand, it might be quite accurate.

Or, to put it another way, the IDRC spends about $150 million a year in government funds without the carping, criticizing, nit-picking, and plain bloody-mindedness that might be brought to bear if the same money went out through public channels, where we could see it.

UNITED WE STAND, AND COLLECT

One autumn day a few years ago, I was sitting at my desk in a downtown Toronto office when I was handed a memo from on high concerning the United Way of Toronto's annual fund drive. The memo announced that a couple of the top officers of the corporation for which I then worked were active volunteers in the drive, and they expected the rest of us galley slaves to come across in suitable fashion. The "or else" was left unsaid. There was a little chart that showed what proportion of my salary would be deemed sufficient, and a lot of unctuous bumph about pulling together to show the grand general public that our staff could give more than any other staff, and a final bit of paper that I could sign after checking off the appropriate slice of flesh to be hacked from the old pay envelope throughout the year.

I thought it was pretty nervy, until I learned that it is almost standard practice; across every major Canadian city (except in Newfoundland, where there is no United Way), similar missives go floating out every year. The United Way is one of the most bumptious arm-twisters in the Western world, which is kind of strange when you reflect that it was established to take the strain out of giving.

The United Way is the successor to the "Community Chest," a term coined in Rochester, New York, in 1919.[10] The idea was to get around the donor fatigue associated with the constant dunning of dozens of charities by gathering them all together—"putting all our begs in one askit" was the way it was phrased at the time. The money would be collected through payroll deductions and would be much more efficient than, say, tag days, while liberating the givers from the constant barrage of charity appeals. Besides being able to turn the constant callers away with five magic words—"I gave at the office"—the donor would be relieved of the burden of having to work out which charities were worthy of his money. That would be looked after by the umbrella group.

In Canada, similar federations sprang up, and for the same reason—to simplify the system, cut costs, and alleviate some of the irritation caused by constantly dunning the donor population. By 1938, nine cities in Canada were involved in these networks, and by 1945, the number had risen to thirty-six.[11]

Companies loved the idea, which, among other things, gave them favourable publicity for their top officers who, then as now, formed the visible front for the campaigns and made solemn speeches about the advantages of community giving as opposed to, say, paying taxes to support social services. "The tax burden would come back, and corporations would end up getting stuck with a bigger piece of the tab" is the way a senior official of United Way of America put it.[12] Much better to shift the burden to the gang on the assembly line. These campaigns are also a safe way to make business contacts and build prestige, to say nothing of making the volunteers, especially those whose role consists mainly of making a few phone calls to buddies and then attending a thank-you dinner, feel good about themselves.

The United Way became a business-oriented organization, and remained so. Today, about seventy-five cents out of every dollar collected by United Ways comes from corporate contributions or employee payroll deductions, which always wind up being credited to the corporation. Every year, when the United Way is announcing that it cannot possibly make this year's target and the television news shows swing their cameras onto the scene at city hall, you will see a corporate bigwig step forward with a six-foot cardboard cheque on which the name "xyz Corporation" or whatever appears in large, large letters. It didn't come from the xyz Corporation. It came from employees, and was topped up by the corporation.

Companies compete with each other under the United Way's "Fair Share" guidelines, which call on wage slaves to kick in an hour's pay per month. Workers who donate this amount are given a lapel pin, usually, and companies are presented with plaques for achieving "maximum employee participation." Ideally, this is 100 per cent, but that is rarely achieved; the plaque gets presented anyway.

The arm-twisting is often brutal. In San Francisco, a memo from a senior executive of the regional telephone company went like this:

> We have tried not to push you where the United Bay Area Crusade is concerned, but, frankly, our results look terrible. We are among the lowest of the low for Fair Share givers. I have bent over backwards seeing that you will be given maximum salary treatment. Next year is another year. Will you please sit down and reconsider your pledge?[13]

Reminds me of that old television ad where the car mechanic wanted you to buy a new oil filter or see your car's engine turn into scrap metal: "You can pay me now, or pay me later."

The United Way publishes guidelines that tell the corporate leaders not to play so rough, but to little avail, given the competitive spur applied by company chieftains who want to ensure that the firm looks good. In Cleveland, a young man under severe financial strain because his wife had been ill pledged $12 monthly to the local United Way through his employer. He was told to push the sum up to $18, and when he refused, he was fired.[14] One of the good—or bad, depending on your point of view—things about the United Way is the fact that its payroll-deduction approach allows it to tap the pay packets of very modest earners. In 1987, half its income came from "people who earn less than $305 a week."[15]

Bear this in mind as you consider the case of William Aramony, currently a guest of the state of Virginia for a period of seven years, with time off for good behaviour, but for twenty-two years the president, chief operating officer, and heart and soul of the United Way of America. A book written by his former friend and colleague, John S. Glaser, makes it clear that Aramony provided much of the muscular hustle behind the organization's annual fund drives.[16]

Aramony wrote a book of his own, before all the trouble started. It was called *The United Way: The Next Hundred Years*, and it was crammed with about as much chest-thumping bravado as a body could stand:

> Campaigns are life-giving phenomena; full of heart, bursting with spirit. Raising money by selling off portions of the world's largest sub sandwich, which happened in Philadelphia, or letting loose 1.5 million balloons, which happened in Cleveland, says something refreshing about the spirit of our movement.[17]

Strangely, the book did not make any mention of the nice little rackets Aramony had set up along the way, and which eventually led to his conviction on twenty-five counts of conspiracy, mail and wire fraud, the filing of false income-tax returns, and "transactions involving criminal property."[18] Hey, an author can't fit *everything* into a book.

Aramony's lawyer told the court that his pay and benefits, which came to $463,000 (U.S.) per annum, were not enough to allow him to keep up with the corporate leaders he had to woo on behalf of the charity. I guess it would be pretty embarrassing knowing that you spent only $100,000 per annum on travel, when the other guys had real money to lay out. To make up for this, Aramony hired a jet to take all his pals to the Super Bowl every January, and dipped into the charitable till to the extent of $1.2 million for personal expenses. Much of this went to pay the bills for a romance that Aramony, then fifty-eight, struck up with seventeen-year-old Lori Villasor in 1986.

Quite a lot of the money squeegeed out of the pay envelopes of factory workers across the United States went to cover the costs of two condos (they used to call them "love nests" in the bad old days) in New York and Florida, where the couple consulted on matters of interest to the charity, thus giving a new meaning to the phrase "Fair Share." Oh, yes, Lori was on the payroll, to the tune of about $80,000, although she testified she only did "an hour or so" of actual work. The condos were actually financed through two spin-off operations Aramony set up to do business with the United Way, but which were actually owned by him and close colleagues, two of whom also wound up as guests of the state.[19] United Way money also paid for gambling jaunts to Las Vegas with Lori and her younger sister, who was given $100 bills to smile for Bill.[20]

Of course, nothing like that could happen in Canada. Or, at least, if it did, we would probably never find out about it. The Aramony case came to light because details of his pay and benefits were on the public record, as part of Internal Revenue Service Form 990, available to anyone who cared to look. The numbers stirred the interest of reporters at the *Washington Post*, who launched an investigation in 1992 that led to his downfall.[21]

We Canadians are shielded from such embarrassments, since we know nothing about our United Ways except what they choose to tell us, and the reporters who cover its annual campaigns do so with an anxiety to please that would sit well with Uriah Heep. After all, their newspaper, television station, or magazine is a proud corporate sponsor of the United Way, and the men and women who cover the beat know it. They get the little note in their payslips, too.

What we can see in Table 1 is that the United Way of Greater Toronto, the thirteenth-largest charity in Canada, declines to divulge to the rude gaze of the public what it spends on fund raising. It does tell us that it spent 80.3 per cent of its income on charitable projects, but that seems low, considering the corporate muscle behind the organization and the fact that raising funds through payroll deductions is done precisely because it is supposed to be so efficient. The cost of raising money through the tax system is about one cent on the dollar; through the United Way, perhaps twenty times that. Which brings up the question posed by Samuel A. Martin in his academic study of charities in Canada:

> Direct taxation is not only a cheaper way of raising money for human-
> istic service, but would it not provide a much fairer and more equi-
> table distribution of the burden throughout society?[22]

The answer, I think, is yes. However, collecting through the tax system
does not involve the dinners, pep rallies, or flattering publicity that attends
the process when it is performed through a charity, and the lack of
efficiency is something the agency is more than willing to sacrifice, on
behalf of the indigent, in return for all that neat publicity.

The United Way in Toronto, as elsewhere in the nation, does a great
deal of good work, and there is no reason to doubt one of the claims made
in its pamphlets:

> Last year alone, 1 out of every 3 people here in Toronto got the help
> they needed from one of over 250 United Way fund charities.
> Whether it was a hot meal, protection from abuse, a caring smile,
> some friendly conversation, a warm bed or job retraining. The United
> Way was there.[23]

This is not, however, the same as knowing that the money is spent in the
most efficient way possible or that a good deal of what the member agencies do should be funded directly from the public purse. I can see no reason
why "protection from abuse" should be dependent on charity; that, surely,
is madness. In the same way, paying money to outfits like "Food for
Thought," a breakfast program for Scarborough schoolchildren, seems
bizarre. Schoolchildren need decent food; it isn't something they should
have to beg for. The academic argument against all these charities is that
they "serve to deflect public and political attention away from the need for
long-standing and urgent reforms in the social security system."[24] If
abused families and hungry children are the responsibility of the United
Way, there is something badly amiss.

Moreover, the United Way has certainly not obviated the need for the
thousands of other charities that swarm the land. The agency's strong
point, the raising of cash in the workplace, has elements of bullying by
some employers about it that make it less than popular around the water
cooler, although nobody wants to say so out loud. The United Way is a col-

lection agency for individual charities who do a lot of good work; but if it loses twenty cents on every dollar it collects, it can hardly be called efficient. At the very least, then, both we and the United Way would be much better off if it were required to give us much more information than it does today about exactly how it goes about its job.

THE HEALTH CHARITIES

At the risk of some overlap, I have made a separate table, Table 2, for the health charities when they go by the name of specific diseases, even though some of them appear in Table 1 as well. Table 2 shows an astounding range of direct government support, from the 81.7 per cent of funding that flows to the Ontario Society for Crippled Children to nil for the Canadian Liver Foundation. Only three of the twelve health charities listed spend more than 80 per cent of revenue on charitable programs (remember that the legal test is that the spending must be four-fifths of the revenue for which tax receipts were issued in the previous year, so there is nothing amiss here), but one of these, War Amps, doesn't show what it spends on fund raising, and another, Ontario Crippled Children, shows neither fundraising nor administration costs.

In most other cases, the charity spends funds through grants to other charities: the Canadian Cancer Society's national office is really a postbox; it receives most of its money from provincial charities and spends most of it through them, so the figures here don't signify much (except the crying need for a single set of books on all these outfits). Four of the twelve decline to tell us what they spent to raise funds; others spent in the millions. Among them, these twelve took in close to $200 million, of which about $122 million was spent on charitable projects; the rest was either used for fund raising, administration, or gifts to other charities, or it evaporated.

There is something drastically wrong with a system that apparently only delivers a little more than 60 per cent of the take to the operating table. It may be just a horrible way of keeping books; equally, it may be that there is a huge amount of waste here. I cannot believe that it wouldn't be simpler, fairer, more efficient, and much more responsible to collect these sums through the tax system and distribute them through the health-care system. As it is, diseases that can show us a cute kid with a shaved head pull in millions, while the ones that cater to drooling old folks do not do so well, although both have exactly parallel, legitimate claims on the financial support of the community.

The appalling danger we have placed ourselves in by depending more and more on charities is that cuteness, not need, may become the criterion for care. David Perry, executive director of the Canadian Tax Foundation, told me, "The trouble is that it is an awful lot easier to raise money for crippled children than for unwed mothers."[25]

MONEY FOR THE SAKE OF ART: CULTURAL CHARITIES

Table 3, which lists thirteen cultural charites, shows that the largest of these is the Canada Council, which received almost $100 million of its $118-million budget from the Government of Canada in 1994, the latest year for which figures are available. It refuses to tell us on the tax form what it spends on charitable programs, but the organization's annual report shows it to be quite lean, mean, and efficient. That same year, it spent $86.7 million on grants to the arts, just over $2 million on "services to the arts," and $787,000 to purchase works of art. In all, the Canada Council spent $20.5 million on grants administration and general administration, and produced a surplus of $6.7 million. I calculate that, had it deigned to fill out the T3010 form completely, the Canada Council would have reported that it spent $111,725,000 in the year, of which $91,204,000 went to "charitable purposes"; that's 81.6 per cent, which is pretty good. Its budget was chopped $10 million for 1995.[26]

But were these really "charitable purposes"? If we want to support the arts out of government funds—and I, for one, do—should they be treated in exactly the same way as cancer research or the Children's Aid Society?

Surely the answer to that is obvious; they should not. Culture and social welfare are entirely separate functions, and the cultural charities slide into this sector only through the vasty vagueness of the "benefit to the community" head. The Canada Council is a benefit to the community, but funnelling a much-needed grant to a starving author or dancer is not the same as supplying funds for a women's shelter. In the rush to slash the share-out to all recipients of government aid, the Canada Council has been dealt with almost as brutally as the Canadian Broadcasting Corporation, and that is a pity, but it is nothing like the pity of what is happening to the food banks, child-protection agencies, and providers of social welfare in general.

I have gathered the financial details on fifteen cultural charities, from the Canada Council to the Toronto Zoo. The Shaw Festival is a charity—and a highly efficient one, too; it gets just over 10 per cent of its funding from governments and raises the rest itself, through ticket sales, sweat-shirts, running a restaurant, any way it can. The Canadian Museum of Civilization, on the other hand, receives 91.6 per cent of its funding from government, which means that it doesn't have to spend much on fund raising, but only 36.4 per cent of its spending goes to charitable projects. Where does the rest go, on paint?

TVO, the Ontario public broadcaster, is almost as dependent on government funding as the Museum of Civilization, and deserves the money it gets (which it will probably lose), but I still don't see why it should be a charity. The spending of public funds on cultural institutions is part of the price we pay for our nationhood. It is money well spent; moreover, unlike any other charitable spending, it is money that returns itself many times over, because events like the Stratford Shakespearean Festival bring in tourist dollars—often, American tourist dollars, which are even nicer—to the community.

These expenditures should be defended on their economic merits, on their national merits, and in the name of art in general, but they ought to be paid through the open channels of departmental grants, and the charities should not be able to give out tax-deductible receipts.

CHARITIES THAT SPEND OUR MONEY ABROAD
Table 4 deals with the largest of the Canadian charities, many of them with international links, that operate mainly outside the country or spend enough money abroad to have been picked up by Revenue Canada's computer. They form the subject matter for Chapter Six.

POLITICS AND CHARITIES
Some of the smallest and oddest charities are shown in Table 5, a table that raises a crucial issue about the charitable sector—politics. One of the sins that bring the auditors of Revenue Canada to life is a complaint that a charity is spending its money on "political activities." Political activities are not charitable, but the trick comes in trying to determine what is political. In a discussion of this point with two people at Revenue Canada, Ron Davis, director of the Charities Division, and Carl Juneau, assistant

director of Technical Interpretation and Communications, I suggested that the distinction was probably that "If I don't agree with what the charity says, it's political; if I do, it's okay."

This drew a patient sigh from Davis, and this comment:

> An organization is political if its purpose is to affect government policy or decision-making directly or indirectly, or to sway public opinion. There is some leeway for charities to become involved in informing the public; for example, a historical preservation group might want to inform the public about the need to preserve old buildings as part of our heritage, and that would be acceptable.

Juneau added:

> We accept activities that are intended to inform decision-makers in some cases; for example, civilization has something to say on the need to adapt buildings better for blind people and the handicapped. We feel that is extremely legitimate.[27]

So, it is all right for an organization that wants to "inform decision-makers" to raise money and hand out charitable receipts, but only in some cases. Which cases?

Juneau replied, "The C. D. Howe Institute and the Fraser Institute provide rational argument based on research, rather than placard-waving."

This struck me as a direct dig against organizations like the National Anti-Poverty Organization or the National Action Committee on the Status of Women, which, so far as any outsider can see, exist for the sole purpose of prodding, poking, and otherwise upsetting decision-makers, and a good thing, too. I asked directly about NAPO. Juneau merely waved a hand in dismissal, while Davis nodded.

I asked if they thought the charitable status of the National Anti-Poverty Organization should be revoked.

Juneau said, tersely, "No comment."

Davis, after a pause, said, "We cannot make these judgments; who are we to say that one thing is okay and the other not?"

The whole conversation left me profoundly uneasy. Political activity is forbidden to charities, except in certain cases where it is done through nicely printed books rather than placard-waving, but there is no one at Revenue Canada capable of saying what is political and what is not, although no one else has been given the job. The governing legislation is singularly unhelpful. The regulations state:

> Whether a particular activity is fundamentally charitable or funda-
> mentally political depends on the facts of the particular situation; it is
> a matter of degree to be judged on a case-by-case basis.[28]

Thus, a charity that lobbies in favour of abortions as a part of family plan-ning is safe, because abortions are legal in Canada, and therefore nonpolit-ical (come again?). In 1991, the courts ordered Revenue Canada to give charitable status to Everywoman's Health Care Centre, an abortion clinic, on the specific grounds that there is no government policy to prohibit abortion.[29] However, lobbying *against* abortions is political, by the same argument, and Human Life International had its charitable status revoked in 1994 on this basis. In a similar case, Greenpeace, an aggressive environ-mental organization, was deprived of its charitable status in 1989 on the grounds of "being an advocacy group,"[30] and Positive Action Against Pornography, which applied for but was denied charitable status in 1988, lost a court appeal on the same grounds. Yet the Smoking and Health Action Foundation, an offshoot of the Non-Smokers' Rights Association, which is a registered lobby that is political, retains its charitable status.

I embrace the views of the Non-Smokers' Rights Association, but its obvious and intended role is to persuade governments to kill the tobacco industry. Not only that, they wave placards, just like NAPO. The difficulty is that we have a rule, which makes sense, that says charities should spend their money on charitable objects, not on politics; but we have no mecha-nism to ensure that the rule is administered evenly. I told Juneau that, on the abortion issue, I am in favour of freedom of choice; but the notion that, simply because abortion is a recognized medical procedure, its use or abuse has nothing to do with politics, strikes me as ludicrous. We parted in an atmosphere of mutual incomprehension.

I remain uncomprehending. The Fraser Institute produces a steady stream of books, articles, speeches, and forums designed to affect politics directly. Indeed, that is almost all it does. The July 1995 issue of *Fraser Forum* carries "The Fraser Institute's Privatization Shopping Lists of

Government Business Enterprises," which urges the federal government to part with, *inter alia*, the Bank of Canada, Canada Post, the CBC, the Canadian Wheat Board, the Royal Canadian Mint, the St. Lawrence Seaway, and VIA Rail. There are separate lists of major institutions that ought to be dumped in every province and territory.[31] The advice, if taken, would transform the nation—badly, to my view; wonderfully, to the institute's. Why isn't this considered political?

Or how about the Fraser Institute's *Critical Issues Bulletin*, produced about the same time, which purported to prove that all the stories we read and hear about famine, scarce resources, and overcrowding in the world are so much banana oil? These are dealt with as "The Myth of Famine," "The Myth of Scarce Resources," and "The Myth of Overcrowding," totally false stories circulated, apparently, by a bunch of starving people crowded around a candle somewhere. The institute's idea is that the whole problem is socialism. Eliminate socialism, and everything will be hunky-dory. Well, it's an argument; but it's a political argument, an argument from an organization whose purpose, in Ron Davis's words, is clearly "to affect government policy or decision-making directly or indirectly, or to sway public opinion."

But the Fraser Institute is considered to be okay, because their stuff purports to be research. As the King of Siam used to say, "Is a puzzlement."

The crown of all this folly, to my mind, was a ruling by the Federal Court of Appeal in 1993 that turned down the charitable-status registration of an organization created to promote national unity on the grounds that it was political.[32] All I can say is, yikes.

GIVING TO POLITICAL PARTIES PAYS OFF

You cannot get a tax deduction for money donated to a charity that meddles in politics, right? However, you can get a deduction, a much bigger one, for a gift to a political party.

When you give to a charity, you may claim a tax credit of 17 per cent on the first $200, and 29 per cent on any donation above that, to a maximum of 20 per cent of your income.[33] But because the provincial tax is affected, the result is a deduction of up to 27 per cent on the first $200, and up to 54 per cent above that if you are in the top tax bracket.

When you give to a political party, however, you are entitled to a credit of 75 per cent on the first $100, 50 per cent from $100 up to $550, and 33 per cent after that, with no limit.[34]

Give $1,000 to a charity, and the tax credit is $266; give the same amount to a political party, and the credit is $466. Which means that Canadians—no, strike that, Canadian MPs—would rather we give to politicians than to charities.

You will also benefit more by donating works of art, sculpture, manuscripts, or other items certified as "Canadian cultural property" than by giving cash. For one thing, their value can be used as a tax credit against your entire income, not just 20 per cent, and you can carry forward the gift for five years[35] to make sure you milk the most out of the system. The rest of us taxpayers will give you back at least half of what you donated. Moreover, you do not have to claim capital gains on the items if they increased in value between the time of acquisition and when you made the donation.

This is just part of the generalized inanity of the tax rules. Take the ground rule that a charity must disburse 80 per cent of its receipted income from the previous year on charitable purposes. Say that the Meadowlark Society for Crippled Children raises $100,000 through donations in one year, all of which is receipted; it must therefore spend $80,000 on charitable purposes the next year, or run the risk of losing its registration. That leaves it $20,000 with which to operate. But say the Society for the Preservation of Popsicle Sticks As Cultural Icons raises $50,000 through donations and clears another $50,000 from bingo. Its disbursement quota the next year is $40,000—80 per cent of $50,000—and it has $60,000 with which to operate.

I guess this isn't supposed to make sense, it's just the way it's done.

6. Our Far-Flung Dollars:
Foreign-Aid Charities

*Never doubt that a small group of thoughtful,
committed citizens can change the world. Indeed,
it is the only thing that ever has.*

—MARGARET MEAD,
Culture and Commitment, 1970

The television picture is hauntingly familiar: a little black girl, stomach
horribly distended, limbs appallingly shrunken, dirty, naked, her crusted
eyes crawling with flies, clutches an empty bowl and weeps in hopeless
despair. The camera pans across to the child's mother, her hands held out
in supplication, then pulls back to reveal a swarm of similar children, in
some refugee camp in some far-off land. You reach for the telephone and
your credit card.

Try visualizing this, instead. A well-groomed, neat, clean young man in
a suit and tie puts down his coffee mug, smiles, and, opening the drawer of

his desk, hands out a press release on the most recent distribution of supplies by the charity that hired him on contract, plus expenses. Not so good for extracting cash from the donors, but just as accurate a reflection of relief aid, and his pay envelope is just as likely a place for your donation to wind up as in that begging bowl.

There is a set of guidelines—charity is full of guidelines—laid down by the Canadian Council for International Co-operation, an umbrella group that represents 115 foreign-aid agencies, most of them charities. The guidelines call for "greater clarity and openness" in fundraising appeals, meaning not so much of the swollen-bellied kids, but when CARE Canada tried to get away from the graphic images, the wallets stayed shut.[1]

The charities that spend Canadian funds abroad represent the dilemma of the charitable approach in its starkest form: to operate effectively when one of the large man-made or natural disasters that mark our age overwhelms some corner of the world requires huge amounts of money, organization, experience, and skill. You need managers, administrators, doctors, engineers, statisticians, transport experts, pilots, drivers, mechanics, and, yes, public relations officers, to handle the necessary information campaign. They get paid the going wage, and they stay in hotels when they travel. If you want professional work done, you pay accordingly. There is not much point in having a gang of volunteers work half a year to prepare the site for a desperately needed village well in Bangladesh if the team brought in to drill it doesn't know their business. And if they do know their business, they will get businesslike pay, in most cases. Similarly, if there is an overwhelming tragedy unravelling in one of the untrod corners of the world, and a battalion of journalists comes in to get the pictures and file the quotes—for salaries about equal to the gross domestic product of the stricken land—the charity on the ground had better have a public relations expert available who knows how to pour a drink, how to schmooze, and where the bars stay open late. But no one is going to give a charity the money to hire a flack, so the only thing any major charity can do if it hopes to contribute much to the alleviation of suffering abroad is to play down the hotel bills and the flack, and haul out the footage of the kids. It is not lying—there are millions of such kids—it is just incredibly simplistic and studiously misleading.

Worse, it is these pictures that attract the emergency budgets of governments, that bring in the official support for the tragedy of the week. It is in response to what television chooses to cover that donors take out their chequebooks, MPs rise howling in Parliament, letters flood the mails, and e-mail communications overwhelm the computers of bureaucrats, and governments find themselves falling in line to send aid—to the Sudan this week, Ethiopia the next, wherever Tom Brokaw *et al.* land the week after that. Pretty soon the din dies down, the pressure eases off, and the cameras move on. The kids, of course, are still there and still suffering, but since we can't really do much about them anyway, in the long run, that is not a present concern. Long-term solutions are not the stuff of charities struggling to get attention, and donations, in their brief moments on the flickering screen, before the TV passes on to another crisis, another crying baby in another land. Within twelve hours of the 1994 crisis in war-torn Rwanda hitting the top of the news lineup on the BBC in London, there were a score of newly minted charities advertising on the tube, flashing telephone numbers where Britons could phone in a donation to assuage their guilt with gelt. One of these telemarketing services took in £12,500 a day, all of which went to pay for the costs of collection, so no money actually got to Rwanda, although the collectors themselves were prevented from starving.[2] There were, and are, several established charities, such as the International Red Cross, to look after such emergencies, but it was the newcomers who collected most of the money.

However, even when the work is done, as it usually is, by honest people who know their job, there is not, and cannot be, any attempt to sort out priorities according to any rational scale of need once the cameras roll and television determines the catastrophe of the week. The flow of money follows after the pictures, and if there are other youngsters elsewhere suffering just as much, that's a darn shame. And this irrational, emotional, wasteful process is simply the logical extension of the charitable impulse. The help is needed, so it would be churlish, to say the least, to ask any rude questions of the organizers trying to provide it. In *Lords of Poverty*, Graham Hancock writes:

> In all Western countries, irrespective of their wealth, and irrespective also of their ideological stance, "overseas development" has been elevated above political debate to become the least questioned form of state spending.[3]

THE MILLIONS SPENT BY AMATEURS

At the very time when every other form of government expenditure is being subjected to rigorous, even brutal, scrutiny, the millions of dollars given to foreign-aid charities to be spent by amateurs go unchallenged. Although there is a provision in law that the receiving organizations must not be in conflict with Canadian foreign policy, not much is done to ensure that this is the case.

In May 1995, Reform MP Val Meredith rose in the House of Commons in Ottawa to raise the issue of the Babbar Khalsa Society of Kamloops, B.C., which had been granted charitable status in 1992:

> This militant organization has been dedicated to the violent separa-tion of the Indian state of Punjab for over ten years. The now deceased founder of this organization is suspected of masterminding the terrorist bombing of Air-India flight 182, June, 1985, which resulted in the deaths of 329 individuals. Can the Minister of Revenue please explain how such a group could obtain and continue to receive charitable status?[4]

The then–revenue minister, David Anderson, responded that most charitable organizations are on the up-and-up, adding, "There may be some activities overseas of some organizations on which I would be happy to receive information on which I can check further." The "deceased founder" Meredith referred to was Talwinder Singh Parmar, who was shot by soldiers in India.

Meredith was back on June 5, with this:

> On Wednesday, May 31, the RCMP named the late Talwinder Singh Parmar and six colleagues as suspects in the Air-India bombing. Today I have provided the Minister with a copy of a 1989 newspaper photo of Parmar holding a rocket launcher, surrounded by dozens of machine guns and rockets. At that time, Parmar said if anyone wanted to commit suicide, he should board an Air-India plane . . .
>
> . . . I have a question for the Minister, which of the above facts does he believe qualifies the Babbar Khalsa Society for charitable status?[5]

Meredith also noted that the Canadian Security Intelligence Service had protested the society's charitable status.

Anderson responded:

> It is the policy of the government of Canada not to support terrorist organizations of any type, whether in the Indian subcontinent, whether in the former Yugoslavia, whether in Ireland or wherever they may be.[6]

A few weeks later, I asked an official at Revenue Canada if there was any investigation into the charity and was told, "No. Why, should there be?"

The evidence is not clear, then, to put it at its mildest, that we have the foggiest notion what is going on within the complex world of foreign-aid charities. On the other hand, it is precisely in this area that a few dedicated workers, with astonishingly little money, can run programs that make an appreciable difference in the lives of the recipients.

One of these successful programs is Sleeping Children Around the World (SCAW, pronounced Se-kaw), which raises money to provide bed kits for children in developing nations. It was the brainchild and remains the lifework of Murray Dryden, now in his eighties, father of two NHL goaltenders, Dave and Ken, and an extraordinary man in his own right. SCAW began almost by accident. Dryden, nearing retirement from a career as a manufacturers' agent in Toronto, was looking around for other projects and had it in mind to bring out a book of photographs of children sleeping; he started with his own grandchildren, then began to take pictures of children in other lands. One day, when he was travelling in Pakistan, he came upon a child in rags, sleeping in the street, and knew he had to do something.[7]

Beds are important, and a comfortable place to sleep is crucial; Dryden knew this from his own memories of the Depression, when he often walked all night for want of a decent place to lay his head. Moreover, supplying bedrolls was something a small organization could handle, unlike, say, trying to distribute food in a distant land. After a series of discussions with his wife, Margaret, Dryden launched SCAW in 1969. They each donated $1,500 to get the project rolling; half of it went to the YWCA in Bombay and half to the Salvation Army in Bandung, Indonesia, along with instructions to buy 100 bed kits. Dryden went out to handle the distribution that summer.

Since then, SCAW has raised nearly $8 million, mostly in Canada—about 20 per cent came from Australia and the United States—and has provided 330,000 bed kits, distributed through local groups, to children in twenty-six countries. Each kit consists of a groundsheet, mattress, pillow, sheets, pyjamas, blanket or mosquito netting (which one depends on the climate in the recipient country), an article of clothing, and personal care items like toothbrushes. The materials are purchased and the work done in the recipient country, providing jobs as well as relief.

SCAW was put on a firm financial footing in 1988, when Dryden turned over to the charity the title to three Christmas-tree farms he owned. Margaret had died in 1985, and this donation was a kind of memorial; it would have pleased her. The proceeds from the sale of two of the farms, invested, provides SCAW with a base of about $220,000 annually; other funds are raised through service clubs, Scout and Brownie groups, and individual donations. The administration costs are covered by the Christmas tree money, and the work is all done by volunteers. SCAW provides tax receipts for individual donations aimed at providing bed kits, but not for such personal expenses as the travel of volunteers, which Dryden doesn't think taxpayers should subsidize.

This is exactly the kind of project that an individual or small group can operate with far more efficiency than any public body, bringing both satisfaction to the workers and donors, and practical help to the recipients. But it isn't going to solve world hunger, is it? It isn't intended to; it is just what can be done by people who have the courage to go out and do it, and also have the administrative savvy—no small point—to do it well.

Another small charity begun with the best intentions was Yes, I Can!, set up by David Adie, a Calgary youth counsellor, to help improve children's self-esteem through sports and cultural programs. To get the project going, the charity launched a Great Wall of China run; the donors would sponsor three Canadians to ramble 2,500 kilometres across northern China, at so much per k. The Beijing authorities demanded an upfront payment of $50,000 to cover the cost of guides, support staff, and fees for the run, but the Calgary group could raise only $30,000. They took off, anyway, and jogged along through sandstorms, high winds, and forty-five-degree heat; they dealt with cliffs, mountains, and rivers, to say nothing of the constant attentions of Chinese military police. The runners and four Chinese companions had gone about 1,500 kilometres before the authorities decided they had to have the other $20,000; when it wasn't forthcoming, they pulled the plug. The project netted minus $10.[8]

SPREADING THE GOSPEL

When drought strikes, volcanoes erupt, famine falls on the land, or war thrusts a million refugees out onto the roads, you need something with a good deal more heft to it than SCAW. Well, we have that kind of charity, too, and Table 4 shows something of the books of the twelve largest of them.

In all, Canadian charities reported spending $1,075,572,073 abroad in 1993,[9] up 14.8 per cent from two years earlier. That is about one-third of what we spent as a national government on Official Development Assistance, mostly through the Canadian International Development Agency.[10] A lot of money. Whether it is wisely spent or wasted is mostly a matter of guesswork. The largest block of funding went to welfare ($393 million) and the second largest to religion ($304 million)—and I wonder how many Canadians know we are sending almost as much money abroad to spread the various gospels as we are to help out in disasters and other welfare projects.

The proportion of money received that gets through to the intended recipients varies from a low of less than 60 per cent, for the Worldwide Church of God, to over 95 per cent for the Canadian Foodgrains Bank (see Table 4). The Worldwide Church of God gives as its aim:

> To carry to the people of Canada and all the world the message which Jesus Christ pronounced and instructed his disciples to take to humanity, a message of warning and instruction in the way human beings should walk.

Strikes me as a bit odd for a charity to tell people how to walk. The Worldwide Church receives no direct government funding but, in the year ending March 31, 1994, wrote $15 million worth of receipts to donors, so it cost Canadians—even those who didn't give and had never heard of the outfit—several million dollars in forgone taxes.

The Canadian Foodgrains Bank, more prosaically, provides "Canadian foodgrains resources for Third World relief and development activities."[11] It receives most of its money from government—almost $18 million of a total of $23 million—and in the year ending March 31, 1994, shifted $22 million worth of foodstuffs, through "Church partner related agencies," to needy recipients in the Third World. It has set up its own monitoring service "to ensure compliance with terms, conditions and policies governing Foodgrains Bank allocation of food assistance." That is because none of the work abroad was done by the charity itself; it hired others, who worked on contract.

Revenue Canada does not make any attempt to count the number of charities that operate abroad, or mainly abroad, nor does the Canadian Centre for Philanthropy. They number several thousand, at a guess, and spend their money on everything from "Culture and Arts Promotion" ($12,653,338 in 1993) through "Protection of Animals" ($2,057,639) to "Temperance Associations" ($58,989).[12]

It is the subsidizing of the religious charities abroad that raises some of the thorniest problems. On the one hand, we have brave priests in Latin America putting their lives on the line for oppressed people—usually against the express command of their own Church, whose hierarchy is nearly always on the side of the oppressors. On the other hand, we have the Missions Fest in Vancouver, bringing together more than a hundred Christian groups with missions around the world, yet banning the United Church of Canada from participation. The United Church's sin was refusing to declare that "the only way to God is through Jesus Christ alone."[13] Bit of a surprise to the Hindu, Muslim, Shinto, and other brothers and sisters in the lands where these folks operate.

WHERE HAVE ALL THE DOLLARS GONE?

I don't object so much to the damn foolishness of these outfits as to the principle of allowing them to charge up their damn foolishness to the taxpayer. In my opinion, carrying the particular word of particular sects into the far corners of the world has done far more harm than good, whether we are talking about our grandparents slaughtering adult Tasmanians so they could put their kids in Sunday school, or our contemporaries pumping *The Watch Tower* into Zambia. Well, maybe I'm wrong, but I don't see why, if I have to help carry the load for something to which I stand in such fundamental disagreement, I cannot find out more about how the money is spent.

A number of questions arise:

1. Do Canadians have the foggiest notion that they are losing more than a billion dollars annually through tax deductions, as well as by paying for direct government grants?

2. If Canadians knew about it, would they object? Or would they save all their gripes about wasting cash in foreign climes when we need it back home for government agencies like the Canadian International Development Agency (CIDA), and forget about charities like World Vision of Canada? This is an international body whose Canadian arm is sending out packages of carrot seeds to raise funds, in hopes that the recipients will return the seeds, along with a donation. World Vision will spend $1 for every $1.50 it raises, according to its own estimate.[14] How would we react to the news that CIDA was blowing a dollar a pack on carrot seeds, in the hope that they would sprout money to help the hungry?

3. Is the foreign charitable sector efficient? You will see in Table 4 that the Watch Tower Society raised $22 million, of which a little more than $14 million was spent on charitable projects; the rest went elsewhere. Isn't that a lot of leakage? Most of this went to "print, distribute and facilitate the printing and distribution of Bible literature and to accomplish every-thing necessary to promote the religion of Jehovah's Witnesses"[15] in Albania, Canada, Colombia, Costa Rica, Estonia, Fiji, Finland, Guate-mala, Hungary, Mexico, Myanmar, Nicaragua, Nigeria, Pakistan, Portugal, Singapore, Turkey, the United States, and Zambia. I guess we cannot object, because we also fork out money through the tax system to allow other religions to spread their hype. My problem here is that I'm not sure whether I want all these soul-chasers to be effective or not, given the way war seems to follow religion into the field. Moreover, I can't help wonder-ing why, if it is considered political to campaign against freedom of choice for abortions in Canada, it isn't political to tell the people of nations that have aggressive state religions to drop everything and sign up for Jesus.

4. If some Canadians want to give money to charities that spend large sums outside Canada, such as the Christian Children's Fund, which spent $32 million abroad "helping children of all faiths,"[16] should other

Canadians be required to chip in? Ron Davis, head of the Charities Division at Revenue Canada, says that:

> There is a feeling that the charitable organization should be able to give a receipt only if the money is spent in Canada; if people want to give money to help abroad, good for them, but why should that be subsidized by other Canadians? . . . Is it normal that we should give to foreign countries? Billions of dollars are flowing out of Canada; the law used to state that all merchandise and services had to be purchased in this country, but no longer.[17]

5. Is there fraud involved in some of these foreign flings? We will never know. There is no effective overseer of the operations of these charities, and we must take what comfort we can from statements like this one in the tax return of the World University Service of Canada (wusc), which spent $6 million abroad, "to foster sustainable human development and human rights in a global context":

> The payments to our agents/representatives represent fees for services rendered. The relationship is governed by a contract. In addition, in most cases, we have field offices in the areas where these representatives work and our employees supervise their performance.[18]

This is the bureaucratic equivalent of "Trust me, I know what I'm doing": maybe they do, but maybe they don't. Canadian University Service Overseas (cuso) spent $15 million outside Canada in the year under review; its total income was $23 million, of which almost $20 million came from government grants, fees, and matching funds. To raise the $2 million in Canada for which it issued official receipts cost $1.4 million, to say nothing of $2.9 million that went on management and general administration.[19] Spending $1.4 million to raise $2 million doesn't make a whole lot of sense until you remember that the burden is being shared with a general citizenry which has no notion of how generous it is.

6. Have we any idea of the effect our charities have in far-off lands? Consider, for example, the charities like Goodwill Industries and the Salvation Army, through which we donate tonnes of clothes every year to

help the poor. The clothing and shoes and other items go on sale in the charity shops here, but anything that doesn't move gets bundled up into bales and sold, for very little, to international dealers who turn around and sell them for several times what they paid. In Toronto alone, as much as 20 tonnes a week of clean, wearable garments are generated through the two dozen outlets of Goodwill Industries.[20] This outpouring fetches about fifteen cents a kilogram for the charity in the first sale, and ten or twenty times that overseas. The bundles are broken up into individual items and shipped all over the world. This has become a huge international business, generating more than $600 million for the private exporters who reap the overwhelming proportion of the rewards.

In Asia or Africa, the goods sell for prices that are high, compared to the money the charity got, but much lower than the same garments can be produced for, locally. Dave Todd of the *Toronto Star* interviewed a New York exporter who exulted:

> I can deliver a pair of pants to the east coast of Africa for 35 cents . . . You can't send a letter to the east coast of Africa for 35 cents. And I'm sending a pair of pants; I mean the merchandise cost, freight, everything is included in there.[21]

The pants may be sold in Tanzania for $6, a huge markup, but much cheaper than the same item produced in the home economy. The result is something no one intended; workers who already make appallingly low wages have them cut or get laid off altogether. Thousands of jobs have disappeared in Third World countries because of the mushrooming import of secondhand clothes from the West, which simply adds to the burdens of the organizations trying to extend a helping hand. Of course, each charity just does what it can; ours are glad to pocket the pittance they get for their bundles of used clothing; making sense of the whole process is no part of their concern. But if giving to help the poor of Canada winds up hurting the even poorer of Asia and Africa, why should the insane process be financed by taxpayers?

Well, the taxpayers don't know, do they?

One of the best, and best-run of our foreign-aid charities, according to the experts, is the Foster Parents Plan of Canada. It conducts programs in thirty-three countries in Africa, Asia, Central and South America through direct sponsorship of individual children abroad by Canadians who contribute a set amount every month. Contributors get a personal satisfaction out of sending their money to a child whose picture they can see. In 1994, Foster Parents raised $33 million in Canada at a cost of $2.8 million, and paid $3.4 million in management and administration.[22] It seems, on the face of it, that if we want to help in the Third World, we would do better to funnel our funds through Foster Parents than WUSC, World Vision, or the Watch Tower Society, but we are supporting all of them through the tax system whether we want to or not.

THE CARE CONTROVERSY

In one of the rare exceptions to the golden silence that governs most of these matters, the CBC, in a television documentary broadcast in mid-1995, alleged that CARE Canada raised money for relief in Somalia, and "The money never got there."[23] The cash, about $367,000 that came welling out of wallets when the tribal massacres hit the television news broadcasts, was spent, the documentary said, on lavish travel and other nonessential costs. A former employee of the charity claimed, in so many words, that "No private donor money was channelled to these projects in Somalia," but there was no hard evidence for the statement, which CARE specifically denies.

CARE Canada is by far the largest of our foreign-aid charities. It is also one of the shyest of these organizations and does not show how much it spends in Canada or abroad, or how much it spends on the purposes for which it was set up. Actually, CARE doesn't tell us what those purposes are on its tax form, or what it spends on management, fund raising, or salaries. In the year ended June 30, 1994, it had an income of $75.3 million, of which $18 million came from government and $39 million from "foreign sources." Most of this was payments and fees from international agencies, such as the United Nations High Commission for Refugees.

CARE International dates back to the period immediately after the Second World War; it was set up to deliver emergency relief in Europe and later shifted its attention to developing countries. Its mission has also evolved into helping the world's poor to achieve economic sufficiency through projects involving forestry, water, and electrical power development. Today, CARE operates in more than fifty countries. The international body has an annual income of more than $600 million[24] and runs refugee camps in places like Zaire and Kenya, and provides drought and famine relief in places like Zambia.

CARE Canada is the lead organization responsible for co-ordinating the parent body's efforts in eleven nations: Angola, Bosnia, Burundi, Cameroon, Croatia, Indonesia, Kenya, Nicaragua, Zaire, Zambia, and Zimbabwe. It also pitches in during emergencies, such as the one that arose when civil war struck in Somalia. CARE's major government funding in Canada is triggered automatically by contracts with CIDA, under which the government agency matches the donations CARE raises from the public. CARE is not the only charity with this privilege, which has the taxpayer putting in one, two, or three dollars—the ratios differ for different charities and projects—for every dollar the group collects on its own. It's a great come-on for donations, but what it means is that if CARE could hoist its private take in Canada by, say, $10 million a year, the taxpayer would have to kick in another $10 million or so, spending public money with no questions asked.

In the year shown here, CARE raised only about $5 million in Canada and spent $1.3 million to raise it. But with government grants, our total contribution to the charity was more than $20 million, so we have a right to inquire into its practices. However, the charity's top officers declined to be interviewed unless the CBC journalists would give them in advance some details about what allegations were being made against the agency and by whom. That was a not unreasonable request; in the course of researching this book, I was asked on a number of occasions to supply lists of questions on controversial aspects. I did so every time, and I cannot think of any reason, other than ambush journalism, which produces fine images of discomfort but not much information, why such a request should be declined. In any event, the CBC wouldn't say what it had in mind, and the charity wouldn't talk. Instead, a CBC reporter waylaid John Watson, CARE's executive director, in a parking lot, with a camera crew and a list of shouted questions about the dismissal of a CARE employee. He looked uncomfortable and answered the queries awkwardly.

Because there was no on-the-record, informed discussion, CARE never did get a chance to explain a number of perfectly innocent items of expenditure that were made to look pretty bad in the original broadcast—such as spending relief money to hire an information officer in Mogadishu.[25] In a press conference called the day after the broadcast, that was explained as a perfectly normal and necessary cost. Then the charity rang down the information window on the grounds that there would be a libel trial sooner or later. Probably we will learn a great deal more about the agency when that trial takes place, but there must be an easier and better way to get information about an outfit that spends millions of our money every year.

Gordon Floyd, director of public affairs for the Canadian Centre for Philanthropy, told me:

> In the CARE case, the CBC was able to show that they collected about $400,000 to feed people in Somalia, and none of it went on food for people in Somalia. Where it went, though, was in making sure people in Somalia got fed.[26]

FOREIGN-AID CHARITIES MUST BE MORE FORTHCOMING

What the CARE case showed was just how complicated is the business of pouring supplies into a stricken area on an emergency basis. It may relieve the couch potatoes in front of their television sets to fire off a cheque or phone in a credit card number in response to the images on the screen, but that it does what needs to be done for the putative recipient is a dubious proposition indeed. Making foreign policy between beer commercials strikes me as a bit strange, but no nuttier than, say, the way we hand money to charitable foundations and hope for the best.

It is no reflection on CARE, or Save the Children, or any other of these well-meaning bodies, to argue that they need to be much forthcoming about where and how they raise and spend their money. It is as much in their interest as that of the general public to ensure that the more than one billion dollars that pours out of Canada each year in response to their urgent appeals is not stolen or wasted.

However, under the present system, many of the charities find it more convenient and less worrisome simply to broadcast the pictures of suffering kids and collar the cash. As with every other segment of the charitable sector, we are placing more and more responsibility in the hands of these organizations, due to the cutbacks to government funding. Without some indication that the money is being wisely spent, there is a good chance that donor fatigue will set in here, as elsewhere, and that won't do the world's wounded any good at all.

It is my view that foreign aid, supplemented by the valiant efforts of charities that fill in the niches neglected by governments, is the right way to deal with the sudden disasters that overcome various corners of the world from time to time. But if the task is to be taken on more and more by voluntary groups, operating either as the paid agents of governments or on a freelance basis, then they must be brought to heel in a systematic and open accounting.

The same may be said for the subject of the next chapter, the charitable foundations.

7. Foundations:
Charities with a Twist

Private charitable foundations are an odd sort of creature. They are really a very roundabout, inefficient way to channel money to worthy causes. They divert funds that would otherwise end up in the public purse into privately-controlled bodies where they are stockpiled for years on end and sometimes made available for private use. A small portion of this money ends up trickling out to causes that the wealthy donors choose to support, often a cultural activity or educational institution that particularly pleases the family. In the process, foundations enable some of the most powerful families in the country to quietly consolidate their economic power in the name of charity.

—LINDA McQUAIG,
Behind Closed Doors, 1987

Nathan Gilbert is a shrewd, cheerful, outgoing man in his mid-forties who radiates charm, energy, and purpose. Interviewing him is a little like interviewing a 500-watt bulb: share the warmth. He is the executive director of one of Canada's most effective charitable foundations, but he isn't anything like what I expected. I have come to his corner office in a central Toronto highrise building expecting to encounter a Suit. Gilbert is not a Suit. A Sweatshirt, maybe, but not a Suit. He is on the telephone when I arrive, and he waves me to one of those sofas into which you sink never expecting to see the sun again, and I look around while he talks to his son. A problem about the youngster's shoes; first things first. The office is large, looks out onto Yonge Street, and contains a clutter of papers, books, pamphlets, magazines, and pictures—lots of pictures—of his family. Oh, yes, and the certificate showing that he holds a degree as a Master of Social Work.

The phone call over, he fetches us coffee, peers at me over the clutter on the coffee table, and says, "Well?"

So I turn on my tape recorder and tell him that I am writing a book on the charitable sector . . .

"Yeah, yeah." He knows that; I told him on the phone.

". . . And I noticed in the *Canadian Directory to Foundations*, put out by the Canadian Centre for Philanthropy, that there is quite a lot of detailed information about the Laidlaw Foundation, and I was just wondering . . ."

A hand comes up like a traffic cop's, waving me into silence, and he is off. I will not get to finish that, or any other, question—I doubt if anybody does, except his kids—because he is ahead of me by about half a mile, every time:

> I give them more than they want, more recent contemporary information, because there is an advantage to the reader to know what we were doing most recently. A lot of foundations do not co-operate with the Centre for Philanthropy, because what the centre's annual listing does is identify that they exist, and who their directors are.

Gilbert throws me a significant glance, which sails right past and goes out the window. He leans forward to explain, "Many of the foundations don't see the tax expenditure side. They see it as their money, private money."

This is the crucial point. Foundations are charitable organizations, with a bit of a twist. What distinguishes foundations from other charitable organizations is that their money comes from just one or a few sources. There is nothing to prevent a foundation from raising funds any legal way it can, but the seed money comes from a family, usually; either in one large lump or in several lumps as members of the founding dynasty write their wills. The lumps are invested, and the income is used to support the chosen causes. By law, the foundation must expend each year, on the purposes stated in its charter, an amount equal to 4.5 per cent of its invested capital, calculated over the previous two years; so if it is to keep going, it must earn enough from investments to meet this target, operate, look after inflation, and, if possible, grow.

Where most charities receive funds mainly from taxpayers, donors, or other charities, a foundation's money comes from the family sock, sheltered from taxes to preserve it, and is dribbled back according to the whims of the folks in charge. I have come to challenge Nathan Gilbert on this very issue: why should we surrender tax revenues to family foundations so they can play with it and spend it how they will? But I never get to put this to him, because he is off again:

> When I started out in this job thirteen years ago, my stump speech was "Whose money is this? Is it the money of a private few to administer on behalf of some transparent statement of public good or is it an extension of private giving?" I think that's an issue that still hasn't been resolved.
>
> Most foundations operate by fiat of the president, who operates the organization out of his or her bottom drawer as an extension of private giving. There are probably fewer than 10 per cent of Canadian foundations that have staff, that are professionally run. If there is any staff, they are probably clerks or administrators tied to the business of the president, and not going to give him any back-chat.
>
> What you get, and I am talking now about some very large foundations with millions of dollars to play with, what you get is a meeting of the family, down to the third generation, to dole out the money. They don't have a clear focus, so they probably get 1,000 or so applications a year. They meet quarterly, and at each meeting, no one has done any real research, so they have a clerical person to organize the list.

They sit around and the clerical person says, "Well, on the first page, does anybody know anything about the organizations on this page? Anyone feel strongly about anything on this page? If not, let's turn to page two." And it's the only way they can conduct their affairs in the time frame they have allocated. It's based on sentiment and who knows whom, not on what needs to be done.

I want to say, Hey, that's my line, but he rolls right over me. "The Laidlaw Foundation," he says, "is a little different; it is relatively unique in Canada."

So it is, and it might be restful, before we look at the tangled and contentious and often screwed-up world of foundations, to probe into one that is about as good as they get.

SITTING ON THE FAMILY NEST EGG: THE LAIDLAW FOUNDATION

The Laidlaw Foundation was set up in 1949 by Robert A. Laidlaw, with money the family made in the lumber business, back in the days when there were still enough trees to cut in southern Ontario to run such an enterprise. Bobby Laidlaw put in $50,000 for the establishment of a foundation "to benefit charitable, educational, and cultural organizations in Ontario."[1] When his brother Walter, also active in the lumber business, died a few years later, he left $5 million to the foundation, which then buckled down to work seriously in the areas that interested family members.

Bobby had been active in the Hospital for Sick Children and in the arts. "He was a builder of the National Ballet," says Gilbert, "one of those who brought Celia Franca and Betty Oliphant over to get it going. He was the type of guy who would pay off the National Ballet debt by just peeling the money off the roll in his pocket and handing it over. Of course, in those days, you were only talking about multiples of hundreds of dollars."

Walter Laidlaw had been active in settlement house work, and the foundation used some of his money to get into the areas of health and social work. Culture and social work remain key activities of the foundation.

Nick and Rod, two of Bobby's three sons, became active in the foundation; a third son was killed during the Second World War. Nick had a background in child psychology and taught at university, while Rod was active in the family lumber business. Nick was the president of the foundation when Gilbert was hired in 1982:

> He was a pretty eccentric guy. On the one hand, he had the patrician quality you would expect from an old moneyed family, and on the other, he had a glint in his eye that made him intellectually generous and curious. He was also very kind. He always wore three watches, and when I asked him why, he said they were all gifts from his children, and he wouldn't want to show any favouritism.
>
> The first time I met him, at the interview for this job, he was wearing a brass hearing trumpet. I can still remember walking into a room with three of these guys and I broke into a big grin when I saw that trumpet; when they asked me why, I said I was debating whether I should bring a megaphone.

Eccentric or not, the Laidlaw brothers handled the foundation from the beginning in a thoroughly professional manner. They segregated a stream of money from the funds to back the family causes—which is all most family foundations ever do—and set about making the best possible use of the rest. Then they hired a professional staff and set up a volunteer research committee, with outside experts like the chief of psychiatry at the Hospital for Sick Children, to tell them where they could get the best results for their donations.

Within ten years, the family's pet projects, such as track-and-field meets in Canada, one of Nick's favourites, were being cut back, and most of the money was going into social work and the arts. The foundation provided fellowships for promising social work students to pursue advanced degrees and financed workshops in child development and mental health, until the department of Health and Welfare took over these areas. In the arts, the idea was to back only new works—especially music, theatre, opera, and dance.

"Nick was always able to make the distinction between the disbursement of personal resources for the things he wanted to support and not to make a claim against foundation expenditures," Gilbert says. "He gave backing to virtually every jazz artist who has come into his own in this country, and track-and-field stars—you used to see them hanging around here with their gym bags, waiting to see 'Uncle Nick,' but that had nothing to do with the foundation."

For nearly four decades, the foundation went along handing out grants in response to beseeching letters and applications, guided by committees of outside experts. Then, in 1987, not long after Nick's death, at a retreat held to ponder future directions, an entirely new approach emerged. There was not, never could be, enough money to fund all the applications, so the foundation should cease being a passive respondent and plan its own programs. In the balsa wood prose of the foundation's annual report:

> Listing charitable disbursements would satisfy the charitable objectives of the Foundation. It would not, however, satisfy the need for measures of outcome, impact or strategy.[2]

Do it yourself, in other words, instead of waiting to be asked for money. Task forces were set up to design new programs in which the foundation would be not just a funder but a planner, organizer, and animator of narrowly defined tasks.

In the arts, this meant concentrating on young and student artists and on the creation of Canadian work, especially among Canada's First Nations. Over the three most recent years covered in its reports, the foundation gave out $1,784,003 in grants, ranging from $74,500 to the Blyth Centre for the Arts to $1,000 to Philip Drube, "For a full evening of four new danceworks on the theme of love and loneliness."[3]

In the social work area, the new approach led to a program called Children at Risk, with a five-year plan to "promote the physical, social, emotional, and material well-being of families within Canada."[4] The three areas of involvement are research, protection, and child and family poverty. During the fiscal years 1991–93, the foundation poured $2 million into studies of child poverty and mortality, workshops on the mental health of Native families and children, and the beginnings of a comprehensive Centre for International Statistics on Economic and Social Welfare for Families and Children.[5]

There also emerged an entirely new project, the Great Lakes Conservation Programme, set up in 1988 under a brilliant young environmentalist, Bruce Lourie, with most of the money, now over $350,000 per annum, going to "innovative projects that have a broad geographical or political impact."[6] Grassroots outfits like Great Lakes are given money to "make information available on toxic use and release and potential toxic chemical accidents," just the sort of hell-raising that governments hate to fund. The project is also active in the Toronto Atmospheric Fund, which was set up with $25 million that came to the city from the sale of Langstaff Farm and is aimed at curbing carbon-dioxide emissions in the region by 20 per cent by the year 2000. Lots of luck.

The family's role in the Laidlaw Foundation has been carefully eased back. (One of the program officers told me, "Actually, the family is rather pissed off," because they have so little say.) The active directors today are people like David Crombie, a former mayor of Toronto; Dr. Lorna Marsden, president of Wilfrid Laurier University and a sociologist by training, and Professor Joyce Zemans, former director general of the Canada Council. The books show $38 million in assets, nearly all in stocks, which produce an annual income of just over $2 million, administrative costs of less than $300,000, and annual grants of just under $2 million.[7] This is a tight and well-run ship. But what is the point of handing out drabs of funding to performers, for example, who get exactly the same sort of funding from the Canada Council? Gilbert defends the cause this way:

> The foundation sector has a unique opportunity, because its account-ability structure is so different, its independence is remarkable. It's not driven by a bottom line; it doesn't have to satisfy customers or electors and think of short-term horizons of electability . . . It doesn't have to be accountable to shareholders in the same way that corporations do; and it doesn't have to raise funds. It can afford to be creative in ways no other sector can, although I doubt many foundations have ever assessed their position of privilege in that way . . . To me, the significant role of foundations lies in being a guarantor in the whole area of democratic pluralism; we can ensure that the marketplace of ideas is broad, that the voices of the timid reach the marketplace . . . So, it's a tall order.

SECRETIVE, SMUG, AND SILENT

A pot of money earned or inherited by a few individuals, some of which would normally flow into the coffers of the hellhounds of Revenue Canada, is instead protected; and the income, and part of the capital, are used each year to back specific projects that appeal to the trustees of foundations. Is it worth society's while to forgo tax revenues because the individual tastes (or weird ideas, depending on your point of view) of the founders will ensure "democratic pluralism"?

It's a thought, and not the worst of them. Nancy's Very Own Foundation, another of my favourites, holds the $7 million and change that Nancy Jackman walked away with when she quarrelled with the rest of her fabulously rich family and departed from the Jackman Foundation. Every year, she gives away about half a million dollars, "To support projects that attempt the removal of systemic discrimination against women and girls on the basis of gender."[8] In 1993, Nancy's gave $100,000 to Mount St. Vincent University in Halifax and $5,000 to Friends of Shopping Bag Ladies in Toronto. Wonderful.

The problem is that these are just two of more than 5,000 foundations, only about 1,000 of which provide a modicum of information to the Canadian Centre for Philanthropy for its annual review, the *Canadian Directory to Foundations*. You can buy the review for $220, plus tax, or consult it at the centre's library in Toronto for free, if you happen to live in Toronto. (The law requires foundations to make out a T3010 form, as it does charitable organizations; the foundations' figures are buried in the mound of 73,000 returns from charitable outfits available through Revenue Canada, so it is not impossible to get information, just damned hard.)

The foundations surveyed in 1993 held assets of $3.99 billion, handed out grants of $346 million, and really didn't tell us much about what they did with all the money. The Carr Foundation supports "Religious Studies at St. Thomas More College in Saskatchewan" and handed out just $6 in 1993; the Chin Foundation was established in British Columbia in 1974 "to accumulate funds for the purpose of constructing a nursing home," which was still unbuilt in 1994. The Campeau Foundation, which seems to have salvaged $5.5 million from the wreck of developer Robert Campeau's empire "to use its resources to foster hope,"[9] didn't do much of anything, dribbling out $140,266 in grants; what is the rationale for a $5.5-million tax shelter that returns less than three per cent to fostering hope?

The typical foundation is not at all the transparent, open, hard-working instrument of social progress represented by the Laidlaw; it is much more likely to be secretive, smug, and silent. When Samuel Martin was conducting the studies that led to his thoughtful book *An Essential Grace*, he circulated a research questionnaire to a large mailing list of foundations and reported the typical reply:

> We do not issue Annual Reports and do not wish to be included in any research your particular group is conducting. I am sure if there is any information you desire in this direction, you will find it easy to obtain.[10]

This "seize by the scruff of the neck and the seat of the pants and heave" approach to providing information to the public made Martin a little tetchy, and in a study remarkable for its generally muted tones, he noted that the criticisms levelled against Canadian foundations include the following:

> They dodge taxes, they are self-dealing, paying exorbitant salaries and fees to family members, lending money to themselves at sweetheart rates, leasing space at outrageous rentals from family members, employing relatives in the summer who are unemployable elsewhere, buying goods and services from family corporations.[11]

Mind, he doesn't say all these wicked things are true, because he doesn't know, any more than anyone else does, what actually goes on in the innards of these babies; he just says that, given the way they behave themselves in general, "No wonder there has grown a misconception, suspicion and even distrust of foundation activities on the part of responsible Canadians."[12] They should have filled out his damn research questionnaire.

The real reason foundations exist is not to be rude to academics, but because, as Teresa Odendahl, the author of an American study of foundations, has written, "Rich people like to make their own decisions about where their surplus money goes."[13]

It has always been thus.

BEHIND TAX-FREE WALLS

Foundations have been around as long as organized charity, if we define a foundation in the accepted way:

> A non-governmental, non-profit organization having a principle fund of its own, managed by its own trustees or directors, and established

to maintain or aid social, educational, charitable, religious or other
activities serving the common welfare.[14]

The phrase "having a principle fund of its own" is the key one.
Foundations have always been used for five main purposes:

+ to buy the founder's way into heaven
+ to wreak revenge on certain family members by leaving them out of the
  sharing
+ to cover up or atone for the misdeeds of the founders, as a public relations exercise
+ to retain control of a company by dumping its shares behind the high
  and tax-free walls of the foundation
+ or simply to allow someone with a lot of money to blow his own horn.

For centuries, foundations have enjoyed the agreeable advantages of
hoicking funds out of the grasping hand of the state and allowing the
donors to control where the money went.

In the first category, buying your way into heaven, we have the bodies
established by the Benedictines as early as the sixth century as a sort of toll
road to heaven. You handed over your goodies, expired, and were wafted to
paradise on the prayers of the brothers. Or, if you weren't, you were in no
position to make a warranty claim. These foundations prospered so might-
ily over the next two centuries that the Byzantine emperor confiscated
their property, on the grounds that they had become too powerful.[15]
Edmund Burke described foundations as "the useful fruit of a late peni-
tence,"[16] and there is an awful lot of fruit strewn down the halls of history.

In the family-revenge category comes George Jarvis, an Englishman
who disapproved of his daughter's marriage and left his huge fortune to
the poor of three villages in Hertfordshire, just to make sure that she and
her scurvy husband didn't get any. The upshot was that so many of the
needy and greedy moved to the three villages to collect that the area was
devastated. In the same vein, Thomas Nash, an eighteenth-century
grouch, set up a foundation to finance the pealing of church bells at Bath;
the bells were to be muffled in a funeral dirge every year on the anniversary
of his wedding and to peal unmuffled on the anniversary of his death to
commemorate his release from his wife.[17]

There is some debate about whether John D. Rockefeller set up the series of foundations established in his name for the reasons given—"To promote the well-being of mankind throughout the world"—or just to try to clear up the odium attached to his name. The oil millionaire and robber baron had always given away large sums to the poor—and paid exceedingly small sums to those who worked for him—so his defenders say that he was really a nice guy. On the other hand, when he found he had an excess of coal at his 7,500-acre estate in the Pocantico Hills section of New York state, he sold 1,500 tons of it to the residents of a nearby town for $8.75 a ton, when the going rate was $7.43.[18]

He founded the University of Chicago, and the University of Chicago duly turned out a gaggle of professors of economics who declared that the immensely wealthy and law-breaking trusts run by Rockefeller and his friends were "sound Christian institutions." Not only that, a professor of English literature declared Rockefeller to be "superior in genius to Shakespeare, Homer and Dante,"[19] so you can't say he didn't get a good return on his gifts, whether he intended to or not. Syracuse University, also awash in Standard Oil money, fired a gifted young instructor in economics who was felt to be sympathetic to the burgeoning unions that were at war with Rockefeller. There is no evidence that John D. ordered the firing, but he would not have been displeased.

The oil baron decided that he had to have some more organized method of dispensing the money that was piling up around his ears, so he hired a former Baptist minister, Frederick T. Gates, to advise him. Gates told him that the way he was accumulating money would "inundate and destroy him and his family," and even wrote Rockefeller a letter in which he declared, somewhat dramatically, "Your fortune is rolling up, rolling up like an avalanche! You must keep up with it!"[20] There was also the fact that the Rockefeller name had become a stench in the nostrils of humankind, thanks in part to Ida Tarbell, the muckrucking journalist who called him "the supreme villain of his age" and went a long way to proving it.[21] While John D. was trying to muscle the charter for his foundation through Congress, *Hampton's Magazine* wrote that "If the Standard Oil Company is a monster; the Rockefeller Foundation might easily become a whole platoon of Frankensteins."[22] Whether to buy some nice publicity, or to sweeten Congress, which was trying to break up the Standard Oil Trust, or just because he was such a nice guy, John D. threw $50 million into the foundation in 1913, following a line of thought which, if nothing else, was candid:

> I believe the power to make money is a gift of God . . . to be developed and used to the best of our ability for the good of mankind. Having been endowed with the gift I possess, I believe it is my duty to make money and still more money, and to use the money I make for the good of my fellow man according to the dictates of my conscience.[23]

Apparently, it was God who told John D. to hire thugs and goons to beat up, shoot, and otherwise inconvenience workers who objected to the conditions in his mines, mills, and refineries. One of the fledgling foundation's early projects involved hiring a Canadian named William Lyon Mackenzie King to study industrial relations. While the future prime minister was still studying, a strike broke out at the Colorado Fuel and Iron Company, culminating in the Ludlow Massacre, in which dozens of union members and their families were slaughtered; many of them burned to death in their company-owned shacks.

The link between the series of nonprofit and nontaxable bodies Rockefeller had set up and his own personal interests became a controversial part of the federal investigation that followed the Ludlow Massacre, and the public furore led, gradually, to outsiders taking control of the charitable group.[24] Today, the largest survivor, the Rockefeller Foundation, with assets of about $3 billion, is active all over the world as a professionally run outfit. Rockefeller's name, it is fair to say, is now surrounded with hosannahs, because so much money has flowed out of his grave and into good works. It is totally in vain that an editorialist wrote in the *Raleigh News and Observer* at the time of his death, "Let us not canonize Standard Oil Rockefeller by putting laurels on his head because he seeks to buy the appreciation of the people whom he has been robbing for a quarter of a century."[25] He has been canonized, in what was probably the most massive public relations campaign in history, through his own creation.

Some of the foundation's projects, such as the re-creation of Colonial Williamsburg in Virginia, are triumphs that have benefited everyone interested in history, so there is that in its favour. Offsetting this is the fact that in 1911, when the U.S. Congress ordered the breakup of the Standard Oil Company, Rockefeller's monopoly, he got around the law by splitting the firm into several pieces, each held by one of his foundations, and went on running the whole empire just as he wanted to.

This brings us to the fourth category of these organizations, those set up to retain control of a company.

The Ford Foundation, one of the world's largest, was established as a family foundation in 1936 by Henry Ford and his son Edsel for just this reason. Under the succession laws of the time, taxes would have gobbled up 91 per cent of the family holdings. Instead, Henry and Edsel funnelled 90 per cent of the company shares, in the form of nonvoting stock, into the foundation, retaining 10 per cent, the only voting stock, for themselves. The foundation paid the tax bill, at a modest rate. The Fords kept complete control over the firm, and, while they lost the income from dividends, which remained with the foundation, they were not hard up for money, anyway. The Ford Foundation today, which is no longer connected to the family, has assets of $6.9 billion, about three times the assets of all Canadian private foundations.[26] Incidentally, one of the reasons there are so many U.S. foundations—more than 20,000, controlling assets of more than $40 billion—is that there is still a succession duty in the United States; in Canada, with no such charge, the need to protect the family funds is not so great.

Other rich corporations looked at how the Fords had made a private family foundation into a vehicle for preserving control of a corporation, saw that it was good, and did likewise. The Krupp Foundation was founded "to preserve the unity of the Fried Krupp enterprise,"[27] so the arms maker could hang onto its millions after the Second World War, and the Agnelli Foundation of Italy, and hundreds more.

Howard Hughes, the interesting but nutty American entrepreneur, sheltered $134 million in company stock in the Hughes Foundation, but not a penny of dividends went into the charity. Instead, Hughes shuffled funds among this body, the Hughes Medical Institute, and a number of his companies, in such a way that he escaped paying millions in taxes.

In Canada, the W. Garfield Weston Foundation was formed with the controlling shares of the baking family's far-flung, $2.6-billion empire, but in 1976, when the law was changed to require foundations to reveal a minimum about themselves, the organization dropped out. The word "charitable" was deleted from the foundation's title, although it still exists and still controls the 250 companies in the empire.[28]

In the fifth category of foundations, personal horn-blowing, my favourite is one set up by John Stuart McCaig in England, which provided ₤2,000 a year "to encourage rising artists" by having them erect statues of himself and his family on his estate.[29] J. B. Duke, the tobacco king, gave money to a small Methodist school in Durham, North Carolina, on condition that it change its name to his, and it gets along famously as Duke University; Cambridge and Oxford Universities both have colleges named Wolfson in response to cash from the Wolfson Foundation, and the trend has grown so popular that I am thinking of leaving some cash to support the Walter D. Stewart urinal back at my old alma mater, Victoria University, since every other chunk of brick, mortar, and porcelain in institutes of higher learning in this land seems have been stamped with someone's name already. Ben Whitaker notes that "At least ninety per cent of all existing foundations today perpetuate the donor's name."[30]

The huge advantage of these benefactions is that the donors get to do what they want, whether it makes sense or not, and the costs are passed on to the foundation. A British donor set up a foundation to pay ₤300 a year to a man "unsuccessful in literature, in the diffusion of my opinions";[31] another funded the Robert Schalenbach Foundation Inc., which still exists, "to keep before the public the ideals of Henry George." An American established a fund, which he hoped would prove his thesis that the French will do anything for money, to pay French peasants to dress up as matadors or hula dancers.

Foundations have been established to support an orchestra, by a man who wanted his son to be a conductor, and to form a ballet company, in which the founder could dance. One that started out in one direction and then changed channels was set up by John Chaloner of New York, to help Americans study art abroad. In 1897, Chaloner was committed to a New York lunatic asylum, probably at the instance of his brothers so they could get control of his wealth. He escaped and fled to Philadelphia, where he was found to be perfectly sane. He then amended the charter of his foundation, giving it three new purposes: to crusade against the lunacy laws, to publish his own poetry, and to keep any of his brothers from ever sniffing a dime of his money.[32]

My least favourite in the I-can-do-anything-I-want-with-my-money sweepstakes goes to the late Mrs. Beryl Buck, an oil millionairess in California, whose will set up a fund to be spent entirely in Marin County, then the richest county, per capita, in the United States.[33] The Buck Trust, with $447 million in the old sock in 1984, gave $25,000 to the Bio-Dynamic French Intensive Gardening School; $20,000 to the Sleepy Hollow Home Owners' Association to hire a swimming coach for a pool used by the association; $169,000 to equip a television studio for the Golden Gate Baptist Theological Seminary; and $300,000 to another foundation to study the possibility of making improvements to three historic forts in the county. This money might otherwise have been frittered away foolishly. In the end, some of the sensible trustees responsible for the funds petitioned the courts to break the binding stipulation so they could spend money outside the county, on the grounds that Mrs. Buck didn't understand the extent of her fortune. They were denounced as "grave robbers" by the good folks of Marin County, and they lost the case.[34]

There certainly have been sensible reasons for setting up foundations, beginning with Andrew Carnegie, who received $500 million for his steel companies from J. P. Morgan (who then injected more than a billion dollars of watered stock into the new U.S. Steel conglomerate) and set about spending it through the Andrew Carnegie Foundation to escape "the disgrace of dying rich."[35] Carnegie gave $43 million to build and equip libraries in the United States, Canada, and Britain; to set up teaching, scientific, and technological institutes, and to fund the Carnegie Endowment for International Peace. By 1913, Carnegie was spending more on education than the federal government of the United States. When he couldn't get rid of all his money, he put the rest into the Carnegie Corporation, which he ran with increasing belligerence and dottiness, squandering some $38 million while achieving very little.[36] When he died in 1919, he was still rich, but he had given it a good try.

EARLY CANADIAN FOUNDATIONS

In 1918, while Carnegie was still at it, the first Canadian foundation was established with the estate, mostly shares in the family business, of Hart Massey, scion of the founder of one of the world's major farm-implement manufacturers. The McConnell Family Foundation, the nation's richest, was not founded until nearly twenty years later, by John Wilson

McConnell. He made his millions by cornering the sugar market with St. Lawrence Refineries and then multiplied them with investments in publishing—he owned four Montreal newspapers and wouldn't allow any of them to print his name or photograph—as well as banking, transportation, and insurance. Today, the foundation controls nearly $400 million in assets and during 1993 distributed sixty-three grants that amounted to $16,072,800; it declines to say exactly where the money went, except that it is interested in "social development, arts and culture."[37]

The Atkinson Charitable Foundation was founded in 1942 with the legacy of Joseph Atkinson, "Holy Joe," founder of the *Toronto Daily Star*, and made its first grant to the Hospital for Sick Children in Toronto for research into hearing defects. Joe had such a problem himself. Soon after came the McLean Foundation, financed by the Canada Packers fortune of J. S. McLean, in 1945, then two foundations set up in London, Ontario, in 1947, to perpetuate the names of Richard Green Ivey and his wife Jean. The Ivey money came from law, insurance, and finance, and went into one foundation for men and another for women, an early and commendable attempt to promote gender equality in this country.

Another dozen families immortalized themselves during the 1950s, from the McLaughlans, Bronfmans, and Molsons in the East to the Donners, Woodwards, and Muttarts in the West. The Donner Foundation was set up in 1950 by William H. Donner, from Indiana, who made a fortune in oil, gas, tin, and steel. It is now our fifth-largest foundation, and third-largest family foundation, with assets of over $81 million.[38] (The Chastell Foundation, founded in 1987 by Charles R. Bronfman, has $133 million.)

The first institutionalization of Francophone family money came with a foundation established by Quebec financier Jean-Louis Lévesque in 1961, to celebrate his fiftieth birthday. The Bombardier Foundation followed in 1967. These remain the only two French-Canadian bodies among the top fifty Canadian foundations.[39] The breed is overwhelmingly WASP, male, and rich, and serves an astonishingly narrow band of tastes, despite Nathan Gilbert's hopeful talk about pluralism. The major funds appear to go (appear to, because no one really knows anything beyond the modicum of material released by the bodies themselves) to health care, education, theatres, museums, and art galleries. However, there is at least one foundation on the left: the Douglas-Coldwell Foundation was established in 1971 in the names of Tommy Douglas and M. J. Coldwell, "To distribute funds for political education and social democracy." Its most recent report showed assets of $657,612 and total grant spending of $0; it is not a threat to the C. D. Howe Institute.

The trickle of foundations became a flood in the 1970s and 1980s, as more and more families discovered the pleasures in being able to hold on to their hard-won cash by the rather elementary process of simply sticking it into an organization with a charitable purpose and spending the income to favour their own pet projects. Today, there are foundations that will undertake to do almost anything, from curing your headache—the Migraine Foundation—to "enhancing the well-being of the citizens of Calgary"—the Nat Christie Foundation. They have grown their own lobbying arm, the Association of Canadian Foundations, which Samuel Martin found to be "rather loosely knit and soporific"[40] until 1981, when the then–finance minister, Allan MacEachen, brought in a series of budget measures to reform the foundations.

There had been a rather nasty scandal in Quebec, involving a feed-mill operator, Antoine Guertin, in the village of Sainte-Pie. Guertin set up the Fondation Ste-Pie in 1960 to support a religious mission in Brazil and persuaded his employees to donate some of their annual bonus to this. They got back tax receipts. The foundation then lent the money each year to the company at interest rates far below the market, and it was only this interest that found its way to the mission. Revenue Canada took Guertin to court, claiming the whole process was a sham, but the federal court found in Guertin's favour in 1981, thus legitimizing all such daft deals.[41]

In an attempt to restore some measure of sanity, MacEachen proposed new rules designed to block self-dealing loans and investments. He also drafted rules to end money transfers between the charities, which they used to evade the rules requiring them to pay out a minimum of 4.5 per cent of their asset base every year (a foundation could get around this by simply slipping money to another, related foundation, bringing it back again, and showing the transaction as a charitable expenditure). Finally, and, most awful of all, he wanted to require the foundations to include capital gains in the income that was subject to disbursement rules.

The way it stood, if a charity made a large capital gain on stocks or real estate in its portfolio, that didn't count; it was the price at which the asset went onto the books that mattered. When this bit of legislation was floating around Ottawa, I spoke to a man who had worked on drafting it for the finance minister; I wondered if the effect of making the foundations pay out part of their gains, and not just their income, wouldn't be to nibble them to death. "Not nibble," he responded, "chew."

That was certainly the way the lobby saw it, and within a few days, foundation director was calling to foundation director across the dismal swamp, and Ottawa was deluged with letters from the kind of people who kick in large amounts of money not only to charities but to political campaign funds. Within a few months, the measure was as extinct as the dodo. In its place came the requirement now in force, that a foundation must base its 4.5 per cent disbursement requirements on invested capital, period. To eliminate self-dealing and favours to relatives, there was a penalty tax on "non qualified investments," which were all transactions not entered into at arm's length, but that died on the Order Paper.[42]

It was an awesome performance, when you think about it. The tax rules had created a new and muscular financial instrument, supported entirely by sheltering the family kitties from the cruelty of having to pay out a portion to the state, the way the rest of us do. And this new financial instrument had become so well dug in to the body politic that it could, by itself, through the exertions of a few dozen men, say to the government, "Thou shall not pass." And it didn't.

The Centre for Canadian Philanthropy lists, in its annual roundup of those who choose to reply to its questionnaire, data on 944 foundations, with total assets of $3,977,527,298.[43] The top fifty of these control 68 per cent of all the assets, leaving the remaining 894 with 32 per cent. Not surprisingly, the foundations follow the same pattern as the corporate sector, with a few giants dominating. We have more foundations in this country than we have hospitals;[44] they employ 36,000 people full-time and 6,000 part-time (many of the family foundations have either a single employee or none at all.) While charities in general receive most of their money from government, the foundations get less than 5 per cent of theirs this way; most of it comes from nest eggs and the income they earn.

Still, we have such interesting situations as the Aga Khan Foundation, set up in the name of one of the world's richest men, to "assist people in low-income countries of Asia and Africa without regard to race, religion or political affiliation."[45] In 1993, it received just over $7 million in government funding in Canada, out of a total income of $18.4 million (Table 5).

The Aga Khan himself made "a discretionary donation" of $1,269,117 (down from $1,302,339 a year earlier), through another foundation in Switzerland.[46] Why should the Canadian taxpayer put in more than five times as much (through CIDA and other agencies) for the great khan to get all the credit?

In addition to the private family foundations, which represent four out of every five of these organizations,[47] there are corporate foundations (of which more in the next chapter); special purpose foundations (like the Hospital for Sick Children Foundation in Toronto, with assets of $109 million); community foundations; service club foundations (there are only four of these, connected with health care), and crown foundations.

COMMUNITY FOUNDATIONS

The first community foundation was set up in 1921, with $100,000 in a personal cheque from W. F. Alloway, a Winnipeg banker who wanted to repay his home city for making him rich. The Winnipeg Foundation is still going strong and is very active in support of social services in the city; among other things, it helps to fund the Harvest Food Bank. While community foundations flourished in the United States, we didn't get another one until the Vancouver Foundation bobbed up in 1943, the Hamilton Foundation in 1954, and the London Foundation in 1979.[48] These bodies, which usually combine social work with cultural support, are not financially significant, except for the Vancouver one, the second-largest foundation in Canada, with assets of $355,602,470 in 1993, and grants of more than $22 million for arts and culture, child welfare, medical research, conservation, seniors, and the environment.[49]

CROWN FOUNDATIONS

Crown foundations are something else again, an often resented outgrowth of yet another wrinkle in the tax law. While individual donors to a charity can claim a tax credit to a maximum of 20 per cent of personal income (as can corporations), if you give to the queen, you can write off whatever you choose to give, up to 100 per cent of your income. This may be a moot point for you and me, but not for a millionaire with a tax problem.

Crown foundations are not directly owned or run by government; they are the offspring of nonprofit organizations mainly funded by government, such as hospitals, universities, or provincial nonprofit organizations. The

Hospital for Sick Children in Toronto has its own crown foundation. If you give money to the hospital itself, you can get a tax credit equal to, but no more than, 20 per cent of your annual income in any one year, no matter how much you give. If you give to the hospital's crown foundation, the kickback can be up to your entire income for the year; in that event, you will pay no tax. Obviously, these bodies are aimed at the super-rich, and the only practical reason for their existence is as a tax-avoidance funnel. When I give my million to a crown foundation, I decide how the money will be spent; otherwise, it will be taxed away from me, and someone else will get to decide where it goes.

Crown foundations have been around for some time—the Wild Rose Foundation in Alberta, the Trillium Foundation in Ontario, and the Institute for Research on Public Policy, a federal crown foundation, are examples. In 1984, a bright lawyer in Vancouver, Blake Bromley, began to agitate for the creation of crown foundations for universities and hospitals, and in the flicker of an eyelash, comparatively speaking, the deed was done. In July 1987, the Universities Foundation Act was passed, creating separate crown foundations for each of British Columbia's institutions of higher learning.[50]

Dr. David See-Chai Lam, formerly B.C.'s lieutenant governor, threw in a million dollars for the Asian Gardens at the University of British Columbia, and the institution has been practically drowning in money ever since. (In the year ending March 31, 1994, the university had revenues of $710 million.)[51] Soon there were similar laws on the books in seven Canadian provinces, allowing schools and hospitals to set up new bodies to receive this bounty.

Without being dog-in-the-manger about it, the other charities are filled with alarm and despondency. A senior officer with a large corporate foundation told me:

> Crown foundations are a real concern. They always have loads of money, so, when a granting agency gets an application from one of them, it is always well-drawn, with a neat set of graphs proving how necessary the money is. Other outfits don't stand a chance.

Fair or not, the crown foundations are here to stay, and in the dog-eat-dog world of charitable fund raising, they are likely to come out ahead, because of the skewing of the tax system. Take the case of Mr. Green Jeans, who has an annual taxable income of $200,000 and a nice pile of capital. If he wants to give, let us say, $1 million to the Alzheimer's Society, he can get a tax credit equal to a maximum of 20 per cent of that, or $200,000. He can spread this out over five years, at $40,000 a year. However, suppose he decides to give the $1 million, instead, to a crown foundation; now, he can write off his entire annual income of $200,000 and spread it over five years to claim *all* of his gift against tax; it won't be his gift, any more, it will be yours and mine as well, but he will be the one who gets his name up in lights.

Where do you suppose Mr. Green Jeans will give his money? Not to Alzheimer's, that's for damn sure.

FOUNDATIONS AND TAX DEDUCTIONS

When I wandered out of Nathan Gilbert's office about two hours after I had entered, with a full notebook, a tape recorder reading "battery low," and my mind in a maze, I was thinking much kinder thoughts about foundations than ever I had thought before. There are, it is clear, a good many foundations, both public and private, that do much good work and that support the optimistic, cheerful and positive note he sounds. However, it still seems to me that if our super-rich want to earn honorary degrees—one of the easiest, though never one of the cheapest, ways to be declared officially intelligent is to pop a few millions into the charitable kitty—or see their names on the front of a hospital, or simply pile up points in heaven, they ought to do it with their own money. A cynical American once remarked that "Philanthropy is tied at the hip bone to tax deductions,"[52] and nowhere is that clearer than in the operation of the foundations.

Anyone who thinks the money that flows from these granting institutions isn't directed in a specific way hasn't been paying attention. Whether it is the C. D. Howe Institute funding paper after paper to prove that private enterprise ought to be left untrammelled to get on with the job, just as its founding members believe, or the Pioneer Fund Institute putting up the cash so that Professor Philippe Rushton of the University of Western Ontario can churn out papers suggesting that race is the key to intelligence,[53] a notion which disappeared from respectable science just about the same time as spats vanished from the world of fashion.

We are marginally better served than the Americans, who give house room and tax concessions to such strange outfits as the Margaret Thatcher Foundation, which has $3 million in the kitty "to promote capitalism in Eastern Europe." The baroness tried to set up a branch in England, but the Charity Commission refused the registration on the grounds that it was "too political."[54] Then there is the Progress and Freedom Foundation, Newt Gingrich, prop., which sponsors the college course and cable-television show that features the U.S. House Speaker. Much of its cash comes from pharmaceutical and cable-television companies, two industries crucially involved in pending legislation before Congress.[55]

Neither of these foundations would qualify for tax-exempt status in Canada, although that is not the same thing as saying we couldn't have them here. We certainly do have our fair share of outfits whose reasons for existing and receiving government support remain vague and problematic.

Philanthropic foundations are not charities at all, in the real sense of helping the poor. A poor person who turned up on the premises of the Ford Foundation or the J.W. McConnell Foundation would be bounced back out onto the street. These institutions exist to protect the money of the elite so that it can be spent as the elite wants it spent, and the rationale is provided by the fourth head of charity—benefit to the community. It is a dubious proposition that allowing Robert Campeau to sock away $5 million is of benefit to the community, and, while it is undeniable that at least some of our foundations do some good, I doubt very much if they could justify their existence against any really prolonged scrutiny of how they spend their funds. Isn't it convenient that they don't have to?

The world's most prestigious foundation, founded with money made by munitions maker Alfred Nobel, flourishes in Sweden, a nation that will not allow charitable donations as deductions from taxable income. At least some of the unfairness of our own system could be cured by simply copying the Swedes in this simple rule, but I wouldn't hold my breath.

8. Cause Marketing:
Selling Beer and Buying Blessings

Today, cause marketing, which includes promotions in which a portion of the purchase price is
donated to non-profits, is the fastest-growing
type of marketing.

—CRAIG SMITH,
Harvard Business Review, SPRING 1994

It's a hell of a life for a tycoon; you rack up a billion or so in profits for your corporation, and everybody jumps on your neck as a blood-sucking capitalist; you don't, and you get the order of the boot. But take heart; there is always charity, which has poured its soothing salve over reputations even more dodgy than your own and which can do it for you, with—and this is the best part—most of the money being laid off on the saps who pay taxes. William Zimmerman, one of the more prominent rogues in the rich gallery of rascals that illumines our history, is described in the *Encyclopedia*

Canadiana as a solid businessman whose successes "brought him a large fortune and enabled him to contribute generously to many worthy causes."[1] There is no mention of hiring clergymen to sell stock in a railway that never got built, or bribing legislators, or the fact that Zimmerman died when one of his trains plunged into the Desjardins Canal in 1857 because a trestle which was supposed to have been built of oak was built of pine instead, with William pocketing the cost savings.[2] The trestle collapse and the crash killed sixty passengers, including Zimmerman, but if you contribute to worthy causes, you are a worthy man, and that's how Zimmerman is remembered.

In our own day, tobacco companies massacre the masses with their cancerous products six days of the week, and on the seventh collect kudos for putting up the tax-deductible cash for ski races, horse shows, and cultural shindigs. After a hard day of fleecing the widow and orphan, the stockbroker wends his way to a five-course dinner at a charity do for which the company bought the tax-deductible tickets at $2,000 a table. If he saves enough on dinners, he can give a large whack to his alma mater to buy himself an honorary degree, thus proving that he is not only honourable but erudite. He will be a "Doctor," imparting more heft to his speeches about the need for the governments whose tax revenues he has helped whittle down to pull in their belts.

We mustn't be too cynical about this; our history and our present both ring as well with the names of generous donors who took little or no credit for what they gave. With very little fuss, Sigmund Samuel, the metal magnate and philanthropist, devoted all the profits from his companies to good works for twenty years before he died. He called his autobiography *In Return* and explained that "A man must show his gratitude if he can."[3] It is undeniable that it is nice to have gratitude appreciated in the form of tax breaks, honorary degrees, and maybe even, if we fork out enough dough often enough, the Order of Canada. Along the way are the warm articles in the newspaper and the cherished "Also seen at the dinner were the lovely Mr. and Mrs. Whatsits; he is the one who is so generous with his money, she with her favours."

The cover line on a British magazine called *Time Out* not long ago contained a querulous question: "Why can't these old farts just hand over the money instead of flaunting their tired egos?"[4] But that would be missing the point, wouldn't it? Just as the politician should strive not merely to be honest but to be *seen* to be honest, the tycoon must be *seen* to be generous, or the company won't get the publicity benefit at all.

And the tycoon who is well-advised can use the occasion to boost the old firm with what could be called charitable leverage. In financial circles, leverage is the process through which a small amount of money can be turned into a large amount by a series of interlocking deals. In charity, the same philosophy can be applied by resisting all pressures to have you donate a few hundred thou to, say, a theatre or art gallery, and then throwing in your doubloons at the last minute, on condition that they name the place after you. Thus, Thomson Hall, in Toronto, perpetuating the name of Roy Thomson on the basis of a last-minute cash infusion of $4.5 million. The concert hall, which cost $39 million to build, was to have been called New Massey Hall.[5] Much more recently, the O'Keefe Centre was renamed on the same basis, going from the celebration of an extinct beer to a live computer company. For a donation of $5 million, spread over six years, it is to become the Hummingbird Centre. But the name is only to last twenty years, at the end of which it turns into a pumpkin. Our art czars have thought up a way to keep milking money out of the tycoons by leasing space instead of selling it, and driving us all nuts.

Given the advantages to be gained by doling out cash in a public way, it is surprising that, on the whole, our corporations are so chintzy. And getting chintzier. In 1946, Canadian firms gave just under one per cent—0.86 per cent, to be exact—of their profits, before taxes, to charity. This rose slowly, to a peak of 1.5 per cent of the take in 1958,[6] then declined to less than one-third of the 1958 level in recent years. In 1993, corporate donations came to $1.2 billion,[7] just under 0.43 per cent of their pre-tax profits; in 1994, profits soared by 192.9 per cent, and charitable corporate donations rose by 5.4 per cent.[8] Company giving accounts for one per cent of charitable revenues, while individuals, with gifts of $8.2 billion, account for about seven times as much.[9]

The larger the corporation, the tighter. Samuel Martin shows that while companies with net incomes of more than $30 million annually are much more likely to make donations than those in the lower strata—they have, after all, much more to slosh around—their giving, measured as a percentage of income, is about one-third of that donated by smaller firms.[10] Foreign-owned companies, our largest, are even more reluctant to part with a loony than the natives; they gave at the border. Of $100 worth of pre-tax income, the foreign firms surrender thirty-five cents to charity; the Canadian ones, eighty cents.[11] To finish the thing off, the amount of money contributed by all our corporations, per employee, has been going down steadily for nearly four decades, even though their tax burden has been shrinking. Martin comments, "Thus both voluntary and involuntary contributions have shrunk considerably."[12]

When you consider that our corporate sector is increasingly foreign-owned, increasingly dominated by large firms, and increasingly sacking employees to raise productivity, it is clear that the miserable amount corporations dribble into charitable endeavours is bound to shrink even further, unless something is done.

Well, by golly, something *is* being done. There is a campaign, launched in 1988 through the Canadian Centre for Philanthropy, which endeavours to persuade Canadians to open their wallets a little wider and to sign up as volunteers a little more often. It is called IMAGINE, all in capital letters, and the Governor General of Canada is its patron. There are two components, a public program directed to individuals, which seems to be chiefly aimed at marketing charities through ads in the Yellow Pages and other promotions; and the corporate program, which actually tries to accomplish something, namely to "help develop a broader and deeper base of corporate philanthropy in Canada."[13]

ONE-PER-CENT CARING COMPANIES

Specifically, the idea is to build a list of "Caring Companies," defined as companies that will pledge themselves to a policy of "donating 1% of average, domestic, pre-tax profit based on the three preceding years."[14] In Phase I, the first five years, IMAGINE reports, it achieved "important success," which it describes in the following canny way:

> When IMAGINE began in 1988, the norm of giving by Canadian corporations was one-half of 1% of pre-tax profits. Now, in a recent survey by The Conference Board of Canada, 70% of Canadian business executives are aware of IMAGINE and its goals. Three hundred and fifty Canadian corporations are now committed to a minimum corporate donation policy of 1% of average, pre-tax profits.[15]

The important success, then, consists of making a lot of noise and signing up a lot of companies that will, praise God, set an example for others. Ergo, the program is to be continued for another five years with, it is hoped, a contribution of $3 million from the federal government to juice it along.

It has taken five years to sign up 350 corporations, during which time the "norm of giving by Canadian corporations" has actually gone down a bit, or, as IMAGINE itself says, "Much remains to be done." If it were doing so well that every blessed firm in Canada became a "Caring Company," we would be back to two-thirds the level of giving that prevailed about half a century ago. What will make the campaign take off, if it ever does, is the increasing use of "cause marketing," also known as "social marketing" or "affinity-program marketing" or (by me) "flogging a dead horse and calling it a thoroughbred." This new approach allows the corporation to mount a campaign of fuzzy warmth, featuring the company logo and a needy kid, in return for allowing a little, sometimes a very little, of the proceeds of sales to slip through to a charity. The average appears to be between one and five per cent of the sales price; given normal markups, that would be from half a cent to under three cents on the dollar. You are not likely to be lured into a purchase or into switching brands for a half-cent discount, but you may well do so when the money is going to a worthy cause. The company ends up with more profits and a better reputation. The lump in the throat and the bump on the bottom line occur together, and induce a warm glow in the boardroom.

Probably the most effective of these campaigns is the one run by McDonald's, the hamburger chain, to support Ronald McDonald Houses, where the families of children in hospital can stay to be near the youngsters. If there ever was a company whose corporate image stood in need of burnishing, it is McDonald's; and if there ever was a campaign that supplied the necessary oil, it is this one. Eat a burger, help a stricken family; french fries and a pop help even more. In one of those wonderful twists that cry out for the satirical pen of Jonathan Swift, McDonald's Corporation agreed, in October 1995, to finance a $6.5-million child-safety campaign to settle charges brought by the United States government that it had failed to report defective playground equipment in its restaurants. The company had installed a device called Tug-N-Turn, a merry-go-round built to look like a hamburger, at 1,200 of its outlets, and 104 children suffered injuries, including broken bones, when shoelaces or clothing got caught at the base of the machines.[16] When the Consumer Products Safety Commission and the U.S. Justice Department filed charges, the corporation agreed to fund the safety campaign. The upshot was what will no doubt be another great PR boost for the golden arches, and you can't do better than that.

Becel Margarine gives money to support Heart and Stroke Foundation fund drives, which is a neat tie-in, because the product is claimed to be less harmful in terms of cholesterol than other spreads. Becel is now the best-selling brand in the land.[17] Optimum Communications, one of the new long-distance phone companies, has come up with a tie-in that is much harder to follow. If you sign up to use its long-distance service, the company will donate 5 per cent of the cost of your calls to the Trans Canada Trail, a cross-country nature ramble planned to open on July 1, 2000, at a cost of $432 million, which is something I guess we need more than women's shelters. The gimmick is that you will help "unify the country with every long distance call,"[18] a claim that is a long distance from making sense.

CALL MOM, HELP US BUY A BOOK

The phone companies have been mud-wrestling for customers for years now, and anything that works rings, you should excuse the expression, the bell. ACC TeleEnterprises works both ends of the line; it has 29 universities and colleges signed up as "affinity partners." When they bring in customers, they get a kickback, and they also get a percentage of every long-distance charge. Call Mom, help us buy a book.

Sprint Canada donates $10 to minor hockey for every new customer signed through a deal with the Canadian Hockey Association. Maybe they should call it Splint Canada, in view of the way we play hockey these days.

And so it goes. Imperial Oil runs full-page newspaper ads of a smiling kid because "We have always believed that Canada's young people are the future of our country, and our greatest natural resource."[19] Beats the hell out of running a photo of the Exxon *Valdez*.

One of the most worthwhile of these tie-ins involves Telus Corporation, a communications giant, and Grant McEwan Community College in Edmonton. Telus polled Albertans to find out what issues they cared about most, and education, health, and job opportunities headed the list. With its expertise in communications technology, it was natural for the company to support research at the college to create a computer program to help nearly blind students. The program enlarges letters on the screen so that anyone with even minimal vision can handle a computer, a skill that opens up job opportunities.[20]

MasterCard and Visa both have "affinity" cards that will slip a little something—viz., one per cent—to a worthy cause, which underlines the point that in most of these cases, the products are virtually interchangeable. If the customer is going to buy something anyway, and there isn't much difference which company he or she buys from, chances are that a charity tie-in will turn the trick. This will cease to be the case when, as now seems likely, every corporation in the land has some sort of kickback scheme with a charity, by which time we will surely have reached the one per cent of profits goal for corporate charitable giving.

Companies edge into these arrangements as carefully as a cat entering an alley full of small boys with bricks. You don't want to project the wrong image. General Motors of Canada Limited, Canada's largest company, had a Jean Days campaign going for a while, which meant that on Fridays, car sales persons in the Toronto area could wear casual clothes to work, in return for contributing $1 to the United Way. (My bank, and I'll bet yours, too, is part of this campaign.) However, the practice was ended in April 1995, when a memo came down declaring that "Senior staff has evaluated the level of dress and has determined that the practice associated with Jean Days is not consistent with our standards."[21] I like to think that the Big Boss told the gang that if you expect to lure the unsuspecting hordes into paying twice as much as they can afford for a piece of machinery that will lose 20 per cent of its value the second they turn the key, you have to dazzle them with dress.

A sign of the great care taken in these matters is the small notice, in the right sort of theatre program, that lets you know which companies have chucked something into the till to allow you to get in for less than you might otherwise pay. Theatre attendees in Canada do not come from the riffraff; this is another of those occasions where the well-to-do get to cut costs for each other at public expense. The big bucks go to large, safe, totally uncontroversial works, every time. The same is true of corporate funding of public television shows, where the ideal is to be splendid but safe. Or, as Dr. Mary Anna Colwell, a sociologist and consultant to the charitable sector, put it at a company board meeting:

Nobody is going to suggest a contribution that is going to be controversial as far as any people on the board are concerned . . . You don't rock the boat in that way within the corporate culture.[22]

Molson's Breweries has supported the battle against AIDS since 1988, but only after checking consumer polls to make sure the tactic wouldn't produce a backlash. A Molson spokesman told Art Chamberlain of the *Toronto Star* that these polls showed that:

AIDS is a mainstream issue, not a marginal one, which is code for a gay issue. We know from our own research that our corporate reputation has been enhanced through our involvement in this area. Our customers like what we are doing.[23]

Molson's held focus groups with university students and discovered that AIDS is of special concern to young people, who are the beer-drinking crowd, and, since all brands taste as if they came from the same horse, looked on this as a way to persuade the crowd to pick Molson's:

Say they're in a pub that has Labatt's Blue and Molson Canadian on tap. When they walk to the bar, they might think, "They're both good beers. They taste pretty much the same. The price is the same. But Molson supports AIDS. Okay, I'll have a Canadian."[24]

Actually, what Molson supports is not AIDS, but the fight *against* AIDS. Never mind, it's only PR.

Corporate sponsorships are tied to selling, either directly or by inducing a warm and receptive feeling in the audience—as in the Texaco opera broadcasts. But there is always a price, either in the ruling out of controversial projects or the choice of projects that are of interest to the narrow group that controls the funds. I hope, but it is only a hope, that Canadian corporations are a little less narrow-minded than the American ones that have developed a practice of "red-lining" groups that are seen to be obstreperous, and denying them loans and grants. The Salt Lake Citizens' Congress, set up to protest the lack of city services, escalating utility rates, toxic sites, and high unemployment in the inner city, went after the banks, the city council, and the telephone company as villains in the degradation of the city. Soon after, one of the activists was fired by the Community Development Block Grant Program and previously pledged grants from funding agencies were delayed or withdrawn.[25]

The only case to make the headlines in Canada that I have found concerned Volkswagen Canada, which withdrew financial support for the Toronto Symphony in 1983 after a number of its musicians attended a "Sound of Peace" concert in High Park.[26] Volkswagen did not want its good name smeared by association with a bunch of people who were in favour of disarmament or other weird things. However, the company reversed it decision when the furore promised to do the corporate image more harm than good. But a giant firm does not have to withdraw funding to make an economic decision; every study of these donations has shown that the money goes exactly where you would expect it to go: to the universities, arts groups, galleries, and museums that have the approval of the upper crust.[27]

It is only natural that the people who hand out the cash want to make sure it gets to the right places. Teresa Odendahl, who spent a number of years studying the "culture of philanthropy," talked to a rich Westerner who told her how his foundation decided to give money:

> We are defenders of the American Way. We believe that it is in danger. So organizations that address themselves to the preservation of the traditional rights, the traditional freedoms, and particularly the traditional responsibility of the great American citizen, we favor.[28]

If the NAACP or a gay rights group applies for funding, it will be wasting a stamp.

SOCIAL MARKETING

The elitist bias of corporate giving, and the attempt to equate charity with financial returns, are among the considerations wrinkling the brows of many of the more thoughtful people in the charitable sector. When I asked Gordon Floyd of the Canadian Centre for Philanthropy about this, he told me:

> The whole trend is to marketing, tying the corporate gift to the company logo. In the past, corporations gave because they felt it was part

of their duty to improve the community in which their employees lived. That has all gone out the window, and now everything is fixed on the bottom line. The results may be good for the corporation, but not necessarily for the community.

What we're really debating here is what sort of value system we want to be guided by as a society; if everything is to be measured in terms of its monetary return, obviously that is quite a different approach than we have had in the past. How do we measure the value of a symphony or a theatre group?[29]

A similar point was raised in even tougher terms by Margot Franssen, the president of Body Shop Canada, a U.K.-based chain of stores selling hair and skin-care products. The company became famous for refusing to test its products on animals and has its own charitable foundation. In a speech to a business conference on social marketing delivered on November 9, 1995, Franssen accused the corporations of hypocrisy, or worse. The speech raised such a fuss that one of the colloquium organizers jumped up and spent twenty minutes pouring oil on troubled waters, suggesting that what Franssen was talking about was mainly "a question of semantics." Well, decide for yourself. Here are some semantic snippets from what she said:

> Throwing bits of food to the food bank makes us feel good but it hasn't eradicated the corporate strategies that caused the problem in the first place . . .
>
> . . . Social marketing is a beginning. It's not an end. All it's really done is tinker with the way the consumers view the company. Instead of offering free gifts with every purchase, it offers feeling good.
>
> At its worst, it's corporate comfort food for customers starved of meaning. It's also very attractive to non-profit organizations in the stingy '90s. What disturbs me is that social marketing will be seen as enough.

CHARITIES AS CORPORATIONS

As well as being tied to corporations in their funding campaigns, charities become corporations when they go out to hustle for dollars, either by extracting fees from the government bodies and other charities for whom they act or by selling goods themselves. For example, look at all the cards, stationery products, and gee-gaws stamped with the logos of charities— about five cents on the dollar gets through to the charitable causes. And the enterprises run by charities themselves, such as the Salvation Army and Goodwill stores, have a considerable advantage over other businesses in that they pay very little in the way of taxes and get most of their merchandise for free or the cost of collection. In Toronto, a sporting-goods retailer told me:

> I see people look into my window, check the prices, and walk on by to the nonprofit store next door, where they can sell the same stuff for less than I paid for it. I can't even complain out loud, because I will be seen to be knocking a worthy cause. It may be a worthy cause to you, but it's a pain in the ass to me.

Finally, the charity companies enjoy an advantage that accrues to all charities: not only do they get most of their work done for free by volunteers, they are able to stiff the salaried staff with wages that would be considered unconscionable in the real corporate sector. The people who work for charities do so, in the main, because they believe in the cause, which is not a solid bargaining position at negotiation time. In recent years, the salaries at the top of the largest charities have risen, apparently, to somewhere within distant touch of those paid in the real world. I say "apparently" because, you will recall, the charity lobby has successfully blocked attempts to make the salaries a matter of public record. (In England, where they are not allowed to be so shy, the managing director of Barnados, the child-help charity, gets ₤55,000 a year, about one-third of what the chief executive of a private corporation of comparable size would earn.) I am told that working for a charity is not quite the sacrifice it used to be, because the level of professionalism required in many cases forces the organization to pay for such services as fund raising, data management, research, and telecommunications at somewhere near the outside rate. As the charities become more professional, this trend will continue, but it will always be true that charity work is modestly paid. Most of the professionals I have talked to grumble about it, but not much; they have a job satisfaction that is lacking in other work.

CORPORATE FOUNDATIONS

Besides the emergence of company charities and charity companies, another new development in the corporate sector is the proliferation of corporate foundations, which allow firms to control the money they donate much more than they could by simply handing it over to a charity. Until the past few years, corporate foundations have been as rare, in the words of Norah McClintock, "as sitting Tories in Chrétien's Ottawa,"[30] and they are still not a major player in this country, as they are in the United States. The *Canadian Directory to Foundations* only shows forty-six of the breed, controlling 1.1 per cent of the assets and 0.7 per cent of the grants given out by Canadian foundations. In the United States, corporate foundations disperse 17.6 per cent of the grants.[31]

We ought to be clear about the distinction, which occasionally becomes blurred, between family foundations and the foundations owned by corporations that bear family names. The Rockefeller Foundation is a family foundation, owned by the heirs of the oil baron's wealth; Exxon, the oil empire, supports a number of corporate foundations, whose shares belong to the company, not family members.

Until recently, we had only a few companies who felt they would get a higher profile out of running their own outfits than by trying to get credit for what they gave to others, including Allstate Insurance, Nelson Lumber, John Deere, and Dominion Securities; they are small potatoes indeed compared to the family foundations. Dominion Securities (now RBC Dominion Securities, since it is owned by the Royal Bank), until recently the largest corporate foundation in Canada, has assets of $6.6 million, or about one-sixtieth of the assets of the McConnell family foundation.[32]

However, when the Royal Bank of Canada started its own corporate foundation in 1992, a number of other companies soon followed. The Royal is one of the founding members of IMAGINE, and its foundation disbursed $14 million in 1993, which was 1.36 per cent of pre-tax profits for the bank, averaged over the previous three years.

In the main, the corporate foundations do exactly what other charities do. They hand out lumps of cash in response to applications in the areas of interest to the trustees. Why do they bother to go through the cumbersome process of setting up a separate body to do what used to be done by a committee of the board of directors? For the usual reason: "When you start a foundation, it elevates your philanthropy and creates more of an image of your company being fiscally or corporately responsible within the community," as Carol Bober of the John Labatt Foundation put it.[33] Don't you love the way these people talk? The foundation doesn't necessarily mean that you *become* more responsible, but that you create that image. In fact, since it takes a lot of expertise, experience, and know-how to spend charitable dollars effectively, the plethora of corporate foundations will undoubtedly lead to more waste; but, as another of the flacks, Susan Young of the Imperial Oil Foundation, noted, "In the public's eye, a foundation has a little more depth of commitment."[34]

Corporate foundations are another way for the companies to compete with each other. Since the competition is in PR, not manufacturing, small is good. Let a thousand flowers bloom. In any field other than charity, the flack who tries to tell us that what the economy needs is more and smaller and less experienced and less efficient outfits to handle money would get a horse laugh, but what these people say makes perfect sense, in the circumstances. It's all soap bubbles, anyway, so why should they give the dough over to someone else to pass out, when they can get more credit by doing it themselves?

Obviously, funnelling a substantial corporate donation to the Salvation Army or Save the Children or some other established and experienced dispenser of funds will provide the best value for money. Equally obviously, this is going to become rarer. The ever-increasing pressure in the corporate sector to produce profits means that inevitably the money that flows to charities is going to go less and less to general community support, which was the original rationale for corporate giving, and more and more to cause-related marketing. At a time when the need for the best use of money has become more important than ever, corporate charity will become more diffuse and less effective.

"Efficient charity" appears to be an oxymoron anyway, as we will see in the next chapter, when we look at how much money remains after the fundraising campaigns are paid for.

9. Fund Raising:
The Begging Bowls

*Most people would be shocked to know what a
small proportion of the donated dollar gets
through, not because anyone is ripping anyone
off, but because the simple reality is that fundraising is a very expensive exercise and you have
to invest a lot of money to raise a buck . . . The
truth of the matter is you have to hire and train
people and put on a big dinner and lay on some
funny entertainment that will eat up fifty cents
out of every dollar, and if you don't do that, you
won't get anything out of them.*

—GORDON FLOYD, CANADIAN CENTRE
FOR PHILANTHROPY, 1995

While standing at the corner of Fourth Street and Fourth Avenue in
downtown Calgary, I saw a maroon minivan pull up to the stoplight. Two

teenagers with long hair, dressed in scruffy clothes and wielding wind-shield brushes, ambushed it. They had been lying in wait and rushed forward to dab their slightly damp brushes on the van's windows. The guy working the driver's side wiped with one hand and held the other out for money. The window rolled down. "Bugger off," the driver said.

"It's for charity," the kid said.

"Like hell it is," the driver said. He looked up, ready to pull away when the light turned to green, but the other kid moved in front of the van, cutting him off.

"Jesus," the driver said. A few seconds later, he produced a loonie to buy his freedom, and off he went.

"Have a nice day," chorused the kids.

I watched them work the corner for about ten minutes, and I calculate that they pulled in about fifteen dollars in that time. Not bad. Some drivers didn't mind, some were mad as hell; but nearly everyone forked out.

It is a scene not untypical of some sorts of modern charitable fund raising: part coaxing, part blackmail, a process that transfers money from one set of pockets to another, without anyone being sure where and how the funds will actually be spent. The teenagers issued no receipts, and the act of giving did not leave their donors feeling uplifted, but the rest of the process was pretty familiar. Still, collecting the cash is the heart of the business, without which most charities wouldn't last long. It absorbs at least as much energy as charitable works themselves, and far more money is spent raising funds, in most charities, than ever gets spent on the objects of the exercise. Therefore, it is important to understand something of the way the system works.

HOW DO I TAP THEE? LET ME COUNT THE WAYS

The fundraising business is complex almost beyond belief, so we will confine ourselves to looking briefly at a baker's dozen of the best-known methods, which I list in order of their estimated effectiveness, starting with the best and moving to the least efficient techniques, according to a number of experts I consulted:

- Face-to-face encounters
- Smiling and dialling
- Payroll-deduction plans

- Begging letters
- Paid advertising
- Bingo, lotteries, and other numbers rackets
- Celebrity stunts
- Banquets, parties, and balls
- Telethons
- All the other Begathons—walkathons, swimathons, car washes, bowl-athons, pie-bakeathons, and whatever else you can dream up
- School whines
- Bake sales, charity auctions, and fetes
- Shaking down governments.

I have left out one of the best and simplest—the church collection plate—because it requires no effort or thought on our part. The only new development in church collections is that beleaguered parishioners, faced with as many as a dozen collections from their churches' far-flung interests, have taken to splitting their gifts. That is, if you used to put ten dollars in the weekly envelope, you now put in five, and then, when you get hit at the end of the service with another impromptu collection, you stick in the other five. I am told, though there are no hard figures to prove it, that the money coming in remains about the same, even with more collections. Going the other way, two legal brothels in Canberra, Australia, raffled off "hour-long interludes" to raise money for the "Flying Doctor" service, but it is not recommended that this practice should spread.

Nor have I listed the Internet, although there are a number of web sites on the computer networks through which you can either receive information about charities or even donate, if you are feeling foolhardy enough to trust your funds to the ether. So far, the Internet is a negligible player in the charity stakes for the simple reason that it is the playground of the young, especially young men, while the most generous donors to voluntary agencies are old women. Perhaps in a decade or two, electronic giving will play a larger role.

There is no end to the variations and mixtures of these fundraising techniques, such as having a celebrity start off your walkathon or a gang of celebrities sign your begging letter, but this will give you the broad idea. In addition, donors sometimes dream up their own peculiar approaches. In Fort Lauderdale, a rich, elderly and ailing couple, Helen and Richard

Brown, committed suicide in December 1994 by gassing themselves with carbon monoxide in their Cadillac Eldorado. This was to preserve their personal fortunes, amounting to $13.9 million (U.S.), for the United Church of Christ, the beneficiary of their wills. They took the suicide route for fear that the money would otherwise be dissipated in medical charges over the rest of their lives. He was seventy-nine and suffering from arthritis; she was seventy-six and afflicted with Alzheimer's disease.[1] Actually, dying is one of the best ways to deliver funds to charities, by way of a will; unless, as happens a regrettable number of times, aggrieved relatives file lawsuits that use up all the funds. The buzz phrase is "planned giving," which allows the donor to designate charitable donations out of his/her estate well ahead of time and get the maximum tax benefit out of the operation by timing when the money flows out and how. As we saw in Chapter Seven, gifts to a crown foundation can be written off at up to 100 per cent of income, and this applies to estates as well as individuals. It seems that the dead, like the poor, are always with us.

However, suicide is not a technique mentioned in any of the dozens of books on fund raising; I cite the Brown case merely to show that the possibilities are endless. So are the possibilities of what P. G. Wodehouse, that master of the exact word, used to call "oompus boompus." Consider the activities of a busy little group called the Foundation for New Era Philanthropy, which persuaded a number of large, eminent, and formerly well-heeled American charities to entrust it with large sums of money, on a promise that the cash would be doubled before they could say "tax deduction." New Era gulled more than a hundred evangelical Christian organizations with a pitch promising that, if they would invest $500,000, it would come floating back to them, like the Biblical bread upon the waters, within four to six months, doubled in size.

Some of the early takers, such as Focus on the Family, an outfit seeking greater influence within the Republican Party, did, in fact, get their money back, doubled, within six months, and invested again. But the scam was basically a pyramid scheme, which depended on an ever-increasing pile of suckers to provide the new funds to pay off old investors, and in due course, it went bust abruptly, in mid-1995, taking with it an estimated $300 million.[2] The victims included, besides the Bible-thumpers, the Academy of Natural Sciences of Philadelphia and the English Language Institute in San Dimas, California. It seems the mishaps that befell Jim Bakker,

Jimmy Swaggart, and other bold evangelists who siphoned the wallets of the credulous in the 1980s have been forgotten, and a new generation is being taught that "let us pray" can have a homophonic meaning.

There are also two main avenues through which fundraising techniques, whether straightforward or dodgy, are employed, and they are nearly always mixed: that is, the volunteer approach, headed by a committee of the charity, and the professional approach. Hiring professionals is expensive but pays off, or charities wouldn't do it. One of the few really fast-growing industries in this nation is fund raising (bankruptcy consulting is another winner); the Toronto *Yellow Pages* lists twenty-four firms under "Fund Raising—Consultants" and another thirteen under "Fund Raising Organizations." The first group includes firms like Charitable Funding Initiatives, or Stephen Thomas Direct Mail Fund Raising, which will, for a fee or a percentage of the take, advise charities on the best way to go about extracting cash from the public. The second group mixes the same consulting expertise with the production of goods which the charity can sell—outfits like Balderson Cheese Company, Bazaar & Novelty Company, or Panda Fundraising Ltd.—"Cookies, Confectionary Items— Giftwrap, Fine Stationery—Scratch 'n Pay Raffle, Garbage Bags—Novelties." You buy a few hundred dozen chocolate bars, cookies, post cards, or packets of cheese; your charity's name is printed on them, and you send out the platoons of engaging kids to knock on doors and make a perfect pest of themselves until the householder caves in and ponies up.

Let us go back through the list of methods, to see what we can learn about how the charities raise funds.

I. FACE-TO-FACE ENCOUNTERS

Ken Wyman, one of the best-known and most-respected professional consultants in the fundraising field, says that the exact technique to be employed by any charity depends on a number of factors, including the degree of development of the charity itself, but, overall,

> The single most effective way, the lowest cost and highest income way, is to go and talk to someone face to face. When you talk to someone, they can ask questions, and they are more likely to give a donation.[3]

Well, you knew that, didn't you? When your neighbour shows up at the front door with a receipt pad in one hand, a pen in the other, and an embarrassed smile on his/her face, you know you are going to have to (a) turn out all the lights and hide under the bed, which won't work, because they'll just come back later; (b) come up with one of the stock, and seldom-believed, excuses—I gave at the office, I never give to charities whose names begin with the letter U, I'd be happy to donate, but I'm in bankruptcy; or (c) grin and give. I have a friend who told a collector who said "I'm here for the Canadian Cancer Society," "No, thanks, we already have some." Not nice. Most of us give something to a selected list of charities, which lets us off the hook to the others when they come calling. The volunteers accept this readily. My wife, who has worked for years for a number of charities, has never had anyone be rude to her at the door, although she notes that she has been lied to by some of the most bare-faced bozos in creation. She has also had, as have many volunteers, the uncomfortable experience of having the donor ask for a receipt for, say, $25, then being handed a folded-up cheque which turns out to be for $5. Embarrassing all around.

Still, this method is the best way to bring in dollars, provided the charity is well-organized and able to tap into a small army of unpaid workers. The costs are minimal—receipt books, stationery, and other minor expenses, along with professional office time for the charity staff. Many charities put on a dinner for the volunteers at the end of a successful campaign, but this is tricky. My wife quit volunteering for the United Appeal in Ottawa because it was wasting money this way (they don't do it, any more), so the charity has to decide whether not giving the dinner will make it seem high-minded, or merely chintzy and ungrateful. A letter of thanks is nice, but you can't eat it or show it your new frock.

An invaluable extra from the door-to-door campaigns is that they give the charity a donor list, and not merely an assemblage of names, but names of people who actually give. This is the modern equivalent of the large X that bums used to mark on the sidewalk in front of generous homes during the Great Depression. Donor lists are the heart and soul of fund raising; large sums of money are paid for them, and there are brokers who sell names for anywhere from $100 per thousand to as much as hundreds of dollars per thousand, depending on the quality of the list. Every time you buy a magazine subscription; send away for a catalogue; answer one of those ads that say "Yes, I'd like to learn more about . . ." real estate, investment, or collectibles; fill out a warranty card; join a political party; sign up for one of the "loyalty card" programs at Zellers, A&P or Air Canada; and, indeed, every time you give money to a charity, your name is going down on a list, putting money into the hands of a broker who will sell you as often as he can. The charities use the same direct marketers as other merchants, and there are currently an estimated 2,500 lists in existence in Canada, with anywhere from 3,000 to 5 million names on them.[4]

These donor lists are the subject of a good deal of rancorous wrangling in charitable circles. Ken Wyman recalls a case where he advised a charity to use a professional fundraising firm which, at the end of the campaign, held onto the charity's donor file, until it was threatened with a lawsuit. "It took us two years to get the list back, by which time it was out of date."

When charities lend their lists to other charities, they usually seed in some phony names, so they can tell if the second charity held onto the list after the campaign ceased. That is, buried among the legitimate donors are a number of names which are aliases for people in the lending charity. If any of these folks get a begging letter from the outfit that has supposedly turned back the list, there is all hell to pay. Hey, be careful out there.

2. SMILING AND DIALLING

Telephone campaigns are not quite as effective as the person-to-person approach but are still considered to be a key tool for fund raising. Like the face-to-face method, this approach depends upon an up-to-date list of potential donors and a squad of tireless volunteers. Again, this technique allows the prospect to ask questions of the charity, although in a regrettably large number of cases, in my experience, the telephoners cannot answer them.

Smiling and dialling has fallen into disfavour because it is so open to abuse. In the first place, this is the method most often used by professional fund-raisers, who may skim off anywhere from 40 to 90 per cent of the take, with 60 per cent as the norm.[5] Oh, yes, and then there are expenses on top of that. You give the charity $50, it gets $5 or $10.

In the second place, telemarketing is fearfully abused. Teams of hard-nosed salespeople, who are paid on commission, operate out of rooms equipped with banks of telephones and computers. They have in front of them a list of potential donors—although, in some cases, the smile and diallers simply go through a computerized version of the phone book—and a sales pitch. Sometimes they stick to the pitch which the charity has drawn up and approved, and sometimes they wing it, with statements designed to wring the money out of donors but which have little bearing in fact.

And they never, ever, tell the target that most of the money will never get to the intended charity. One of the most controversial telemarketing schemes involves wheelchair basketball. Typically, a smile and dialler will offer the recipient of a random telephone call the opportunity to support the disabled by purchasing a book of tickets, for about $40, to a game, with a sweatshirt thrown in for free. What the doner doesn't realize is that, in many cases, only about 10 per cent of the money collected ever gets through to the charity, while 90 per cent is eaten up by the expenses and fees charged by the companies that do the soliciting. The wise response to any such phone call is to ask the caller to send along a brochure with the organization's charitable number on it. Many of these firms have no such number.

A code of ethics is supposed to cover these matters, promulgated by the National Society of Fund Raising Executives in the United States and the Canadian Society of Fund-Raising Executives in Canada. The code specifically prohibits working on a percentage basis because it is so expensive and open to abuse, but this is one of those voluntary sanctions with which, and two dollars, you can ride the subway. Ken Wyman's mother got a telephone call from a smile and dialler asking for a donation to a charity she had never heard of. When she said no, the caller said, "Can I put down that you might consider a donation?" She allowed reluctantly that she might, at some time, consider a donation. Soon after, she got an invoice in the mail, which she did not pay. Wyman notes, "Many people would have just gone ahead and paid the 'invoice,' and the canvasser would have received a commission."[6]

Often, the telemarketers are selling something besides the opportunity to hand over cash. One common gimmick is a circus or other live performance, to which you are invited to buy tickets on the understanding that a share of the gate will go to the charity. Again, by the time all the expenses are taken off, the amount that squeaks through to the worthy cause is a small percentage of what you gave. In a typical Canadian case, the phone callers raised $360,000, and the charity got one-sixth of this.[7]

There are a number of common-sense rules to follow if you insist on giving money to smile and diallers:

- Ask the caller if he or she works for the charity, or for a fund-raiser. You will usually be rewarded with the click of a descending phone; occasionally, you will be passed to someone else, who can answer your questions.
- Ask how much of your donation, purchase, whatever, will go to the charity. Ditto.
- Ask for the charity's Revenue Canada number. Many of the telemarketers represent unregistered charities. You may still want to give, but you should know that you will not get a tax-deductible receipt.
- Request printed information about the charity before you give.
- Do not, under any circumstances, give a telemarketer your credit card number.

But I have a much simpler rule: Don't ever give money in response to a telephone solicitation. The method may work well for charities, but it is fraught with inefficiency, dumbness, and danger.

3. PAYROLL-DEDUCTION PLANS

Payroll plans based on a percentage of salary, or an hour's pay per week, are used mainly by the United Way, as described in Chapter Five. They are very cheap to operate, since the money is collected with awesome automatic efficiency as part of the payroll system. The charity itself says that campaign costs run to between ten and fifteen cents on the dollar,[8] but you will see in Table 1 of Appendix 1 that, in the case of our largest United Way, overall costs eat up about twenty cents on the dollar. This is pretty good—just about what the Income Tax Act calls for—but it is accompanied, as I have already argued, by arm-twisting by some employers that makes the phrase "voluntary contribution" sound quaint.

4. BEGGING LETTERS

These are the slick, constant, dunning appeals we get from dozens of charities every year. They usually contain about nine-tenths sentiment and one-tenth information. The difficulty, from the donor's point of view, is that we all know that there are more worthy causes out there than we can possibly support. So the marketers sign up the best copywriters they can afford to squeeze money out of us through guilt, compassion, anxiety, whatever works. One approach, called "If you don't give money, we'll shoot this dog," shows a begrimed kid in a horrific setting and states that you can bring a smile to this tear-streaked face or turn your back and walk away. It works quite well, but does not solve the dilemma that most of your money may go up in smoke. You want to know more before you shell out.

I read in several of those newspaper articles that tell you to "Give to charity—and give to yourself" that the wise giver, in light of the need to be well-informed, should write to the charity and ask for the information contained in its T3010 form, so I did that. The first thirteen charities that sent me a begging letter got a letter back, asking for particulars and enclosing a stamped, self-addressed envelope. One, Amnesty International, replied as requested, and within three weeks; there was even a card and a note inviting me to call for any other information I required. Three others —the CNIB, the Canadian Cancer Society of Ontario, and the Heart and Stroke Foundation—told me, within three months, to address my request to Revenue Canada. The CNIB and the Canadian Cancer Society sent along packets of information, from which it was impossible to tell whether they are efficient charities. (Of course, I was cheating; I already had the numbers on all of them from Revenue Canada.)

The difficulty is that it costs a charity an average of three dollars to send out a tax receipt[9] and at least that much to send out the information I requested, even with my own stamp enclosed. So, we cannot expect the charities to give us this information, and most of them won't. On the other hand, if we all start besieging Revenue Canada for T3010s, we will close the place down. Say, there's an idea. A few Canadians can use the service, but if we all want to be intelligent givers, we will choke the system. Revenue Canada has a toll-free number (1-800-267-2384) which you can call to request forms from a disembodied voice, but if we all get on the line, we won't get anything but a busy signal. What is more, we will send the department's budget through the roof, just trying to keep up. There are more than five million of us who take charitable deductions through the income-tax system; if we all request the financial poop on, say, ten charities before making a decision, entire forests will be destroyed just to provide the paper.

There is an answer to this dilemma, and we will meet it in Chapter Eleven: it is called a Charity Commission.

5. PAID ADVERTISING

Expensive, and only moderately effective. The least efficient ads are the ones on television. The problem, according to Ken Wyman, is that the element of polite coercion is removed; the distressed stare and the energetic squeeze are absent. That is not the way he put it, of course. He said, "The least effective way to raise money is to put an ad on TV or radio because you don't have to do anything and the ad will go away by itself within a few seconds."[10] An announcement in a newspaper or magazine hangs around the house, radiating guilt-inducing distress until you chuck it out, but a television ad is soon swallowed by another pitch for breath mints, beer, or psychic healing at only ten dollars a minute.

6. BINGO, LOTTERIES, AND OTHER NUMBERS RACKETS

This organized fleecing of the unwary is the subject of the next chapter.

7. CELEBRITY STUNTS

The Joe Carter Golf Classic, held at the Glen Abbey Golf Club in Oakville, Ontario, set out to raise money for two charities, Ronald McDonald House and the Canadian Cystic Fibrosis Foundation, on the name of the famous Blue Jays outfielder. Each foursome paid $2,750 to play, and corporations paid $1,250 to have a little sign stuck up at a hole, so you would expect the tournament to produce a bonanza for good causes. Well, it produced a bonanza, all right—$83,000—but only $15,000 got through to the charities. There were greens fees ($21,500), meals for the participants ($9,000), a fee ($15,000) for the Toronto sports agency that organized the event, and other incidentals, such as drinks, limousines, and gratuities. The golf course did 40 per cent better than the charities, which caused Joe Carter to say he was "extremely disappointed."[11]

Many celebrity events do better than this—Joe Carter's boss, Cito Gaston, sponsored a golf tournament that raised $50,000 for the Sick Children's Foundation, on outlays of $120,000—but this is not far off the average. By the time the event is lined up, advertised, and staged by professionals, with all the incidentals paid for, it is very rare for half the money to trickle through to the intended target.

To put it at its kindest, a great many celebrity events are publicity stunts, at least as much as they are charitable fund-raisers. And as fund-raisers, their chief advantage is that they usually generate publicity for the charity, which may lead to donations long after the event is over.

8. BANQUETS, PARTIES, AND BALLS

Many years ago, when the earth's crust was still cooling and my wife and I were in the social swirl in Ottawa, mere playthings of an idle hour, we got caught up in an organization called Children's International Summer Villages. It was, and still is, a noble project, which sends eleven-year-old children from a vast array of countries to camp together every summer, to promote international understanding. (Eleven is considered to be the ideal age; the kids are old enough to carry their memories into adult life, but the gonads have not yet kicked in to complicate camp life.) The job for us socialites —isn't it always thus?—was to raise the dough for the trips—to Japan, Guatemala, or wherever. (In the case of our son, Craig, to Kitchener, Ontario; exotic, but not too exotic.) About 80 per cent of the energy that went into raising money was gobbled up by the annual CISV Ball, held every April, attended by as many of the Ottawa nobs as we could stiff with a ticket. The year my wife and I got involved, someone—not us—was foolhardy enough to ask how much actual cash the event had produced the previous year.

$175.00.

Upon which, after much grinding of teeth, committee meetings, and sulks, we canned the ball and put on a bazaar instead, which raised about six times the cash for about one-third of the outlay of time and energy.

The ball chairperson was numb with incomprehension. "The ball isn't about raising money," she wailed, "it's about raising profiles!"

Just so. Oscar Wilde once described the fox hunt as "the unspeakable in full pursuit of the uneatable": a charity ball sends the overfed and overdressed in pursuit of publicity, on the excuse of aiding a charity. There are all the pictures in the newspapers and the mentions in the society columns, and the parties before and after the main event to plan and then rehash the grand evening, and to bitch at each other, to say nothing of showing off the new duds.

Charity balls are falling into disfavour, these days, because the lower orders are getting above themselves and tend to poke fun at the sight of their betters spending, and writing off, hundreds of thousands of dollars to raise nickels for the downtrodden.

Readers with strong stomachs can get a wonderful insight into the way this racket works by reading gossip columnist Rosemary Sexton's insider account in *The Glitter Girls*.[12] The Brazilian Ball, the Toronto season's most vulgar annual display, contains some of the baser elements of an alley brawl, except of course that the alley thugs can't write their bandages off on their income taxes. In one dustup, someone had the nerve, the immortal rind, to ask Anna Maria de Souza, the ball's originator, whether, since the money didn't go to Brazil, despite the name, the Dixon Hall Music School couldn't be cut in on the action. Sniffing, Anna sent that year's take to the University of Toronto. The music school, bloody but unbowed, decided to try for a share of the pie when the next ball was held. "The next year," Sexton reports, "the women of Dixon Hall came back to Anna, grovelling. Please may we have the ball another year. No, replied Anna. Nor is Dixon Hall likely to find itself a potential beneficiary ever again."[13]

Another of Sexton's heroines, and the recognized queen of the socialites, is Catherine Nugent, described as "an intellectual," who likes to drop names, as in "One of her schoolfriend's fathers was a close friend of D. H. Lawrence and was with him in Egypt when he wrote *The Alexandria Quartet*,"[14] which, as we all know, is about a bawdy Egyptian gamekeeper. Nugent is also quoted as going to a meeting of the Writers' Development Trust in the 1990s where "Dylan Thomas was reading."[15] Dylan Thomas died in 1953, so that must have been quite a sight.

When Charles and Di were brought in for the 1991 Brazilian bunfight, there was a good deal of pushing and shoving for position, and a scene in which one of the grand socialites screamed at one of the organizers, "We've paid $25,000 and you've put us in the second row!"[16]

All good clean fun, or rather, dirty fun, but these affairs are a huge waste of time, money, and effort, and the whole process, in an increasingly straitened economy, leaves behind a sour taste. This is especially the case when we read of the eight-course spread where "cakes shaped like Fabergé eggs, encrusted in silver" were brought in to decorate the tables at a Russian tea held to thank the volunteers for a charity brawl. The serfs served lobster, sturgeon, and "an incredible array of desserts," sluiced down with champagne served in gold-rimmed crystal. The gold-monogrammed plates were flown in from New York and set upon red moiré tablecloths. Sexton was startled when her original story on this affair drew a critical letter to the editor of the *Globe and Mail* from Svend Robinson, the NDP MP. In response, she interviewed one of the organizers, who pointed out that "It was put on so we could all relax and have fun after a difficult year."[17] They feel the same way in Bosnia.

As overblown as the events are the numbers released. After one Brazilian Ball, the mainstream newspapers were told, and duly printed, a net take of $1.25 million; actually, that was the gross. *Frank Magazine*, which won't ever get invited, I'll bet, said the real figure was $350,000.[18]

I suppose there is no real harm in the super-rich vying with each other in fancy dress, but I cannot for the life of me see why the taxpayer should subsidize this nonsense, and even the ballsters are beginning to hear the rumble of tumbrel wheels in the adverse publicity these events generate.

In the place of banquets, we are beginning to get "hunger dinners," where the attendees who pay for a repast on behalf of a South American charity will get a plate of rice and beans, with a glass of water into which a small amount of cocoa has been stirred to represent the dirty water in the target country. In a variation on this theme, seven diners at a table will get a plate of plain rice, and the eighth a huge serving of lobster and steak; sharing out is part of the evening's entertainment. This is marginally better than the glitter girls, but like most charitable events, it is of much more benefit to the donors than the donees.

9. TELETHONS

The major problem with the long, intensely boring television marathons is that they cost so much to stage. Once the airtime, production facilities, artists' fees and/or expenses, and other incidentals are looked after, a 30 per cent return on the money involved is considered good; so when the event's Gorgeous Faces tell you that, by George, we've made our target of three million, remember that this is not what the charity will see. (Variety Village and some other charities get around this by having almost everything, including airtime, donated.) Another problem is that it is becoming more and more difficult to get the folks who succumb to the living-room pitch to part with the promised money once the fever dies. In one New York telethon, the Sickle Cell Foundation received pledges of $800,000, actually collected $217,000, and wound up losing $78,000 because the show cost more than $300,000 to put on.[19] Richard Carter, an American author, described the average telethon as "An interminable orgy of uncertain entertainment and bathos, with its processions of the afflicted and other carefully-planned vulgarities."[20] But they mean well.

10. ALL THE OTHER BEGATHONS

There are walkathons, bowlathons, swimathons, pie-bakeathons, car washes, skipping contests: in short, there is almost no form of human activity which cannot be turned into a charity event by persuading people to sign up for so much per mile, pin, length, crust, wash, or skip. I look forward to the inevitable day when hookers, taking their cue from Australia, will join the parade with a form of endurance contest that will bring money raising to new heights. The disadvantage of all these activities is that, again, they do not collect much money for the time and effort expended. However, if there are no expenses—when high school kids wash cars, they take nothing and hand over everything they make—I think such events are of benefit, because every dime counts. They also teach both participants and sponsors something about joint community effort, so that, even if they are not tremendously effective, they are worthwhile.

11. SCHOOL WHINES

The same cannot be said, alas, for the practice of rounding up schoolchildren and siccing them on their own parents, neighbours, and perfect strangers, armed with bundles of chocolate bars, citrus fruit, cheese, raffle tickets, and other junk. Jane Christmas, writing in the *Globe and Mail*, put it nicely:

> Fund raising has become, for many child-based organizations, a kind of be-all and end-all. It's guerilla warfare cloaked in wild-eyed innocence. It's a battle for your sentiments as the organization trots out its uniformed troops of scrub-faced youngsters armed with a grownup's responsibility. In short, it's one of the circles of hell you want to avoid.[21]

It is also a monumental waste of time, so much so that the Alberta Teachers Federation, as already noted, passed a resolution in 1995 calling on teachers to refuse to take part in these pirate raids, whose end objects are as likely to be a school junket as anything charitable. About 90 per cent of the cash involved goes to buy the products—which often have a short shelf life and leave the school with a basement full of rotting food or out-of-date calendars.

12. BAKE SALES, CHARITY AUCTIONS, AND FETES

Ken Wyman warns that these events usually raise very little money, "once you consider the cost of the items," to say nothing of the time involved:

> I would rather take the same money and hold an auction in which you receive, say, a pie a month from old Mrs. McGillicuddy for a year, or a bowl of chili delivered to your doorstep once every few weeks. You would make much more money.[22]

13. SHAKING DOWN GOVERNMENTS

When I put this one down as the least effective fundraising technique, I don't mean necessarily from the point of view of individual charities, I mean overall. Shaking down governments to support causes leads to naughtiness that ought to be avoided. I call to the stand Patti Starr, who has written a book, *Tempting Fate*, which is a combination funny read, political treatise, and how-to manual on the art of milking governments for money. Starr, who spent two months in jail on a series of charges in connection with funds paid to the National Council of Jewish Women, in which she was hyperactive, describes in loving detail how it was done. In brief, the charity examined legislation to discover where money was available to the bureaucrats and politicians, then fashioned applications in such a way that they would suck in the cash. Truth never came into it:

> The proper fulfillment of grant criteria is often in the eye of the beholder. With some creative thinking, helpful bureaucrats, political contacts, and a worthwhile project to be funded, nothing is impossible.

Thus, when the charity wanted to produce a video to help the disabled cope with their problems, Starr applied for a Wintario Grant, which was supposed to provide financing "to enhance the citizenship participation of Ontario residents in a multicultural society." Are the disabled not citizens? she argued. And, with help from Premier David Peterson, a political crony, she got the money.

Starr's world fell apart when, in her headlong way, she became involved in a nasty political battle with a number of bureaucrats and politicians. Soon, stories were being leaked to the press about the charity's conversion process, which turned money legislated for one purpose into other channels. She was convicted of eight minor counts but still can't see that she did anything very wrong—or very unusual. The case seized upon by the authorities, who actually had a rich crop to choose from, involved a capital grant for improvements to the charity's national headquarters. Starr writes, "The grant application included figures for donated labor and material which were not forthcoming and which were never intended to be forthcoming." Or, to put it another way, the numbers were faked. Then, there is this summary:

> I was the driving force behind that grant—and many others obtained for my community over the past twelve years. I had looked for loopholes that would allow us to apply for funding that would otherwise have been out of our reach. Matching grants with "in kind" donations was a common practice. Simply put, for every dollar the government put up, the organization had to match it . . . my defence was, and still is, common knowledge, along with common practice.[23]

The argument is that cheating is so much a part, and a known part, of the business of extracting money from governments that either she should not have been charged, or everyone else who does the same thing should be—which would give our crowded courts a merry old time, indeed.

I think she has a point. The whole charitable sector is run with such supreme sloppiness that about the only discernible rules are No Opium Smoking in the Elevators and Bury Your Own Dead.

UP IN SMOKE

The end result of all of these fundraising methods is the collection and expenditure of huge amounts of money; in many cases, a good deal less than half goes to the intended charity. In California, the attorney general released a study in late 1995 indicating that seventy cents out of every dollar raised through professional fund-raisers went for payments to the pros. In the most outstanding case, an unnamed professional collected $10.9 million for a children's charity, not a cent of which was spent on children;

it was all eaten up by administrative and fundraising costs.[24] In another American case, the Vietnam Veterans' Memorial Fund spent $4.4 million (U.S.) to raise $7 million to build and maintain a memorial in Washington.[25]

Canadians are protected, as usual, from facing such hard facts by the elemental shyness of our charities and the benign neglect of our governments. When *Front & Centre*, the magazine put out by the Canadian Centre for Philanthropy, tackled this subject in an article entitled "Dollars and Sense: Finding Out What Fundraising Costs,"[26] it provided almost no information about what fund raising costs. Instead, there was a lively exchange among charioteers as to whether it mattered a damn. "Absolutely," said David Lowe of the World Wildlife Fund, while Robert Duck of Boys & Girls Clubs of Canada riposted, "Fundraising costs have little relationship to how effectively donation dollars are being spent." Apparently, these issues are "difficult for the public to understand."[27]

The problem the charities have is that, since they are so bashful about revealing information about themselves, there is no other measure available than the ratio between what they take in and what they spend on the objects for which they were, in theory, formed. And it is not such a bad measure, is it? Most of us would rather give ten dollars to a good cause which spends one dollar of it on fund raising, management, or other oddments, than to another cause where five or six dollars goes up the flue.

In the income-tax forms I have examined, we have the Missing Children Society of Canada (see Table 3), which raised $1,126,876 and spent $577,272 on fund raising, $498,676 on "fund-raising agents" and $116,019 on management and administration.[28] The money actually spent on charity—$463,808—came to just over 40 per cent of that collected.

The Kid's Help Foundation raised $3,333,046 but spent $2,118,393 to collect it, along with another $457,458 on management and administration.[29]

You will see from the tables in Appendix 1 that the percentage spent on charitable objects ranges wildly. Some of this has to do with the way these organizations keep their books, and some with what kinds of work they do: a charity that is supported mainly by government funding doesn't have to spend to gather its own funds. The only firm conclusion to be drawn is that we have a very loose and bizarre system which sets out to aid the hurting and helpless but sometimes ends up spending more money scrabbling around in the search for funds than it ever delivers to the people in need of help.

However, the vagaries of the regular fundraising world pale in comparison with the blackjack methods our governments employ against us in the name of charity, as we will see in the next chapter.

10. A Tax on the Stupid: Gambling and Charity

The young people are the ones who become addicted to it and it's going to become in fifteen years from now a social epidemic. Alcohol and drugs will be nothing to it, and this is what the charitable organizations are pushing.

—TIBOR BARSONY, CANADIAN FOUNDATION ON COMPULSIVE GAMBLING, 1995

The Royal Diamond Casino is part of the Plaza of Nations in downtown Vancouver. Inside, under the clusters of pointy lights against a green baize ceiling, the white-fronted, black-bow-tied croupiers move with mechanical ease to scoop the chips from tables ranged along three sides of the large room. The fourth side is given over to a small refreshment stand and a large fish tank, replete with goldfish. The tank dwellers are not suckers, only the players. There are about eighty charitable donors here this night, laying down their gifts at tables for blackjack, baccarat, roulette, and something called "Canadian Craps," played by rolling large, fuzzy, dice-shaped cushions down what looks like the inside of a coffin. Real, ivory-dice crap-shooting is illegal, so we make do with this version. There is a large banner across the top of one wall wishing everyone good luck, as there always is in these joints. What it means is, don't whine when you get cleaned out; we didn't mean to be mean. This is one of eighteen privately owned charity casinos in British Columbia, a province which funnelled $117 million into charities during 1994, out of gross revenues of $250 million from bingos, casinos, and lotteries.[1]

Outside, sheltering from the drizzle under an overhang, stand two women in their early thirties, dressed in blue jeans that probably fit a few years ago. One of them is blubbering.

"Stevie is going to kill me," she moans. "He is going to beat the living shit out of me."

Her friend says, "It was your money, wasn't it?"

"Oh, shit, no. It was the rent money. It was the goddam rent money, and this is the third time. He is going to beat the living shit out of me."

"Well, I dunno," says the pal. "Want to stay at my place?"

I think of approaching the two women with the good news—at least part of the rent money will go to charitable causes. Under British Columbia law, the casino operators can keep only 40 per cent of the profits; the rest goes to the province, which shares it with the charities. Would she like to pass the word on to Stevie? But I decide to hold my tongue for once; it might not be taken in good part.

Welcome to the world of charitable gambling, where, under the excuse that a portion of the swag goes to good causes, our governments have turned themselves into bookies and croupiers, vacuuming the suckers with the kind of pitch that used to give snake-oil salesmen and carnival touts a bad name: "Come one, come all! You have to speculate if you want to accumulate! Roll up, roll up! Place your bets and fear nothing!"

The games are all rigged, of course, but in the nicest way. That is, you will be beaten by the odds, not by a fixed wheel or a deal from the bottom of the deck. You have to lose, or the government cannot win; and if it cannot win, it cannot turn over part of the loot to charities while keeping the rest for itself. This is the kind of racketeering that used to be conducted by gents with bent noses, photographed with large numbers across their chests; now the practitioners are politicians and bureaucrats who wish to drive home to us a moral lesson for all seasons: work stinks—the real rewards flow, with God's grace, to gamblers. Since we have constructed for you a society in which honest labour brings in very little, and that retractable at almost any time, about the only chance you have for financial security is based on sheer dumb luck.

Our most respectable citizens are touts for the slickers, led by a bevy of lobbies centred on the charities that want to make sure (a) that the activity increases as fast as possible, (b) that the government won't tax it, and (c) that as much as possible gets through the funnel to the voluntary organizations. At the national level, the Canadian Coalition Against Taxing Charities joined forces with the Canadian Society of Fundraising Executives and the Canadian Centre for Philanthropy to raise merry hell when it looked as if Finance Minister Paul Martin was proposing to slap a tax on winnings from lotteries, raffles, and bingos. They are taxed in the United States, and the Province of Saskatchewan levied a 4 per cent tax on $48 million in provincial gaming until it was bullied into withdrawing the tax in early 1995. Martin also retreated.[2]

In Ontario, the Ontario Charitable Gambling Coalition was established in 1991 "to secure and enhance, through fair and equitable gaming practices, the capacity of charities to raise the funds necessary."[3] It started modestly, with a handful of organizations including the Kidney Foundation, Variety Clubs, the Canadian National Institute for the Blind, and the Canadian Mental Health Association. Three years later, the CNIB and the Variety Clubs dropped out, but others joined, and the name was changed to the much slicker Charities 1st, which omits the G word and sounds better. Today, there are twenty-nine member charities, ranging from the Alcohol and Drug Recovery Association of Ontario, through the Easter Seal Society, Ontario Division, to the Spina Bifida and Hydrocephalus Association of Ontario, all out there shouting "Ante up!" Or, more correctly, "When you do ante up, we want our cut."

There are six major channels nationwide for rustling the rubes: raffles, charity casinos, bingos, lotteries, "break open" tickets, and electronic slot machines (called VLTs, for video lottery terminals, soon to be the dominant medium for parting the public from its cash). These activities are nearly always run by professionals who kick back a share of the proceeds to a charity (except in the case of VLTs), and there are regulations stating what the share will be, but none to ensure that the rules are followed. For example, Ontario law provides that when a charity casino is operated under provincial licence, the charity must provide volunteers, who will ensure that all goes well. In fact, what often happens is that a professional operator will approach a charity and offer, say, $10,000 for the use of the charity's name. Then, the operating company will run the show, provide staff in the name of the charity, and dole out what it considers to be the charity's share, according to its own set of books. From the point of view of the voluntary organization, this is manna from heaven; you don't have to do anything, just bank the cheque.

If you believe that, in these circumstances, the division of funds is fair and equitable, then I have a bridge you might want to buy.

Another wrinkle in the casino racket arises from the prevalence of these outfits on First Nations reserves, where they are legal without having to surrender any of the profits to charity. It is hard not to think that this comes under the heading of revenge for the wrongs the First Nations have suffered at the hands of the rest of us.

Canadian governments took up the numbers rackets because of the force of examples from abroad—especially the United States, our moral beacon—and the claims of sheer necessity. Our grandparents thought that gambling was a sin, which didn't stop it, of course, but did deny it state sanction. I can remember, as a junior reporter, writing stories about the Irish Hospital Sweepstakes, which were illegal in Canada, but for which the *Toronto Telegram* newspaper, my employer, always staged a free bumper breakfast. When the lists of those who had drawn tickets on horses in the race were passed to us by the Irish embassy, we invited all the Toronto-area ticket holders down to the Royal York Hotel, fed them, and locked them in a banquet hall to listen to the race on the radio. (This was before television.) If the winner was a local, we were in a position not only to get an interview with the giddy champion but to deny the same to those rascals over at the *Toronto Star*.

The Irish Sweepstakes were given an extra zip by the fact that selling the tickets (but not owning them, or collecting on them) was illegal; they came wafting into our homes in packets mailed from Ireland, rife with promises like the Publishers Clearing House letters of today, and you activated the tickets by sending in the money. There was one chance in thousands that you would draw a horse in the race, one in millions that it would win and you would get a share of the grand prize, which usually worked out to about $140,000 per share. It seemed quite harmless, and at least some of the money presumably went into buying a bedpan for a hospital in Ireland. However, I was somewhat taken aback when I did a story based on interviews with those who had won the $140,000, ten years on, and discovered that most of them had not been made happier by their good fortune, and many of them were downright miserable.

Those were the days of innocence and comparative modesty, labels that apply, in our own day, only to the raffle sector of charitable gambling. This hasn't changed much; the Kiwanis, a school, a church, or another well-meaning group hustles the local merchants for a few prizes and sends the squads out to sell tickets. Or, more grandly, the prize is a car, a boat, or a trip for two to some exotic locale. There is never a lot of money at stake, and the causes actually get most of what is collected. In the village where I live, we ran a (quite illegal) raffle to help pay for a new firehall nearby, which produced a little money, no envy, and quite a lot of fun.

Other gambling events have evolved more drastically. I can remember when bingo was something that took place in church basements to raise a few dollars to help the needy. Cork chips or corn kernels were the markers on dog-eared cards, and the priest—for it was the Catholic churches that were the heady gamblers on bingo—was often the caller. The prizes were mostly toys, ash trays, movie tickets, kitchen utensils, and junk; if you won a cash prize, you were expected, but not required, to turn at least some of it back to the church. Bingo was a social occasion; now it is a national addiction, played in huge commercial halls with flashing lights and electronic equipment, and prizes that run into the thousands of dollars. There is very little talking or socializing, and nobody seems to be having any fun any more, but that is because the stakes are so high. Shut up and play. When a gang of robbers hit a bingo hall in Hintonburg, Ontario, in March 1995, the incident barely interrupted play.[4]

I could not come up with a firm national figure for bingo gambling, but it runs into the billions annually; in Ontario alone, where there are 250 commercial operations counting the cash, the total for 1994 was $1.2 billion.[5] In Ottawa, where I went to check out a few of the sixteen halls devoted to the activity, there are 207 games a week. I was told that there is a considerable population who do nothing but play the game and that the halls fill when the welfare and pension cheques come in.

Almost no one playing in the halls knows or cares that charities benefit from a slice of the proceeds. This is not about giving; it is about getting.

On the horizon is something called TV Bingo, which would allow clients in any hall anywhere to participate in one humongous game, with a grand prize in the $50,000 range.[6]

BINGOGATE

Bingo has given us our first really ripe charity gambling scandal, which led to the resignation of Mike Harcourt, the NDP premier of British Columbia.[7] It seems that the Nanaimo Commonwealth Holding Society (NCHC), for years directed by Dave Stupich, a former NDP MLA, held bingo games to raise money for charities during the 1980s—i.e., before Harcourt became premier. However, quite a lot of the proceeds, perhaps as much as a million dollars, went not to the charities but to expenses connected with the New Democratic Party coffers. In fact, charities apparently got only about 20 per cent of what they were entitled to under the terms of the agreement governing the games; the rest went to pay for some injudicious and failed real estate schemes, and to cover NDP costs in the Nanaimo area. In 1994, the NCHC and three related groups pleaded guilty to a series of charges; the society was fined $55,000 and ordered to repay $100,000.[8] No individuals were charged; apparently the racket had been performed by automation.

The opposition parties, as oppositions will, raised a fuss and said there was much more to it than that. The government replied, as governments will, that it was all under control: a forensic audit has been ordered, all wickedness has been punished, and why don't you guys sit down and shut up? But they didn't and wouldn't, and neither would the RCMP, which, on October 12, 1995, raided seven locations, including the Stupich home, and began drawing up charges.[9] Next, the forensic auditor, Ronald Parks, reported back that the NDP had indeed profited illegally from bingo, and so had David Stupich. The rumour mill began drumming out stories that Harcourt was going to be made to walk the plank, although he said, and no one has ever shown otherwise, that the whole series of events were a mystery to him. The *Vancouver Sun*, one of those damn needle-nosing newspapers, went after what came to be called Bingogate with fervour and turned up a lot more dirt. An outfit called the Burnaby Purpose Youth Society, later the Lower Mainland Purpose Society for Youth (where do they get these names? let us call it LMPSY), was set up in 1983, with, as its guiding light and executive director, an NDP militant, Lynda Fletcher Gordon. It was to run charity bingos, with the money going to help youth.

Almost at once, the provincial gaming commission ran into difficulty with LMPSY, which seemed to have difficulty accounting for what had happened to all the money it received. The regulators were asking for a lot of bothersome stuff, like receipts and accounts. The charity was some put out when it was asked to use a cash register to keep track of things, and told the investigators to do the other thing, which resulted in an increasing pile of paper back at headquarters, including a plaintive note, in 1987, that read: "Would it be possible to ask for a breakdown of where the moneys were spent?" LMPSY sucked in more than a million dollars before the regulators finally stepped in, in 1988, and found that most of the funds had taken a detour on their way to helping youth. According to the fattening file on LMPSY, "While $252,000 was donated from the bingo to charity in the last 11 months, approximately $10,000 can be shown to have been spent on the kids . . . The society is a shell."[10]

All of this stuff was in the file when, in March 1992, guess who was appointed to the gaming commission and made vice chairman? No, really? Yes, really. Lynda Fletcher Gordon herself. This was all kept away from the rude public gaze until the *Vancouver Sun* finally winkled the files out of the government under provincial freedom-of-information legislation. At this point, the government looked at it and fired Gordon, on November 16, 1994.[11]

Harcourt's critics said that if he didn't know about all this tomfoolery, he should have; and if he'd appointed Gordon to the gaming commission without having her background checked, he should look for a new line of work. Which he did, on November 15, 1995.

What we can learn from all this is that when huge amounts of money are sloshing around, the potential for wickedness abounds, and charitable causes are no exception.

LOTTERIES: NO "SKILL OR PLAY" NEEDED

Lotteries are bigger than bingo, although, astonishingly, not all that much. In Ontario, for example, while bingo took in $1.2 billion in 1994, the

Ontario Lottery Corporation had gross revenues of $1.9 billion.[12] Nationally, the 1994 lottery total was $5.5 billion, of which governments were able to grab $1.5 billion. Internationally, lotteries pulled in $130 billion (U.S.),[13] as citizens shelled out from Montevideo to Moscow, on the grounds that they might as well be absolutely broke. The Americans spent $24.5 billion this way in 1994 ($35.5 billion Canadian), which is less, per capita, than our own total.

"The lottery," notes *The New Columbia Encyclopedia* with a sniff, "is distinguished as a form of gambling by the absence of any element of skill or play."[14] Lotteries to finance public works have been around for centuries—British author John Cohen records one in 1566 to finance a water supply for London,[15] and lotteries helped to colonize Virginia, buy guns to defend Philadelphia during the American Revolutionary War, and build Harvard University.

However, the last National Lottery in the United Kingdom was in 1837: "They were stopped because of widespread fraud," according to the Department of National Heritage.[16] And, on this side of the Atlantic, they were choked out later in the century because they had been taken over by various mobs, which led to a good deal of naughtiness, such as shooting, stabbing, fixing the results, and making off with the loot.

The bans did not cause lotteries to disappear but did curb them and gave them a proper modesty. Lotteries began to make a comeback in the United States in the 1950s, when it was discovered that a certain amount of control could be kept over the naughtiness by having the state itself run them and keep quite a lot of the money. The first statewide lottery was in New Hampshire in 1963, and today, there are government-run lotteries in thirty-six states and the District of Columbia.[17]

Canada resisted the temptation throughout the nineteenth century, although a rash of lotteries broke out in the 1920s, through which army and navy veterans raised funds for welfare organizations.[18] They were illegal, but not uncommon. A bill to legalize them and establish a Hospital Sweepstakes reached second reading in the Senate, but was rejected on the grounds that legalized gambling threatened the nation's morals.[19]

Further attempts to remove the ban on lotteries came to nothing until 1968, when Montreal Mayor Jean Drapeau invented a "Taxe Voluntaire" to help pay off the debt left behind by Expo 67, our centennial bash.[20] This scheme, which looked like a lottery, walked like a lottery, and paid off like a lottery, was quite illegal and was condemned by the courts, although no further action was taken. To set things right, Drapeau persuaded the federal government, then led by Pierre Trudeau, to amend the Criminal Code in 1969, making legal what was already being done. This led to the creation in 1970 of the first state-run lottery corporation in Canada, Loto-Québec. Loto-Québec in turn begat the Olympic Lottery in 1974, again to raise money for Drapeau, whose city was hosting the 1976 Olympic Games on the basis of his promise that it could never lose money. Siphoning the suckers was a better way to finance athletics than collecting taxes, it seemed, and the Olympics, which cost $1.4 billion to stage, did lose money after all. (Montreal is still repaying the debt.) After the games, the Olympic Lottery became Loto-Canada, which ran from 1976 through 1979 and netted $161 million, of which $129 million went to the Olympic Games, $4 million to the 1978 Commonwealth Games in Edmonton, $8 million into the federal Fitness and Amateur Sport program, and $20 million to the provinces.[21] The provinces got their share because they had jumped into the lottery game themselves, Manitoba in 1971, the four western provinces as a group in 1974, Ontario in 1975, and the Atlantic provinces in 1976. They kept saying it wasn't fair for Ottawa to muscle in this way; rubbishing the rustics ought to be done closer to home.

In 1979, when Joe Clark was, briefly, prime minister, and anxious to placate the provinces, he took the federal government out of the game in return for payments to Ottawa from the emerging provincial lottery corporations. This was protection money, of a kind that Al Capone would have recognized: Pay up, or I'll be back. The agreement signed in August 1979 "stipulates that the Government of Canada will not participate in the sale of lottery tickets."[22] The payoff amounted to $24 million in 1980 and has gone up steadily since, with a lot of argy-bargy on both sides. In 1994, the total federal take was $49.5 million, of which Ontario paid $18.6 million,[23] on top of $20 million in Goods and Services Taxes.

There are now government-owned lottery companies in every region— the Atlantic Lottery Corporation, Loto-Québec, the Ontario Lottery Corporation, the Western Canada Lottery Foundation, and the Interprovincial, which runs the nationwide Lotto 6/49.

When Ottawa tried to rejoin the game in 1984, with a new national sports lottery called the Canadian Sports Pool, to help finance the 1988 Winter Olympics, the provinces raised merry hell. They went further and leaned on the network of retailers not to handle the tickets, with the result that the feds lost millions and bowed out of the racket.[24] Now, they must rest content with their protection money while the provinces get the rest. Ottawa retains the corporate shell of Loto-Canada, however, for much the same reason that Al Capone had a couple of his bruisers stroll up and down outside one of the protected night clubs, to persuade the owners of the value of keeping those contributions coming.

The largest, fattest of these money machines is the Inter-provincial 6/49, the "Saturday night fever," which depends on players picking 6 numbers out of a combination of 49, and in which the odds of winning are just under 14 million to one, or, as the statisticians like to point out, a little less than the chance of your being struck by lightning twice. Nice if it comes off, though; the payoff on one jackpot in 1994 was $19.9 million, shared by a group of butcher-shop workers.

The 6/49 combination is the most popular internationally, in part because the odds are so long that the grand prize may not be won, in which case it gets carried forward to the next week, building up the bundle, the suspense, and the sales, all at once. In Britain, which plunged into lotteries for the first time in 1994, one jackpot reached $80 million in December 1995; it was shared by three winners, who thus got a mere $26 million each. Darn. In the United States, jackpots of this size are not uncommon, but because the money is taxed, it is paid out in the form of an annuity rather than a lump sum, to keep Uncle Sam's share to a minimum. There is a gigantic cheque with the total written onto it for publicity shots, then you go home and get a monthly stipend for twenty years instead. Just part of the general flim-flammery.

Aside from being a vicious swindle, sucker bait, and a persuasion to the plebs that work is pointless, there is something to be said for these giant jackpots as an entertainment tax. My mother used to buy a ticket on the 6/49 on Thursday, spend Friday and Saturday dividing up the money among her children ("Walter didn't write; he only gets a million"), and chuck away the bent stub on Sunday morning. I'm sure she got her money's worth.

The lottery corporations keep making up new games to keep the unwashed interested, with dandy names like LOTTO Super 7, Instant Millions, Pick Three (a daily lottery), Wintario, Lottario, and Encore. Then there are the copies of other gambling games, like Instant Keno and

Instant Bingo, in which the chances of winning are higher but the prizes lower, and all the sports lotteries, like PRO Line and Sports Select, which make your bookie look like a choirmaster.

Ontario flirted with the idea of a "Cleansweep" lottery in 1991, which would have dedicated the money to cleaning up the environment. However, this came under criticism for "leaving environmental protection to the whims of gamblers,"[25] and was dropped. All the wiseacres agreed that it is much better to leave to the whims of gamblers such lesser matters as heart transplants or the protection of abused children.

The lotteries are growing at several times the rate of the Gross Domestic Product, proving that money is not in short supply, after all. In Ontario, the gross revenues of the lottery corporation shot from $759.5 million in 1984–85 to $1.886 billion ten years later, an increase of 248 per cent.[26] During this period, the GDP advanced at less than 2 per cent per annum; the net effect is a huge transfer of funds to a sector of the economy which is entirely nonproductive.

Out of the huge cash flow thus generated are paid all the costs for commission salespeople, administration, marketing, ticket printing and handling, and, of course, the prizes. Retailers get a commission of 5 per cent for every on-line ticket printed on a lottery terminal and 8 per cent for other tickets, such as scratch-and-win games. They also get commissions for cashing small prizes—2 per cent for on-line games and 3 per cent for others—plus a bonus that can go as high as $1,500 for selling a jackpot ticket. In Ontario, during 1993–94, payments to 11,000 retailers came to $126.9 million.[27]

Next come the costs for brand marketing ($22.7 million); ticket printing and running the computer-ware ($44 million); and operating costs, including administration ($109.7 million).[28] The largest expense is the prizes, $941.5 million, or 49.9 per cent of the total sales figure. Then there is, and this I do not understand, a figure of $48.1 million set aside for "unclaimed prizes," which can be collected up to a year after the draw (how could you not know?). No income tax is paid on the winnings, needless to say. After deducting all that and a handful of minor items, such as interest charges, rent, and the GST, the Ontario Lottery Corporation netted $602 million, or 31.9 per cent of the gross, and $563 million of this was passed through to the Ontario government. It went to the Trillium Foundation, which is funded mainly this way, and the departments of

Culture, Citizenship, Environment and Energy.[29] The Trillium Foundation got $17 million, which it passed out in turn to dozens of other charities. Among the government departments, culture got $73 million, citizenship $1.1 million, and, oh, yes, food banks got just under $17 million. Most of the rest went into general revenues. All this double handling insured that the bureaucrats were kept busy, busy, busy, which we all like to see as part of our new lean and mean administrations.

To put it another way, in Ontario, as in other provinces, the lotteries are a tax on the stupid which pays off at about 30 per cent and ends up being dumped, in large part, right back into the same hopper where it would have gone had it been collected through the tax system, at a much lower cost. Along the way, a number of totally undeserving people become millionaires and don't have to pay taxes on their winnings, because God must have chosen them not to have to share in the costs of the society that so solaced them. We learn from this that it is good not to work and even better not to share.

One of the many problems associated with lotteries by people foolish enough to worry about such things are the grossly misleading ads, which, under slogans like "Imagine the Freedom," paint fantasies and dream sequences to move the product. The instant lotteries are pushed by headlines that urge the reader to "Go hog wild for an instant" or, more revealingly, "Don't think for an instant." If the liquor boards ran ads urging the customers to "Get blotto for an instant," there would be hell to pay, but the lottery floggers are above criticism because it is all just good, clean fun. Apparently, people have all kinds of fun just playing the game—"I wish everyone could get the thrill of going across the row of numbers and circling every one," says Linda. "It's incredible!"[30] I stood beside a middle-aged woman at a booth in Oshawa, Ontario, and watched her buy forty-eight quick-pick tickets, play them all, tear them all up, then burst into tears.

The law says that no one under the age of nineteen may play any of these games, which is one of the rich jokes of our time. A survey of 1,000 Windsor, Ontario, high school students conducted in 1994 found that 86 of them played PRO Line weekly and 82 of them played scratch-and-win games.[31] In response to a newspaper column complaining about the lottery preying on youths, Don Pister, supervisor of media relations for the Ontario Lottery Corporation, wrote a letter to the *Toronto Star*, in which he commented, "People can legally play lotteries at age 19, and if they are old enough to play they are old enough to win."[32] Actually, a two-year-old could play; what he meant, I assume, is that if the province is witless enough to allow the corporation to skin teenagers, don't blame him.

The Canadian Foundation on Compulsive Gambling commissioned a survey in the fall of 1994, which showed that the prevalence of gambling among teenagers was four times that among adults. This means either that we are headed for an epidemic of the stuff or that teenagers are bigger suckers than the general adult population. Either way, it ought to ring alarm bells.

The newest market ploy is to put lotteries on the telephone, which would effectively insert a twenty-four-hour-a-day gambling casino into every household in the land, whether we wanted it or not, and ensure that the kiddies would get a chance to blow the mortgage money along with the grownups. The Coeur d'Alene Indian tribe, in northern Idaho, are trying to launch a lottery that would sell tickets all across the country, over the telephone or computer modem, and collect the money through credit cards.[33] They have been blocked, so far, by state legal action, based on a fair injection of humbuggery. Idaho has argued before the courts that the phone lottery would violate laws against interstate gambling, which is ironic, since the state welcomes outside suckers to play in its weekly contests. It seems at least as likely that concern about competition for the large but limited number of gulls available for plucking—and, perhaps, a dab of racism—may be as much responsible for the opposition to a national telephone lottery as concern about the sanctity of interstate gambling laws.

In all likelihood, cable television, telephones, and computers will become outlets for national and international lotteries, with ever-more billions evaporating while we complain about the lack of finances for schools and hospitals. One of the direct effects of increased charity gambling appears to be a drop in the money available to charities. This is hard to measure in North America, because lotteries have been around for so long and no one ever thought to keep tabs. However, in the United Kingdom, the launch of a National Lottery on November 19, 1994, led to a measurable drop in charitable donations, as the money was switched to gambling. The National Council of Voluntary Organizations put the shortfall during the first year of the National Lottery at ₤339 million[34]—about $729 million Canadian—although there is some debate about the exactitude of this number.

In fact, British studies showed that spending on entertainment, dining out, confectionary sales, and soft drinks all fell as the nation went nuts over the lottery, which sucked ₤4.09 billion out of British pockets in its first ten months. Of this, ₤1.1 billion went to the Good Cause Fund, for distribution to five causes, including sports, culture, heritage, charities, and the Millennium Commission, a body set up to provide a massive national blowout for the turn of the century.[35] A pound of lottery spending is divided this way: 12 pence to government, off the top, 49 pence to prizes, 23 pence to the five Good Causes, and 16 pence to the operator, a private company called Camelot, for costs and profits. There are also costs in connection with the board that administers the grants, so that when all is said and done, charity actually gets 5.6 per cent of the gross[36]—₤229 million out of ₤4.09 billion, a good deal less than it lost in dropped donations. Among the good causes to benefit from all this largesse were a ₤13-million award to Winston Churchill, namesake and descendant of the Grand Man, for family papers, and ₤3.6 million to a community trust to build sports facilities for Eton School (which will share them with the community; Eton only has exclusive access to the new stadium 13 per cent of the time).[37] Much better than wasting the cash on orphans.

The outpouring of funds through the lotteries has led, naturally, to attempts to further cut back government funding for charities. Simon Hebditch, policy director of the Charities Aid Society, told me:

> It will be impossible to resist the temptation to cut government funding because of the lottery money. The arts council gets perhaps ₤80 million from government and twice that from the lottery; the minister is going to say, "Why should we give?"[38]

Moreover, the huge slab of money pulled out by lotteries goes mainly into the bank accounts of the new millionaires. The Treasury Department solaced itself with the notion that, while this "must have reduced the economy's growth," it was not possible to measure the impact,[39] so why worry? Economist David Mackie of the J. P. Morgan merchant bank commented, "Billions have been taken out of the economy and put into the bank. People have been very reluctant to acknowledge this."[40] In Canada, the subject has never even come up.

It is probably too late to make any estimate as to how much money the lotteries are actually costing charitable organizations in this country, because we cannot measure how much they might have received without them. Perhaps we don't want to know. It is bad enough to consider that, in all probability, charities are worse off as a result of all this insanity.

SCRATCH-AND-WIN: MIND-NUMBING SIMPLICITY

The scratch-and-win games, so attractive to the high school crowd, and the "break open" cards, also called "Nevada tickets," to salute their origins among the sin bins of the American West, only cost fifty cents, and you collect at once, which is why the kids love them. They are most popular in Ontario, where the provincial government, through an order in council, authorized municipalities to issue licences to local charities in 1993. Within eighteen months, there were 7,000 outlets hauling in $700 million annually.[41] They are of a mind-numbing simplicity; you break them open and find out if you won. The tickets are sold in boxes of 2,184, with $800 in prizes per box, the top prize being $100. There are 224 prizes in each box— four $100, four $25, four $10, twelve $5, and two hundred $1; thus, the chances of winning something are 224 out of 2,184, or one in 9.75. Hey, it's only money. Your chances of winning on a slot machine, by the way, are generally around one in 1.2, since most slots are set to return $84 out of every $100 bet,[42] so the Nevada tickets may be seen as a one-armed bandit with a two-fisted grip.

There is no mechanism to allow the provincial gaming control commissions, which are responsible for the licensing procedure, to check into the operations for fraud; the law, dear innocent, assumes that the charities' boards of directors would detect any hanky-panky and call in the cops.

Never mind, some of the money does go to charity. I asked Glenn Thompson, executive director of the Canadian Mental Health Association, Ontario Division, how much? He told me that in 1995, the CMHA grossed $971,930 from the tickets, of which more than half went to "ticket purchases and the time of the people who operate in these companies," i.e., the outlets. "In the scheme of things, not a large amount of money."[43] Still, better than a kick in the ass with a frozen boot if you accept the business of a mental health association battening on the frailty of suckers. In favour of the Nevadas, it must also be said that at least they are not as bad as VLTs, which are especially attractive to a generation brought up on video games.

THE VLTS: TERMINALLY ADDICTIVE

Video lottery terminals are illegal under federal law for use by the charities, because they are defined as slot machines, frowned on in the Criminal
Code, but there is nothing to prevent the provinces from running the rackets and keeping the swag, with an argument that at least some of the
money goes to good causes in the end. Nine provinces have already paved
the way with local laws to make them okay. In the tenth, British
Columbia, the government was willing, but the people were not. The NDP
under Premier Harcourt tried to force video lottery terminals down the
craw of municipalities by passing legislation to disallow local bans on the
machines, but the attempt came to a crashing, probably temporary halt in
1995. The loot promised, $120 million,[44] from 5,000 machines installed in
bars, hotels, and bus stations around the province, did not seem enough to
offset the demonstrable fact that the terminals are particularly addictive—
terminally addictive, you might say—especially to the youngsters. In addition, critics advanced the argument that the VLTs are simply wrong, in part
because the money disappears with such blinding speed. While they are
supposed to be games, an experienced player can spit away his money in
two seconds—as fast as with a slot machine. The game pays off in credits,
which can be cashed or, more usually, converted into more plays, and a
mesmeric state overcomes many of the addicts, who just keep banging
away until they are cleaned right out. These dangers galvanized opponents
in British Columbia into mounting a fierce campaign against the VLTs
through lobbies like Vancouver Citizens Against Gambling Expansion.

When forty municipalities representing two-thirds of the provincial
population announced that they didn't want the damn things, the legislation died. Government Services Minister Ujjal Dosanjh sighed that he
found it "very worrisome" that these "negative opinions" could stall the
march of progress in lotus land, while all around—in Washington State, for
example, or Alberta, where there are already 6,000 VLTs chuckling to themselves—more enlightened electorates worked on the principle that hell, if
it makes money, who cares if it destroys a few hundred thousand lives?

Not to worry, time will bring the terminals to the folks whether they
want them or not, because in the collision between rights and revenues,
there is always only one eventual winner. In British Columbia, the top
anti–organized crime organization, the Coordinated Law Enforcement
Unit, estimates that there are already 10,000 illegal VLTs operating.[45] They

will doubtless buttress the argument that heck, if we can't beat 'em, we might as well join 'em.

The newest convert to VLTs was the Harris government of Ontario, which introduced the necessary legislation as part of its 1996 budget. Part of the reason given was an estimate by the Ontario Provincial Police that there were already 20,000 illegal gambling machines in the province, pulling in $500 million on which no tax was paid.[46] Quite a lot of money, on which no tax is paid either, is also made selling illegal drugs and child pornography, without inciting governments to jump into these rackets. The Ontario legislation will allow up to 20,000 *legal* VLTs on premises licensed for the purpose.[47] They are expected to extract $460 million annually from provincial wallets, of which $260 million will go to the province. At least Ontario is setting aside some money—about 2 per cent of the take—for a fund to help fight problem gambling, which is more than you can say for most provinces.[48]

Ontario law will also give some of the proceeds directly to charities. Finance Minister Ernie Eves estimated that this will amount to about $100 million annually, while $46 million will go to the operators.[49] If the province wanted to raise $100 million for charities through the tax system, which is much more efficient, there would be hell to pay; but the VLTs are seen as costing nothing—unless you count the ruined lives of the addicts.

On a per capita basis, Ontario will actually have fewer VLTs than any of the prairie provinces. The machines were introduced in Alberta in 1991, Manitoba in 1992, and Saskatchewan in 1993. There is already a machine in almost every bar, pub, or lounge between the Ontario border and the B.C. border—in addition to Alberta's 6,000, Manitoba has 5,300 VLTs and Saskatchewan 3,600. Despite the chiding of naysayers who bleat that this is the equivalent of selling crack cocaine to kids,[50] the governments are hooked. Saskatchewan made $80 million out of this one brand of gambling in 1995, more than it made in uranium royalties. In Manitoba, the VLTs churned out $577.2 million, of which $120 million became provincial revenue; and in Alberta, a staggering $1.5 billion in VLT revenue produced $357 million for the province.[51] It also produced a number of personal tragedies, but who's counting?

In Alberta, the money thrown into VLTs has reportedly cut the take from charity bingos.[52] There's a nice irony for you. The governments hook the charities on gambling revenue, then grab it for themselves.

WE NEED THE MONEY: END OF ARGUMENT

It is the uncounted and uncountable personal disasters that have fanned at least some resentment against the whole gamut of charitable gambling gimmicks. In Alberta, a Lac La Biche truck driver killed his wife and himself after an argument over his use of VLTs; a female accounts clerk enlisted the help of her daughter to steal $178,500 from her company so she could feed the machines; a Calgary man, who lost his house and family over his gambling habit, converted his entire weekly paycheque into loonies and blew it through a VLT in one sitting.[53]

In essence, the argument comes down to this: the charities that promote gambling say that they need the money and that we can't stop progress. The naysayers, who include a number of charities like the Mennonite Central Committee in Alberta and the Salvation Army everywhere, which will not accept funds gained this way, state that gambling is addictive and that the money comes at too high a price.

Glenn Thompson, the thoughtful executive of the Canadian Mental Health Association in Ontario, represents the first view. He told me:

> It's a very demanding time for charities, because government funding is being reduced and contributions are declining, so everyone is looking for other approaches . . . I think people who quite justifiably have quite a worry about addictive behaviours reach the same conclusions as the prohibitioners did in the 1920s. They say this is a bad thing, so no one should be able to gamble. We crossed that Rubicon many years ago when government began to fund some of its services through lotteries.
>
> People who go to a doctor, you could say, or go to a hospital, have some piece of their services being provided by the lottery ticket they bought last weekend.

In short, our love is here to stay. Or, as Thompson put it when I suggested that a government would be loath, I assume, to stage drinking contests because that would up the tax take:

> Again, you can go and have a look at the revenues from the sale of alcohol and have that same debate. It is addictive to some. When a government is taxing, those who smoke and those who drink will get taxed more heavily . . .

... Some people say drinking is wrong, but that is a judgement that I wouldn't make for the whole population, either about alcohol or about gaming. It is not a new debate ... but one thing certain is that less money is going to come from government and more from somewhere else, and the debate is, Where is that somewhere else?

It is a reasonable thing for money to come from gaming. This organization has taken the position that that is a viable way to obtain funds ... The question of whether it is right or wrong is not an evaluation our boards would get into.

He believes the moral strictures against gambling are as misplaced as were those against alcohol, when it was banned earlier in this century:

I am old enough to remember my parents talking about prohibition days, and it's a little like the prohibition argument that because some people become alcoholics, no one should have alcohol.

Thompson doesn't worry about the danger of criminal activity increasing with the upsurge in gambling, because "these things are very closely regulated," as is the sale of alcohol. He concludes with the clincher: "The vast majority of people don't find gambling unpalatable."[54]

The contrary argument is put by Tibor Barsony, executive director of the Canadian Foundation on Compulsive Gambling, Ontario, with more passion and less grammar:

Some of these charities are themselves addictive related so how do you justify raising money to aid an addictive behaviour by adding to another addictive behaviour? And gambling is an addictive behaviour, this is well-established. How could a charity which is trying to do something good for a segment of the population justify this?

Is this morally accepted? Would this charity who finds it acceptable to raise money through bingos think it was all right to raise money through drinking contests? ... Would they justify the problem drinking they create by, "Oh, well, it raises money?"[55]

Barsony says that a number of studies sponsored by his group and others show that anywhere between one and three per cent of the population is prone to become "pathologically addicted," which means that the more you increase gambling, the more addicts you create. In Ontario, one survey found that 84 per cent of the populace had gambled within the past year, and that 10 per cent, nearly one million, had problems as a result.[56] However, Barsony notes, there is very little money set aside to cope with this new problem—"I asked for some help with research, and they would-n't give me sixty cents"—which costs a large, but immeasurable, amount of money, besides ruining lives. Barsony adds:

> With the legalization of gambling, more and more people are trapped. Why do I care? For the same reasons I care about alcoholism, child abuse, and other social problems . . . It's devastating, hundreds of thousands of people are affected, you get criminal behaviour, bro-ken families, bankruptcy . . .
>
> . . . Money is the substance as alcohol is the substance to an alco-holic, and it produces a tremendous impact on embezzlement and fraud.

Barsony also believes there is a huge shift of money away from productive purposes to gambling, which is bound to have a severe impact on the econ-omy. He concedes, however, that gambling is here to stay:

> We are too far into it. I don't know if there is a point of return before disaster, just as a person has to reach a point of personal low before he can recover from alcoholism, has to recognize that, we as a society have to reach a low point to realize what this gambling age is doing to us . . .
>
> . . . You can't stop it, the backers are not there. The industry has demonstrated to the general public that we can't exist without it; there will be no change until the devastation is visible, and then there will be a public outcry.[57]

The nub, then, is that whether we like it or not, we are going to have more gambling because we are not willing to levy taxes to supply the services society must have; no politician has yet been defeated for pushing VLTs. It appears, in fact, that governments see themselves as having no choice but to turn citizens into suckers to balance their books. In Manitoba, a

Conservative government facing an election in 1994 switched $145 million into general revenues from a "special lotteries transfer" to produce a balanced budget. Jeffrey Simpson of the *Globe and Mail* wrote:

> No politician will apparently make the argument against reliance on gambling revenues—that the revenues are regressive, that gambling brings with it social costs which the state must bear, and that if people want public services, they should be taxed to pay for them.[58]

The charities, presented with new costs they cannot meet, are divided as to whether it is unfortunate, or merely inevitable, that a part of the price we will pay is in the devastated lives of those members of society who are compulsive gamblers—to say nothing of the increase in crime which can be attributed directly to gambling.[59] However, if there is one thing we have learned from the past, it is that the weakest members of society are always considered fair game when it comes to setting priorities for saving government funds.

The time has come, then, to see if we cannot fashion at least some defences suitable for the dangerous new world into which our charitable sector—and all of us—are now moving.

III

SOLUTIONS:
AN END TO WASTE,
GREED, AND FRAUD

If you are concerned about the optimal use of tax expenditures and optimal justice to society, you have to be aware that the charitable system does-n't deliver either. If you are feeding a few people or providing shelter for a few people in the win-tertime, that is neither efficient nor an answer to the problems of poverty.

—DAVID PERRY, CANADIAN TAX FOUNDATION, 1995

11. The Case for Regulation

Voluntarism is no substitute for services that can best be delivered by government, particularly if coverage, equity, and entitlements are valued.

—R. M. KRAMER, *Voluntary Agencies in the Welfare State*, 1981

I have been looking for Terry Nagy for quite a while, but the son of a gun is as elusive as an eel. I phoned, wrote, left messages, even went around to see him at the office listed for his charity, but he wasn't there. I wanted to talk to him because he represents, to my mind, the simplest, most direct, cheapest, and, it may be, most effective way to raise money for a charity. You stick a whole bunch of little containers on the counters of banks, restaurants, shops, waiting rooms, whatever, with an appealing label, and wait for the money to roll in. In Terry Nagy's case, the cause is the AIDS Society for Children, which went into the money-collecting business in December 1994 and received a charitable number, allowing it to give out tax-deductible receipts, in February 1995.[1]

The pamphlet the society puts out is quite impressive and lists all the various departments of the organization. There is a Volunteer Office, an Outreach Department, a Development Office, and a Research Department ("Undertaking Technical, Statistical and Scientific Research for a cure and understanding of HIV/AIDS for children"). There is also a Building Fund, scheduled to raise $10 million to provide housing for the families of AIDS sufferers.[2] I called around, hoping to have a look through the facilities, check out the labs, and consult some of the doctors, researchers, or statisticians, at the address given on the pamphlet—6 Clarence Square, Toronto, Ontario. This is in a building in a square that opens off the foot of Spadina Road, and there is not, in case you were thinking of dropping in, anything anywhere at 6 Clarence Square to indicate the vast and humming hive of activity suggested in the literature.

What there was, on the day I got tired of receiving no answers by mail or phone, was an office on the ground floor of 6 Clarence Square, labelled TCC Courier Co. The company is owned by David Winn, who is listed along with Glenn Stonehouse, "a courier and student," as a director of the charity. Inside, a young woman named Evelyn told me that she does some work, sometimes, for the charity, and sure, she would be glad to show me around.

It didn't take all that long. The hub of this thrumming empire consists of a windowless cubbyhole, about eight by eight feet square, one desk, a filing cabinet, a calendar, and a pile of pamphlets which Health Canada distributes free, titled *We need to know about AIDS*, and which the charity hands out to those who ask for information. Evelyn said that "Things are rather slow right now." There had been plans for a Bowlarama, but that didn't come off. Maybe it would be rescheduled. Terry wasn't in, and hadn't been in for a while, but if I left my name and number, he would be sure to get back to me. (And maybe he will; that was only a year ago.) Another idea was to get tickets for Toronto theatres at a large discount and sell them, with some of the money going to charity; possibly he was busy working on that.

In its first four months of existence, the AIDS Society for Children— "Being There for the Families in Our Community" (but not, alas, for needle-nosing journalists who drop in unannounced)—raised about $170,000,[3] and it certainly hasn't squandered any of it on high-class digs. Trouble is, outsiders seem unable to find out exactly where the money went, and other groups working in the same sector are a mite perturbed.

Carol Yaworski, executive director of the Toronto Committee on AIDS, told me, "As far as I know, not a nickel they have raised has actually been spent on providing services to kids."[4] Of course, she might not know. Nagy has resisted all attempts to persuade him to co-operate with other AIDS-related charities or with the umbrella group, the Canadian AIDS Society. "He was more than reluctant to accept advice," says Yaworski, "he was resistant."

Well, who cares? Perhaps Nagy has a better approach than the mainstream AIDS charities, which will become clear in due course. However, Yaworski points to a number of problems:

> We initially heard about them when we began to receive calls from corporations who were being approached for donations, and we hadn't heard of them. I phoned him [Nagy] and it became very clear that he hadn't done any consultation with other organizations working with children, he just went ahead and set this up.
>
> We suspect that they have raised a fairly substantial amount of money, and if that money doesn't go to the kind of services it's advertised to go to, that reflects on the rest of us.

So, the first concern is that if the AIDS Society for Children doesn't do what it says it can do, other charities will suffer. As Yaworski put it, "Donors . . . saw 'Children' and they saw 'AIDS' and they wrote a cheque. Now, they're probably not going to write a second cheque."

Another problem, Yaworski says, is that existing charities in the same field need help and co-operation, not competition:

> There are legitimate AIDS charities who work with children on a shoestring. There is one group that picks up children in Dunville and drives them to the Hospital for Sick Children in Toronto, and they're doing it with virtually no money and it's very demoralizing for them when an organization like this comes along.

Anyone who donated to Nagy's charity's building campaign is in for a bit of a shock. The money was to go to purchase a property at the corner of Jarvis and Isabella Streets in downtown Toronto, just around the corner from Casey House, an AIDS shelter, and refurbish it as a sort of Ronald

McDonald House for the families of AIDS victims. The building, which is still for sale as I write this, belongs to a law firm, Outerbridge, Miller, Sefton, Wills & Shier, whose senior partner, George Miller, told me that he was approached by a real estate agent on behalf of Nagy: "I frankly didn't take it all that seriously. I think he was trying to get allotments under the Residential Housing Act under the NDP."[5] Which allotments are now as evanescent as a politician's promise.

Perhaps all we learn from this is that established charities don't like it when a newcomer comes sniffing around their turf, threatening the small pool of available cash. But I think there is more to it than that; I think we learn something fundamental about the way in which money can be raised by a charity in this country.

Terry Nagy lists himself as a "self-employed financial agent." He has no apparent expertise in the area of AIDS or in health, social services, charitable funding, building, or administration. Yet all he needs to set himself up in the business of handing out charitable receipts is a number, which he got from Revenue Canada after filling out a two-page document. Then he bought a consignment of counter-top boxes, had them printed with evocative phraseology, and he was in the collection business. We will be able to learn, in a couple of years, from the charity's T3010 form—if that form is correctly filled out—whether most of the collected cash went to administration, salaries, or the research, development, housing, and other advertised programs. Whether he has done any harm, which the other charities in the same line of work seem to think, or simply not done much good, it seems a bit simple-minded, does it not?

DON'T BLAME CHARITIES FOR THINGS THEY CAN'T DO

There are so many problems connected with the collective decision we have made to dump more responsibility for social welfare on the charitable sector, while giving it less money, that it is easy to become discouraged. The vastness of the sector, its inefficiency, its waste and fraud, and the simple, uncontestable fact that it cannot adequately perform the task we have shoved off onto it, invite despair. But it would be quite wrong, it seems to me, to blame charities for things that are not their fault. It is not the fault of the volunteers that governments have abdicated their responsibilities and buggered off, leaving behind a note that reads, "Here, you do it. Oh, and by the way, I've just cut your funds." Nor is it the fault of the vast majority of honest charitable organizations that some rogues and rascals are among them. Nor that gambling, sanctified by the state, is offered to them as about the only way to replace the funds that have vanished with the dew.

Even if it gave us some comfort to heap coals of righteousness on the charities, that would not affect the fundamental fact that they are here to stay, and for good reasons.

In the first place, they give enormous aid, comfort, and pleasure not only to millions of recipients here and abroad, but to millions of givers. Always have, always will. Probably more to the latter than the former. In the second place, there is no question of manufacturing more money for the stricken sectors of society by diverting it from charities. I have argued—I think I have proved—that a system that eats up somewhere between 20 and 90 per cent of its substance just surviving is not efficient, and that when government spends five dollars for every dollar spent by the voluntary agencies, there is a vast waste of public funds. The tax system is a fairer, far more efficient way to raise funds for social causes, but that fact is not merely unacknowledged, it has become almost irrelevant. We won't increase taxes, because we have been convinced that government is already too big, that taxes are already too high, that the social contract is a myth, and that in a modern global economy, it's every man for himself, as the elephant said to the chicken. But cutting government support even more to the charities will not mysteriously cause dollars to flow out of the ground; it will just make things worse.

There is a belief among the optimists of the charitable sector, comparable, in my view, to the belief that the Easter Bunny can be counted on to deliver chocolate eggs on April lawns, that we are moving towards a new form of social service delivery, called "the third sector." (The phrase dates back to the Reagan years.) Government is the first sector, business the second—or vice versa, it makes no matter—and the voluntary sector is the third.

Gordon Floyd, the engaging and energetic director of communications for the Canadian Centre for Philanthropy, is a strong believer in the third sector:

I'm convinced this is where the action is going to be in the next decade. Just as it was the public sector in the 1960s and the private sector in the late '70s, now it will be the not-for-profit sector . . . I see massive shifts in responsibility, most of it indirectly . . .

. . . When you cut welfare, unemployment insurance, and support for hospitals and education, it is the voluntary sector that picks up the pieces, whether it is through food banks or neighborhood support or whatever. The shift is going to be massive, but it is mostly unacknowledged as of now.

Not merely unacknowledged, I would have said, but almost invisible, except insofar as governments are transferring funds which they used to administer themselves into contracts with charitable organizations, adding, in the name of efficiency, another layer of administration to the mix. Or, as Floyd puts it:

We were trying to deliver a whole lot of programs through government that we weren't prepared to pay for, and a lot of us have been looking for solutions to what were seen as systemic problems. There is a strong argument to be made that these programs have not delivered what we thought they were delivering, and maybe we should look at more targeted programs with communities, where people and the community get together to find out where the greatest needs are, and meet these selectively. Instead of having universal programs delivered by professionals, you have targeted programs delivered by amateurs— an engaged citizenry.

Probably what we are moving towards is a society in which we have a much more engaged citizenry, and we will be less inclined to pass a whole series of measures to meet particular problems.[6]

Or, to put it another way, why not turn the blood supply over to the Red Cross, and see what happens? Bad example. Well, never mind. Either Floyd is right, and we are moving to a grand future in which the third sector will take on much more responsibility with a new surge of joy and efficiency, or he is wrong, and the volunteers will have to do more with less any way they can.

In either case, we come up against the problems of waste, fraud and inefficiency. If the $86 billion we spend annually through the charitable sector results in the loss of some $30 billion into the black hole of overhead, there is a problem. And if the general public gets to know how much goes missing, the result will simply be a further withdrawal of support for the charities. Henry David Thoreau wrote, "There is no odour as bad as that which rises from goodness tainted."[7]

He might have added, "And there is nothing that makes the customers slam their wallets shut faster than goodness tainted." In an interview with *Front & Centre*, the Canadian Centre for Philanthropy's magazine, pollster Michael Sullivan addressed this issue. Sullivan is vice president of Decima Research, which has done surveys for IMAGINE on the attitudes of Canadians towards giving and volunteering. He never used the word "spooky," but he might well have:

> The motives of people in the charitable sector are still believed to be good motives . . . But if the public starts to question this, if they believe that the sector is spending too much money on fundraising, if they believe that the sector is spending too much money on administration, if you get a couple of scandals in that direction, it could be pretty devastating.[8]

Further on, he says Canadians "don't have a clue about the size or scope of the charitable sector. They just don't know." That, so far, has been the sector's protection, but it is no long-term solution. That must come from greater, not less, exposure, what Gordon Floyd calls "constant and effective accountability." Unless Canadians are convinced that the sector is operating with some efficiency and minimal waste and graft, they will not give, and we will all be the worse for it. The answer is a Charity Commission. A Charities Aid Foundation would be nice, too.

THE CHARITY COMMISSION FOR ENGLAND AND WALES

In England and Wales (Scotland goes its own way), the Charity Commission dates back to 1853. As we saw in Chapter Two, there were charity commissioners as long ago as the sixteenth century, but these were local; the national board was set up much more recently. When I first heard about it, my mind flashed back to those scenes from Dickens, where a few fat men feast on ham hocks while, in the background, a mob of boys hold out their gruel bowls and beg. The commission was the registrar of charities and, in theory, the sector's overseer, fulfilling the roles assigned in Canada, more or less, to Revenue Canada. For decades, the commissioners muddled through, in a thoroughly British fashion, until it became obvious that a major overhaul was necessary. In 1986, the Public Accounts Committee of the House of Commons discovered that while there was, as in Canada, a legal requirement for every charity to submit accurate accounts annually, only about 10 per cent of them ever did so. The MPs asked, "If nine out of ten charities don't submit their books, does that mean there is a massive amount of fraud?" Gosh, we don't know, the commissioners said.[9]

The upshot, in due course, was a thorough investigation, a White Paper, and new legislation, the Charities Act 1993, which has taken three years to implement in full. The new Charity Commission, headed by five commissioners appointed by the home secretary and housed in three centres—London, Liverpool, and Taunton, Somerset—is the Mary Poppins of the voluntary sector: stern, efficient, but kindly in intention. It has a number of responsibilities, but the heart of the matter is one simple phrase: "The Charity Commission's task is to seek to preserve the integrity of charity."[10] The job is divided into four separate tasks:

- Maintaining a public register of charities
- Investigating misconduct and the abuse of charitable assets, and taking (or, in some cases, recommending; i.e., call in the cops) remedial action
- Proffering advice to charities to make them more efficient
- Providing plans and orders to modernize the purposes and administration of charities, and to give the trustees additional powers.

Two of the tasks, the first two, involve regulation and correction; the other two, help and supervision. The commission has no mandate, and no desire, to run the nation's 178,000 charities; it does have a mandate to make the system work efficiently and in such a way that the public will have confidence that their money is going where it is intended to go. Anyone can walk in off the street into one of the offices and get the lowdown on a charitable group instantly off a computer, with a commission employee on hand to help; or write for details, or plug into a modem, or call on a telephone. Or they can write to the charity and ask for a copy of its accounts; it is a criminal offence to refuse such a request. Unlike Revenue Canada, which has neither the staff nor the mandate to enforce compliance rigorously, the commission is muscular, in a quiet way.

I asked Richard Corden of the Charity Commission how it would respond to a charity that established itself for one purpose and spent the funds otherwise, which, as we have seen, is perfectly all right in Canada. He replied, "If you set up a dog charity and put on an opera, we would get you to stop it, and then investigate to see whether you ought to make personal restitution."[11] Ah, but how, exactly, would the practice be stopped? Mostly by moral suasion:

> It would be extremely rare that we couldn't stop it by speaking to the charity trustees. If they continued, our line would be, "Every penny you spend as trustees is a breach of trust, and you will have to pay it back out of your own pocket along with any monies the charity might have lost." Our aim would be to make sure the charity's financial position was the same as it was before the breach of trust started.

In one spectacularly successful case, the Salvation Army was persuaded by a group of financial wizards that it could make more than bank interest on its considerable bank balances and turned over ₺6 million (more than $13 million), with a hope and a prayer, for investment in various commercial papers. The money rose up and wafted away, leaving the Salvation Army bereft. With a curse—Darn!—and a bang on the drum, the godly suckers called in a law firm and the investigation branch of the Charity Commission, to go after the vanished funds. Over two years, in a search that spread across thirteen countries, the sleuths recovered all the money, interest on it from the beginning, and the costs of the pursuit, including legal costs. It was, says Corden, "A complex fraud, a long investigation by us and vigorous action by the Army to get back every penny." Criminal prosecutions for fraud are under way as I write this.

In another case, the Welsh Heart and Handicapped Children's Society was running a series of lotteries, the profits of which disappeared into "paying wages and providing employees with cars to ensure the continued sale of tickets," with the result that only 3 per cent of the money was spent on charity. "We pointed out to the trustees that the operation of a lottery is not a charitable activity," and the trustees "took the decision to wind up the charity."[12] In the right hands, moral suasion is a potent persuader.

The Charity Commission has a staff of 550 and an annual budget of ₺25 million. It earns about ₺2 million in fees and receives the other ₺23 million from the Home Office.[13] In return, the commission examines in detail 12,000 charities a year; in 1993–94, it "protected" charitable property valued at ₤25 million.[14] "Protected" is a tricky phrase; the commission makes a calculation, when it catches either sloppiness, maladministration, or outright fraud, as to how much money was either recovered or saved by its actions, and calls that "protected." The figure is estimated to rise to ₤45 million by 1997–98 as the investigators get better at their work, even though the staff is due for a slight decrease.

Well, I'm impressed. Not only does the Charity Commission in effect pay for itself, its presence has two other wondrous results. One is to signal to charitable trustees that someone up yonder knows if you've been naughty or nice, which must do something to curb the small percentage of rascals. The other is to signal to the general public that they can expect efficiency and accountability out of the sector.

Janet Morrison, director of policy for the National Council for Voluntary Organizations, says, "The main advantage of the Charity Commission is that it instills a level of public confidence, without which there is a danger that people will simply stop giving."[15] In the United Kingdom, as in Canada, "The public's propensity to pay tax is not there; you will always vote for more education, but not the taxes." But at least in the United Kingdom, it is reasonable to suppose that, if new money can be pried out of private pockets, it will not simply be wasted or defrauded away.

The major drawback to the Charity Commission, according to a number of the charity workers I spoke to, is the usual complaint about forms and form-filling. "It may look wonderful to you," said one man who helps a London children's charity keep its books, "but it's an unholy pain to the people who have to fill out the forms." Only charities with incomes above ₤1,000 are required to register, but that isn't much, and the cost and trouble of keeping books of the sort demanded by the commission is considerable.

That is no doubt a shame, but it is a reasonable trade-off for greater efficiency and probity in the system. (The other charities, besides small ones, that are exempt from the commission's gaze are universities, grant-maintained schools, and most national museums and galleries, which come under other supervisory boards.) The result is bound to be, in the end, that smaller charities will be folded into large ones or disappear entirely. This may not be an altogether bad thing, even if it leads to the vanishing of the Benevolent Association for the Relief of Decayed Tradesmen.

TOWARDS A CANADIAN CHARITY COMMISSION

In short, I believe we ought to have something like the Charity Commission in Canada, with five regional offices, the same rigorous mandate, and the same capacity to chide, correct, and aid the charitable sector. We won't pay for it out of taxes, I guess, but it could be paid for either out of a direct levy on the provincial lotteries, by taking over half the protection money now paid by the provinces to Ottawa through the lottery corporations, or by charging the charities a fee, based on assets, for this regulatory and advisory service. This would work in much the way we finance the Canadian Deposit Insurance Corporation for our financial institutions by an all-but-invisible charge on deposits.

My choice would be a small hit on either the lotteries themselves or the prizes. If we blow $5 billion on the damn things every year, a tax of one-half of one per cent on the gross, or of one per cent on the prizes, would provide a pool of $25 million to run a Charity Commission. That ought to be enough, if the English and Welsh can supervise more than twice as many charities with £23 million.

Probably the simplest way to handle the matter would be to have the Charity Commission draw up its annual budget and submit it for payment to the provincial lotteries, which could pay it on the basis of their own assets or annual revenue. This is how the supervision of banks and insurance companies has been financed at the federal level for decades. My objection to this method is that the regulator is being paid by the very group it is supposed to supervise, but nobody else seems to think this worth bothering about; so, if it is okay for the banks, it is okay for charities. The lotteries could work out exactly how to meet their obligations by themselves; the main thing is to get some sort of rational system in place without adding to the cost to the general taxpayer.

THE CHARITIES AID FOUNDATION

We might also do well to copy the Charities Aid Foundation. This is a body set up by the National Council of Voluntary Organizations, a more muscular version of the Canadian Centre for Philanthropy, which works for charities, companies, and individuals in Britain, with a staff of 200 in Kent and London.[16] The CAF passes donations to charities, helps them with investments, commissions and publishes a vast array of statistics and studies, and organizes conferences and seminars, as well as making grants

of its own with money donated to it. It helps corporations by setting up
CAF company accounts and also helps individuals with CAF charity
accounts. There is even a debit card for regular charitable giving, and the
CAF operates the nation's largest agency for payroll giving, called "Give As
You Earn." In 1994–95, personal donors funnelled more than ₤38 million
through the CAF and about the same through companies.[17] Finally, there
are trust funds, now over ₤330 million, invested with CAF by the charities,
through which the voluntary groups do much better than they would by
leaving their money on hand with the banks. The foundation, which
charges fees for its work and invests on its own behalf, actually made an
operating surplus of ₤1,335,000 during 1995.[18]

Probably the finest, and most necessary, and easiest to copy of all the
Charities Aid Foundation projects is its annual publication of charity statistics, *Dimensions of the Voluntary Sector*.[19] This volume presents an amaz-
ingly detailed insight into charities, with articles, research papers, and,
most importantly, detailed financial information on the top 500 fundraising charities, as well as on the large community trusts and foundations.
The tables contain far more detail than is available in the T3010 forms in
Canada, including income sources, expenditures, management and fundraising costs, investments, assets, sales, corporate support, and government
grants and fees. The survey sells for ₤20, which, with corporate sponsors,
covers most of the costs, but most libraries carry it, so anyone can find out,
either through this publication or the Charity Commission, a great deal of
information about charities generally, as well as about all the most important voluntary groups, their donors, and supporters.

This is a sort of Domesday Book, except that it is regularly updated to
show what has happened since the last time, and the charities all know
that their level of efficiency is going to be compared by intelligent givers
with that of other major organizations. In the United States, where there
are two major foundations devoted to collecting and releasing information
about charities, the data available to the general public is not as complete
as this, but at least some can be found. In Canada, the situation is pitiable.
The Canadian Centre for Philanthropy's brave attempt, *A Portrait of
Canada's Charities*, contains a lot of general information on the sector, collected four years ago, but names no names. Most of us want to know,
before we write a cheque to Muscular Dystrophy, or the Alzheimer

Society, or any other good cause, what they did with the money last time. As of now, we have no ready way of knowing.

It is as if we were determined in this country to make no distinction between voluntary groups that do well, abide by the rules, watch every dollar carefully, and reach out to the community, and those that are sloppy, dumb, or just plain crooked.

Perhaps that was acceptable, or unavoidable, in Victorian Canada, but if we do not move, soon, to make our charitable sector more accessible, more accountable, and more responsible, we cannot expect ordinary people to devote the extra time, money, and effort required to make up for the retreat of government.

The vast and powerful charitable industry is regulated, in theory, by Revenue Canada and its registration system, which is a flea bite on the hide of an elephant, and by provincial regimes that are even less visible and effective. In Ontario, where one-third of Canada's population lives, the task is left to the Official Guardian, the office also responsible for looking after orphans. When it seems that public moneys are at stake within the narrow confines of the enabling legislation, the office can go before a court and demand an accounting. In one of the rare cases where this oversight clearly worked to the benefit of charities, the province intervened in the 1994 takeover of Maple Leaf Gardens in Toronto. Steve Stavro, a grocery tycoon and an executor of the will of Harold Ballard, majority owner of the sports complex, bought control of the Gardens from the estate, in a secret deal, for $34 a share, or $75 million.[20] Ballard had left money to a number of charities from the residue of his estate, but under this deal, there was to be very little residue, and thus very little for the charities. The province argued that an open auction for the shares would have brought a higher price and more for the charities, so a lawsuit was launched against Stavro. It was dropped in 1996 when he agreed to a complex deal that will ensure at least $30 million in funds for the charities, which include the Salvation Army, Princess Margaret Hospital, and a number of other organizations.[21] It was, I think, a signal victory, but it was not the same thing as having a regulator in place to work with the charities, not only to keep them in line but to help them when they need it.

In Alberta, there is more rigorous legislation, under a new Charitable Fund-Raising Act, which requires the registration of charitable bodies that raise more than $10,000 within the province and the release of financial information on request. Only registered charities may use professional fund-raisers, and they, too, must be registered.[22] Thus, we have moderately effective legislation in one province, although it has not been tested in court. Alberta was elbowed into passing the new law when its Public Contributions Act was thrown out by the Supreme Court of Canada because it required prior authorization before a fundraising campaign could be carried out; this was, sigh, a violation of the Canadian Charter of Rights and Freedoms, which, under Section 2(B), the freedom-of-thought section, apparently makes it okay to flim-flam the folks. I asked a lawyer who has worked in this area for a number of years what he thought of the regulatory regime in Canada's charitable sector, and he replied, "What regulatory regime?"

Everyone who looks at this subject comes to the same conclusion: without better regulation, charitable donations will decline. Here is the view of Donald Bur, a lawyer with the Ontario Law Reform Commission, which has been studying philanthropy in Canada, that parallels almost exactly what Janet Morrison told me in London:

> Charities are going to be much more important, but on the other hand people are not going to have as much money, and there's going to be rising demand, along with less inclination to give to charities. I think it's a number of things, primarily an attitude that you start to look after yourself, therefore you don't look after your neighbour as much as you did in the past. People are going to have less money, people are more insecure about their jobs and their income, so it's going to be more difficult. You have to have a system so that people can be confident in giving to charities. We have to create a system that will give that confidence, so that when people give money, they know where it's going to go to.[23]

A LAST WORD

In case you haven't noticed, I believe there are a few flaws in the way the charitable sector works. I believe the raising of a substantial portion of the cost of social services through this sector is wrong, dumb, and dangerous. David Perry, the long, lean, worried-looking executive director of the Canadian Tax Foundation (itself a charity), puts it this way:

You spend the money through the tax expenditure system, inefficiently, and it's the same money that you would spend through government, except that you have almost no accounting for it . . .

The conventional wisdom says the private sector can do things a lot cheaper than government can, and there is some truth to that, but not in the case of charities. The feds average about 1.1 per cent in costs to raise cash; no charity can come anywhere near that.[24]

However, I do not believe there is anything like a national will to reverse the process we have been going through for at least the last decade, which means that, like it or not, we are stuck with Lady Bountiful again, even if she flubbed the job last time.

In the circumstances, all a body can do is to try to work with what is available. If we don't want to go back to the welfare state and the social contract, then we must at least make better use of the mammoth resources now being poured into charity.

The first step along this route ought to be the establishment of a Charity Commission and a Charities Aid Foundation; the alternative is bound to be increasing disillusion, doubt, and despair.

Notes

CHAPTER I   THE KINDNESS OF STRANGERS

1 *Front & Centre*, March 1995, p. 8. This magazine is the publication of the Canadian Centre for Philanthropy, which is the most reliable source of information on charities in general in Canada.

2 *Toronto Star*, October 2, 1995, p. A1.

3 *Toronto Star*, November 5, 1995, p. A14.

4 *Toronto Star*, October 3, 1995, p. A4.

5 *Registering your Charity for Income Tax Purposes*, Revenue Canada, Ottawa, p. 4.

6 Ibid., p. 6.

7 Ibid., pp. 7–8.

8 *Hansard*, June 5, 1995, p. 13237.

9 Drache, Arthur, *Canadian Taxation of Charities and Donations*, Toronto, Carswell, 1994, pp. 8–14.

10 *Charities Division: Delinquent/Voluntary/Cause*, 1995.

11 *Ottawa Citizen*, April 22, 1995, p. B1.

12 Interview, August 20, 1995.

13 Revenue Canada figure, interview, August 29, 1995, Charities Division.

14 Sharpe, David, *A Portrait of Canada's Charities*, Canadian Centre for Philanthropy, Toronto, 1994, p. 5. This is the only comprehensive review of charities done to date; it ought to be an annual, although, as the work of the charity lobby, it almost never mentions a charity by name.

15 Ibid., p. 5.

16 Ibid., p. ix.

17 Sharpe, p. 41. A Decima Research survey in 1991, sponsored by the Canadian Centre for Philanthropy, found that 43 per cent of Canadians fifteen years of age or older had done some volunteer work in the previous year.

18 Derived from Table 9 in Sharpe, p. 22.

19 Ibid., p. 37.

20 Ibid., p. 19.

21 Ibid., p. 27.

22 *Globe and Mail*, September 15, 1995, p. B3.

23 Sharpe, op. cit., Table 9, p. 23.

24 *Financial Post*, December 9, 1994, FOCUS section, p. 26.

25 *The 1995 Canadian Global Almanac*, edited by John Robert Colombo, Toronto, Macmillan, 1995, p. 193.

26 *Toronto Star*, January 24, 1994, pp. A6, A21.

27 *Toronto Star*, January 26, 1995, p. E2.

28 *Toronto Star*, December 10, 1995, p. D4.

29 *Edmonton Journal*, May 23, 1995, p. 1.

30 We do not keep a tax expenditure budget in Canada, although the Americans do. When he was finance minister, John Crosbie insisted on such a summary, on the sound grounds that money forgiven through the tax system is money spent just as surely as if it were doled out in grants. That lasted one year, produced a number of alarming statistics on the amount of gravy ladled onto the plates of Canadian corporations, and was dropped. This figure is derived from the Department of Finance, very gingerly. The Canadian Tax Foundation believes it is probably too low. Still, a billion here, a billion there, it soon adds up to real money.

31 This is where the loonie you threw into the Sally Ann bucket or deposited in one of those little cartons by the cash register in a restaurant shows up. The Canadian Centre for Philanthropy worked backwards to get this figure, going from the receipts shown by charities and then deducting the amounts shown in official receipts issued by the charities, as recorded in their income tax forms.

32 *Globe and Mail*, September 15, 1995, p. B3.

33 Revenue Canada press releases, April 1994.

34 Interview, November 16, 1995, with Glenn Thompson, executive director, Canadian Mental Health Association, Ontario Division.

35 *Dimensions of the Voluntary Sector*, Charities Aid Foundation, London, 1995, p. 81.

36 *Globe and Mail*, February 6, 1996, p. A7.

37 Sharpe, op. cit., p. 5.

38 Ibid.

39 A study done by Prof. Robert Thompson of McMaster University in 1993 for the Canadian Centre for Philanthropy shows that Canadians gave about one-third less, in proportion to their incomes, than they did in 1969.

40 *Toronto Star*, December 14, 1995, p. B3.

41 *Toronto Star*, April 2, 1994, p. A4.

42 *Toronto Star*, April 11, 1996, p. A12.

43 *Toronto Star*, February 6, 1996, p. A6.

44 The figures in this paragraph are from *Child Poverty in Canada*, Report Card 1994, and are derived in turn from Statistics Canada, the National Council of Welfare, Human Resources Development Canada, and the Centre for International Statistics.

45 O'Reilly, John Boyle, *In Bohemia*, stanza 5.

CHAPTER 2   GOD'S LADDER

1 Quoted in Bakal, Carl, *Charity USA*, New York, Time Books, 1979, p. 22.

2 Ibid., p. 19.

3 Quoted in Whitaker, Ben, *The Foundations*, London, Methuen, 1974, p. 46.

4 Ibid, p. 47.

5 *The New Columbia Encyclopedia*, New York, University of Columbia Press, 1975, p. 1028.

6 *Satire X.*

7 Matthew 19:6.

8 Quoted in Bakal, op. cit. p. 21.

9 Ibid., p. 22.

10 Daltrop, Anne, *Charities*, London, B. T. Batsford, 1978, p. 15.

11 Ibid., p. 8.

12 Quoted in Durant, Will, *The Reformation*, New York, Simon and Shuster, 1957, p. 39.

13 Ibid., p. 40.

14 Bakal, op. cit., p. 22.

15 Quoted in Coulton, G. G., *Social Life in Britain from the Conquest to the Reformation*, Cambridge, 1938, p. 203.

16 Quoted in Durant, op. cit., p. 340.

17 Bakal, op. cit., p. 23.

18 Bindoff, S. T., *Tudor England*, London, Penguin, 1951, p. 95.

19 Ibid., p. 107.

20 Bakal, op. cit., p. 23.

21 Bindoff, op. cit., p. 226.

22 Whitaker, op. cit., p. 35.

23 Tawney, Richard, *Religion and the Rise of Capitalism*, London, Holland Memorial Lectures, 1922, p. 49.

24 Perkins, Thomas, *Of divine or religious worship in Works*, London, 1605, unpaged.

25 *The Statute of Charitable Uses* 1601 (43 Elizabeth I, c. 4).

26 Jordan, W. K., *Philanthropy in England 1480–1660*, London, Allen and Unwin, 1959, p. 36.

27 Daltrop, op. cit., p. 21.

28 Ibid., p. 26.

29 Jones, M. G., *Hannah More*, Cambridge University Press, 1952, p. 39.

30 Daltrop, op. cit., pp. 28–29.

31 *The Deserted Village*, Line 51.

32 Quoted in Bakal, op. cit., p. 23.

33 Quoted in Leonard, E. M., *The Early History of English Poor Relief*, London, Cass & Co., 1965, p. 303.

34 Friedlander, Walter, *Individualism and Social Welfare*, New York, Free Press of Glencoe, 1962, pp. 81–83.

35 Malthus, Thomas, *Essay on Population*, London, 1798, Chap. IV.

36 Daltrop, op. cit., p. 42.

37 See Bryden, Kenneth, *Old Age Pensions and Policy-Making in Canada*, Montreal, McGill-Queen's University Press, 1974, pp. 20–21.

38 Dicey, A. V., *Law and Public Opinion During the Nineteenth Century*, London, Macmillan, 1962, p. 233.

39 Whitaker, op. cit., p. 39.

40 Ibid.

41 Daltrop, op. cit., p. 39.

42 Hobbes, Thomas, *Leviathan*, Part 1, Chapter XIII, 1651.

43 Dubinsky, Lon, *Philanthropy, the Power of Benevolence*, CBC Transcript, Toronto, 1985, p. 3.

44 Daltrop, op. cit., p. 41.

45 Quoted in Daltrop, op. cit., p. 43.

46 Magnus, Sir Philip, *Gladstone, A Biography*, New York, E. P. Dutton, 1954, p. 108. 108 Magnus reports that one of the women Gladstone rescued was a twenty-year-old prostitute whose admirer had provided her with her own carriage and horses, and when she gave up the job, the man who ran the livery stable where these were

kept threatened to sue Gladstone for the balance of her account.

47 Whitaker, op. cit., p. 39.

48 Quoted in Daltrop, op. cit., p. 57.

49 Quoted in Ludwig, Emil, *Bismarck*, translated by Eden and Cedar Paul, London, George Allen & Unwin, 1927, pp. 550–551.

50 Daltrop, op. cit., p. 62.

51 Ibid., p. 58.

52 Grigg, John, *Lloyd George, the People's Champion, 1902–1911*, London, Methuen, 1978, p. 194.

53 Quoted in Daltrop, op. cit., p. 62.

54 Beloff, Max, *Wages and Welfare in Britain, 1914–1945*, London, Edward Arnold, 1984, p. 263ff.

55 Martin, Samuel A., *An Essential Grace*, Toronto, McClelland & Stewart, 1985, p. 54.

CHAPTER 3 MAPLE LEAF RAGS: THE GOOD OLD DAYS

1 Bakal, op. cit., p. 25.

2 Martin, op. cit., p. 57.

3 Ibid., p. 58.

4 Neatby, Hilda, *Quebec: The Revolutionary Age*, Toronto, McClelland & Stewart, 1977, p. 239.

5 Ibid.

6 Ibid., p. 234.

7 Minville, Esdras, "Labour Legislation and Social Services in the Province of Quebec," *Report of the Royal Commission on Dominion-Provincial Relations*, Ottawa, King's Printer, 1939, pp. 45–46.

8 Quoted in Stewart, Walter, *But Not in Canada*, Toronto, Macmillan, 1976, p. 104.

9 Ibid.

10 Wright, Esther Clark, *The Loyalists of New Brunswick*, Hansport, N. S. Lancelot Press, 1981, p. 101.

11 See Stewart, Walter, *True Blue: The Loyalist Legend*, Toronto, Collins, 1985, p. 155ff.

12 Ibid., p. 164.

13 Martin, op. cit., p. 61.

14 Quoted in Martin, op. cit., p. 67.

15 *St. John Daily Sun*, October 13, 1902, quoted in *Philanthropy, The Power of Benevolence*.

16 Martin, op. cit., p. 64.

17 Ibid., p. 62.

18 Ibid., p. 69.

19 *Ontario Legislature Debates*, December 19, 1868.

20 MacInnis, Grace, *J. S. Woodsworth*, Toronto, Macmillan, 1953, p. 53.

21 Ibid., p. 64.

22 Finkel, Alvin, *Business and Social Reform in the Thirties*, Toronto, Lorimer, 1979, p. 82.

23 Bryce, R. B., "The Canadian Economy in the Great Depression," in *Interpreting Canada's Past*, edited by J. M. Bumsted, Toronto, Oxford University Press, 1993, Volume Two, p. 468ff.

24 Struthers, James, *How Much Is Enough?* Toronto, University of Toronto Press, 1994, p. 84.

25 Ibid., p. 85.

26 Berton, Pierre, *The Great Depression*, Toronto, McClelland & Stewart, 1990, p. 51.

27 Ibid., p. 132.

28 Bryce, op. cit., p. 469.

29 Martin, op. cit., p. 75.

30 Berton, op. cit., p. 358.

31 Quoted in Bryce, Table 1, p. 473.

32 Bryce, op. cit., p. 471.

33 See "A Riotous Time Was Had by All," in *But Not in Canada*, op. cit., p. 8ff.

34 Haliburton, T. C., *Sam Slick*, 1836, Chapter xv.

35 Struthers, op. cit., p. 83.

36 Quoted in Berton, op. cit., p. 132.

37 *Bennett Papers*, Vol. 811, p. 50359, Sir Charles Gordon to R. B. Bennett, January 6, 1934.

38 Finkel, op. cit., p. 88.

39 Bryce, op. cit., p. 481.

40 Quoted in Struthers, James, "Shadows from the Thirties," in *The Canadian Welfare State*, edited by Jacqueline S. Ismael, Edmonton, University of Alberta Press, 1987, p. 10.

41 Struthers, "Shadows from the Thirties," op. cit., p. 10.

42 Fraser, Blair, *The Search for Identity*, Toronto, Doubleday, 1967, p. 18.

43 Ibid., p. 19.

44 Struthers, "Shadows from the Thirties," op. cit., p. 13.

45 Ibid.

46 Ibid.

47 Ibid., p. 14.

48 Ibid.

49 Ibid., p. 4.

50 Tom Kent, a key policy maker during the Pearson years and into the early Trudeau years, has an excellent description of the genesis of these plans in his book *A Public Purpose*, Kingston, McGill-Queen's University Press, 1988, p. 129ff.

51 Bryden, op. cit., p. 5.

52 Kent, op. cit., p. 316.

53 *The Welfare State in Historical Perspective: European Journal of Sociology* 2 1961, p. 228.

CHAPTER 4 GOODBYE WELFARE: A VERY MEAN SOCIETY

1 Interview, August 29, 1995.

2 Interview, May 17, 1995.

3 Interview, August 29, 1995.

4 *Report of the Royal Commission on Taxation*, Ottawa, 1966.

5 Quoted in Kierans, op. cit., p. 145.

6 *Annual Report of the Minister of Industry, Trade and Commerce, under the Corporations and Labour Returns Act, Part I, Corporations*, p. 76.

7 Ibid., p. 133.

8 Quoted in Stewart, Walter, *Shrug: Trudeau in Power*, Toronto, New Press, 1971, p. 171.

9 Kent, op. cit., p. 426.

10 Kierans, Eric, and Walter Stewart. *Wrong End of the Rainbow*, Toronto, Collins, 1988, p. 134.

11 *The 1995 Canadian Global Almanac*, op. cit., p. 239.

12 See Hurtig, Mel, *The Betrayal of Canada*, Toronto, Stoddart, 1991, p. 152.

13 Canadian Manufacturers' Association, *Year-End Review and 1996 Outlook*, Toronto, 1995, p. 3.

14 *Toronto Star*, December 24, 1995, p. D2.

15 Ibid.

16 Witcover, Jules, *Marathon: The Pursuit of the Presidency*, New York, Viking, 1977, p. 98.

17 Ibid.

18 *New York Times*, August 18, 1988, p. 4.

19 *Toronto Star*, December 22, 1995, p. A27.

20 *Toronto Star*, February 11, 1996, p. A10.

21 *Toronto Star*, December 19, 1995, p. A28.

22 Ibid., p. A20.

23 *Toronto Star*, October 3, 1995, p. A7.

24 *Globe and Mail*, September 14, 1995, p. A7.

25 "Feeding Canada's Poor: The Rise of Food Banks and the Collapse of the Public Safety Net," in *The Canadian Welfare State*, op. cit., p. 126.

26 Ibid., p. 137.

27 Ibid., p. 127.

28 Ibid., p. 135.

29 Interview, April 27, 1995.

30 *Globe and Mail*, February 7, 1996, p. A1.

31 *Globe and Mail*, February 9, 1996, p. 7.

32 *Toronto Star*, December 8, 1995, p. A3.

CHAPTER 5   TAKING A CHARITABLE VIEW

1 *Toronto Star*, January 2, 1995, p. A12.

2 Sharpe, op. cit.

3 *Vancouver Sun*, June 7, 1995, p. A6.

4 *Montreal Gazette*, June 30, 1995, p. B2.

5 Telephone interview, November 7, 1995.

6 *The New Columbia Encyclopedia*, op. cit., p. 2288.

7 T3010, p. 3.

8 *Globe and Mail*, May 18, 1995, p. A11.

9 T3010, p. 3.

10 Bakal, op. cit., p. 407.

11 Martin, op.cit., p. 219.

12 Quoted in Bakal, op. cit., p. 408.

13 Ibid., p. 409.

14 Ibid.

15 Aramony, William, *The United Way: The Next 100 Years*, New York, Donald I. Fine, 1987, p. 48.

16 Glaser, John S., *The United Way Scandal*, New York, John Wiley, 1994.

17 Aramony, op. cit., p. 48.

18 *New York Times*, June 23, 1995, p. A14.

19 Ibid.

20 *Globe and Mail*, April 5, 1995, p. A10.

21 *Washington Post*, February 16, 1992, p. A1.

22 Martin, op. cit., p. 142.

23 Pamphlet, The United Way of Greater Toronto, 1995.

24 Riches, Graham. *Feeding Canada's Poor*, Toronto, University of Toronto Press, 1987, p. 147.

25 Interview, April 28, 1995.

26 *38th Annual Report*, Canada Council, p. 33.

27 Interview, August 20, 1995.

28 Section 87–1 (8) of the Income Tax Act, Charities Division.

29 Drache, op. cit., pp. 1–17.

30 Rosemary Speirs, Ottawa columnist for the *Toronto Star*, asked Revenue Canada about this, and was given, almost word for word, the explanation I got in connection with NAPO: "There's a difference between waving placards in the streets and conducting factual research." *Toronto Star*, January 25, 1996, p. A21.

31 *The Fraser Forum*, July 1995, pp. 11ff.

32 Drache, op. cit., pp. 1–17.

33 *Your General Income Tax Guide and Return*, 1994, p. 32.

34 Ibid., p. 34.

35 *Gifts and Income Tax*, Revenue Canada, 1994.

CHAPTER 6 OUR FAR-FLUNG DOLLARS: FOREIGN-AID CHARITIES

1 *Montreal Gazette*, June 30, 1995, p. B2.

2 *The Times*, August 8, 1994, p. G2.

3 Hancock, Graham, *Lords of Poverty*, London, Macmillan, 1990, p. xiv.

4 *Hansard*, May 4, 1995, p. 12192.

5 Ibid., June 5, 1995, p. 13237.

6 Ibid.

7 Gill, Audrey, "Happiness Is a Comfortable Bed" in *Maturity* Magazine, May/June 1995, pp. 6–8.

8 *Globe and Mail*, October 15, 1994, p. A12.

9 *Canadian Registered Charities Financial Growth Analysis by Year, Sector & Category for Line 910 of T3010 Return*, Revenue Canada, Statistical Services Division, March 8, 1995, p. 69. Line 910 deals with spending outside Canada.

10 *The 1995 Canadian Global Almanac*, op. cit., p. 203.

11 T3010 form, p. 3.

12 *Canadian Registered Charities*, p. 69.

13 *Toronto Star*, February 12, 1996, p. A15.

14 *Montreal Gazette*, June 30, 1995, p. B2.

15 T3010 form, p. 3.

16 Ibid.

17 Interview, August 20, 1995.

18 T3010, p. 3.

19 Ibid., p. 2.

20 *Toronto Star*, November 13, 1995, p. B5.

21 Ibid.

22 T3010 form, pp. 1–2.

23 CBC TV, May 30, 1995.

24 *Montreal Gazette*, June 30, 1995, p. B2.

25 *Vancouver Sun*, July 1, 1995, p. A4.

26 Interview, July 19, 1995.

CHAPTER 7 FOUNDATIONS: CHARITIES WITH A TWIST

1 *Laidlaw Foundation Report, 1991–1993*, p. 3.

2 Ibid., p. 8.

3 Ibid., p. 22.

4 *Improving the Life Prospects of Children and Youth*, Laidlaw Foundation, Toronto, undated, p. 3.

5 *Laidlaw Foundation Report*, op. cit., pp. 16–17.

6 Ibid., p. 32.

7 Condensed Balance Sheet, 1994.

8 *Canadian Directory to Foundations*, Canadian Centre for Philanthropy, Toronto, 1994, p. 206.

9 Ibid., various pages.

10 Martin, op. cit., p. 260.

11 Ibid., p. 261.

12 Ibid.

13 Odendahl, Teresa, *Charity Begins at Home*, New York, Basic Books, 1990, p. 44.

14 *Philanthropic Foundations*, Russell Sage Foundation, 1953, quoted in Whitaker, op.cit., p. 29.

15 Whitaker, op. cit., p. 30.

16 Quoted in Whitaker, op. cit., p. 50.

17 Ibid., p. 52.

18 Abels, Jules, *The Rockefeller Billions*, New York, Macmillan, 1965, p. 277.

19 Josephson, Matthew, *The Robber Barons*, New York, Harcourt Brace, 1934, p. 324.

20 Quoted in Whitaker, op. cit., p. 53.

21 Tarbell, Ida, *History of the Standard Oil Company*, New York, Macmillan, 1925, p. 288.

22 Abels, op. cit., p. 272.

23 Quoted in Josephson, op. cit., p. 325.

24 Abels, op. cit., p. 276. The Federal Commission on Industrial Relations that studied the strike commented that "The funds of these foundations are largely invested in securities of corporations dominant in American industry . . . The policies of these foundations must inevitably be coloured if not controlled to conform to the policies of such corporations."

25 Ibid., p. 330.

26 *Canada's Charitable Foundations*, Toronto, Canadian Centre for Philanthropy, 1994, p. 315.

27 Whitaker, op. cit., p. 54.

28 Linda McQuaig has an intriguing description of this development in *Behind Closed Doors*, Toronto, Viking, 1987, p. 52ff.

29 Whitaker, op. cit., p. 50.

30 Ibid., p. 48.

31 *Transactions of the British Social Science Association*, 1859, p. 69.

32 Whitaker, op. cit., p. 52.

33 Nielsen, op. cit., p. 255ff.

34 Odendahl, op. cit., p. 10.

35 In his collection of essays *The Gospel of Wealth*, Cambridge, Belknap Press, 1962, Carnegie wrote: "This then, is held to be the duty for the man of wealth: to set an example of modest, unostentatious living, shunning display or extravagance, to provide moderately for the legitimate wants of those dependent on him, and after doing so, to consider all surplus revenues which come to him as simply trust funds, which he is called upon to administer."

36 Ibid., p. 136.

37 *Canadian Directory to Foundations*, 1994–95, p. 189.

38 Ibid., p. vi.

39 Ibid.

40 Martin, op. cit., p. 272.

41 Ibid., p. 261.

42 Ibid., p. 274.

43 *Canadian Directory to Foundations*, Table 2, p. vi.

44 Sharpe, op. cit., p. 11.

45 T3010 form, Notes to Financial Statements, p. 1.

46 Ibid.

47 *Canadian Directory to Foundations,* Table 4, p. viii.

48 Martin, op. cit., p. 264.

49 *Guide to Canadian Foundations,* Toronto, Canadian Centre for Philanthropy, 1994.

50 Vale, Norma, "Crown Foundations, Are They Fair?" in *Front & Centre,* July 1994, p. 2.

51 T3010 form, p. 1.

52 *Foundations, Giving and Public Policy: Report and Recommendations of the Commission on Foundations and Private Philanthropy, Chairman Peter G. Petersen,* Chicago, University of Chicago Press, 1970, p. 12.

53 Rushton has a new book out, called *Race, Revolution and Behaviour: A Life History Perspective.* Rosie DiManno, in a review in the *Toronto Star* on March 22, 1995, claimed that all it proved was that "Philippe Rushton has penis on the brain." Perhaps they should give her a grant.

54 Interview, November 5, 1995, with Richard Corden, Charity Commission.

55 *Toronto Star,* March 13, 1995, p. A21.

CHAPTER 8   CAUSE MARKETING: SELLING BEER AND BUYING BLESSINGS

1 *Encyclopedia Canadiana,* Toronto, Grolier, 1975, Volume 10, p. 408.

2 Myers, Gustavus, *A History of Canadian Wealth,* Toronto, James, Lewis and Samuel, 1972 edition, Vol. 1, pp. 195-199.

3 Colombo, op. cit., p. 522A.

4 *Time Out,* November 1995.

5 *Globe and Mail,* January 13, 1982, p. A17.

6 Martin, op. cit., p. 228.

7 Sharpe, op. cit., p. 19.

8 *Corporate Profits,* Statistics Canada, 61-008, 1994, p. 50.

9 Ibid.

10 Martin, op. cit., Table, p. 232.

11 Ibid., p. 234.

12 Ibid., p. 230.

13 *Imagine—Making a Difference,* Toronto, undated booklet, p. 19.

14 Ibid.

15 Ibid., p. 25.

16 *Toronto Star,* October 14, 1995, p. E2.

17 *Toronto Star,* November 10, 1995, p. D1.

18 *Toronto Star*, October 26, 1995, p. B1.

19 *Toronto Star*, April 29, 1995, p. A7.

20 *Financial Post*, December 9, 1994, p. 26.

21 *Toronto Star*, May 1, 1995, p. B1.

22 Dubinsky, op. cit., p.17.

23 *Toronto Star*, January 26, 1995, p. E1.

24 Ibid., p. E2.

25 Odendahl, op. cit., p. 51.

26 *Canadian News Facts*, 1983, p. 1049.

27 Sharpe, op. cit., Tables 9, 10, 11.

28 Odendahl, op. cit., p. 47.

29 Interview, July 19, 1995.

30 *Front & Centre*, July 1994, p. 14.

31 Ibid.

32 *Canadian Directory to Foundations*, op. cit.

33 McClintock, Norah. In *Front & Centre*, July 1994, p. 14.

34 Ibid.

CHAPTER 9   FUND RAISING: THE BEGGING BOWLS

1 *Minneapolis Tribune*, December 12, 1994, p. 1.

2 *Los Angeles Times*, June 5, 1995, p. A4

3 Interview, November 22, 1995.

4 *London Free Press*, February 11, 1995, p. E1.

5 The Attorney General's Department in Massachusetts conducted a detailed investigation of telemarketing schemes for charities, which found that the typical return to the charity was in the range of 20 to 30 per cent.

6 *Toronto Star*, January 6, 1996, p. A2.

7 Ibid.

8 *Financial Post*, December 9, 1994, p. 23.

9 This is the estimate of the Canadian Centre for Philanthropy.

10 Interview, November 22, 1995.

11 *Globe and Mail*, February 25, 1994, p. C10.

12 Sexton, Rosemary, *The Glitter Girls, Charity and Vanity: Chronicles of an Era of Excess*, Toronto, Macmillan, 1993.

13 Ibid., p. 35.

14 Ibid., p. 45.

15 Ibid., p. 61.

16 Ibid., p. 66.

17 Ibid., p. 124.

18 Ibid., p. 212.

19 Bakal, op. cit., p. 351.

20 Carter, Richard, *The Gentle Legions*, New York, Doubleday, 1961, p. 131.

21 *Globe and Mail*, March 27, 1995, p. A20.

22 Interview, November 22, 1995.

23 Starr, Patti, *Tempting Fate: A Cautionary Tale of Power and Politics*, Toronto, Stoddart, 1993.

24 *Orange County Register*, December 20, 1995, p. 13.

25 ABC Television newscast, November 11, 1994.

26 *Front & Centre*, January 1995, p. 1.

27 Ibid.

28 T3010 form.

29 T3010 form.

CHAPTER 10   A TAX ON THE STUPID: GAMBLING AND CHARITY

1 *Front & Centre*, March 1995, p. 7.

2 Ibid.

3 *First News*, newsletter of Charities 1st, Ontario, Volume 1, Issue 1, p. 4.

4 *Ottawa Citizen*, March 23, 1995, p. B3.

5 Ibid.

6 *Toronto Star*, November 23, 1995, p. A4.

7 *Vancouver Sun*, November 16, 1995, p. 1.

8 *Globe and Mail*, October 13, 1995, p. A13.

9 *Toronto Star*, November 16, 1995, p. A36.

10 *Vancouver Sun*, November 17, 1994, p. A2.

11 *Vancouver Sun*, November 18, 1994, p. A18.

12 *Annual Report*, Ontario Lottery Corporation, 1995, p. 3.

13 Goodman, Robert, "The Grand Illusion," in *The Wilson Quarterly*, Autumn 1995.

14 *The New Columbia Encyclopedia*, op. cit., p. 1614.

15 Cohen, John, *Chance, Skill and Luck*, London, Penguin, 1960, p. 62.

16 Fax to author, October 20, 1995.

17 *USA Today*, June 6, 1995, p. 2A.

18 Martin, op. cit., p. 292.

19 Ibid.

20 Colombo, John Robert, *Colombo's Canadian References*, Toronto, Oxford Univer-

sity Press, 1976, p. 384.

21 *Globe and Mail*, January 11, 1995, p. A18.

22 *Annual Report*, Ontario Lottery Corporation, 1995, p. 20.

23 Ibid., p. 16.

24 Martin, op. cit., p. 293.

25 *Toronto Star*, June 11, 1994, p. A2.

26 *Annual Report*, Ontario Lottery Corporation, 1995, p. 4.

27 Ibid., p. 11.

28 Ibid.

29 Ibid., p. 17.

30 *Winners Information News*, Ontario Lottery Corporation, July/August 1995, p. 1.

31 *Toronto Star*, June 11, 1994, p. A2.

32 *Toronto Star*, November 27, 1995, p. A16.

33 *USA Today*, June 6, 1995, p. 2A.

34 *London Independent*, November 4, 1995, p. 2.

35 Fax reply to my questions from Roy Payne, Information Office, Department of National Heritage, October 20, 1995.

36 Figure provided by the National Council of Voluntary Organizations, November 1995.

37 Ibid.

38 Interview, November 5, 1995.

39 *London Independent*, November 3, 1995, p. 23.

40 Ibid.

41 *Toronto Star*, November 5, 1994, p. B8.

42 Cardoza, Avery, *Winner's Playbook*, New York, Gambling Research Institute, 1995, p. 30.

43 Interview, November 17, 1995.

44 *Globe and Mail*, May 15, 1995, p. A4.

45 *Vancouver Sun*, May 25, 1995, p. A2.

46 *Kitchener-Waterloo Record*, May 7, 1996, p. 3.

47 *Globe and Mail*, May 11, 1996, p. D2.

48 *Toronto Star*, May 6, 1996, p. A18.

49 Ibid.

50 *Toronto Star*, January 1, 1996, p. A11.

51 Ibid.

52 *Calgary Herald*, October 3, 1995, p. A4.

53 Ibid.

54 Interview, November 17, 1995.

55 Interview, July 26, 1995.

56 *Toronto Star*, August 11, 1995, p. A2.

57 Interview, July 26, 1995.

58 *Globe and Mail*, April 14, 1995, p. A18.

59 *Winnipeg Free Press*, February 4, 1995, p. A15.

CHAPTER II   THE CASE FOR REGULATION

1 Revenue Canada, September 21, 1995.

2 The AIDS Society for Children (Ontario), *Our Mission*, pamphlet.

3 *Toronto Star*, April 18, 1995, p. A6.

4 Interview, October 5, 1995.

5 Interview, October 5, 1995.

6 Interview, August 17, 1995.

7 Quoted in *Foundations, Giving and Public Policy*, op. cit., p. 11.

8 *Front & Centre*, May 1994, p. 3.

9 Interview, November 6, 1995, with Richard Corden, Charity Commission.

10 *Charities and the Charity Commission*, Charity Commissioners for England and Wales, May 1995, p. 2.

11 Interview, November 5, 1995.

12 *Report of the Charity Commissioners*, 1994, p. 15.

13 *Home Office Annual Report*, 1995, p. 114.

14 Ibid., p. 20.

15 Interview, November 6, 1995.

16 *An Introduction to the Charities Aid Foundation*, undated pamphlet.

17 *Charities Aid Foundation Annual Report*, 1994/95, p. 4.

18 Ibid., Consolidated Balance Sheet, p. 10.

19 *Dimensions of the Voluntary Sector*, Charities Aid Foundation, London, 1995.

20 *Toronto Star*, April 6, 1996, pp. B1 and B3.

21 Ibid., p. B1.

22 *Regulation of Charities in Alberta*, Canadian Centre for Philanthropy, "Summary Report," March 1995.

23 Interview, October 17, 1995.

24 Interview, April 25, 1995.

The Facts:
Tables on Charity Finances

Cautionary Note: These tables have been composed by analysing the tax-return form called T3010, which each charitable organization is required to file annually with Revenue Canada. Some charities take this very seriously, others do not, with the result that there is a good deal of latitude in the figures. I have tried to signal some of the more obvious cases below, but a far better solution would be to have a uniform code of accounting policies enforced on the charities.

—WS

Table 1 CANADA'S TOP 25 CHARITIES, BY REVENUE

Name	Revenue	Received from Government	% from Government
All dollar figures $'000			
1 Canadian Red Cross Society	461,951	310,014	67.1
2 Ontario Cancer Treatment & Research Foundation	158,065	139,482	88.2
3 International Development Research Centre	152,759	142,000	92.9
4 Canada Council	118,491	99,335	83.8
5 Legal Services Society of B.C.	101,055	95,732	94.7
6 Grey Sisters of the Immaculate Conception	98,622	2,438	2.5
7 World Vision Canada	95,672	14,867	15.5
8 TVO (Ontario Educational Television)	83,949	70,178	83.6
9 CARE Canada	75,330	18,525	24.6
10 Children's Aid Society of Metropolitan Toronto	71,088	68,303	96.0
11 Ontario Arts Council	49,262	43,084	87.4
12 Metro Toronto YMCA	64,634	29,208	45.1
13 United Way of Greater Toronto	47,254	56.9	1.2
14 Catholic Children's Aid Society of Toronto	45,899	44,037	95.9
15 Alcoholism and Drug Addiction Research Foundation	44,103	40,480	91.8

Table 1 (continued)

Spending	Spent on Fund Raising	Management, Administration	Spent on Charitable Projects	% of Revenue Spent on Charity
		All dollar figures $'000		
455,183	8,688	6,930	191,384	41.4
154,372	NIL	3,534	150,837	95.4
127,890	NIL	12,966	114,924	75.2
112,505	N.A.	22,708	not shown	not shown[1]
101,894	NIL	7,236	93,657	92.6
93,652	4.3	NIL	93,547	94.8
94,769	11,173	7,480	94,283	98.5[2]
83,683	1,929	8,211	65,680	78.2
		no figures shown by charity		
70,815	NIL	6,250	64,565	90.8
44,177	N.A.	7,189	1,625	3.3[3]
59,320	441	NIL	58,517	90.5
43,772	4,245	1,540	37,987	80.3
45,768	NIL	6,387	39,380	85.8
44,800	NIL	4,837	39,962	90.6

Table 1 *(continued)*

Name	Revenue	Received from Government	% from Government
	All dollar figures $'000		
16 United Israel Appeal of Canada, Inc.	42,476	NIL	0
17 Metro Toronto Association for Community Living	40,777	30,787	75.5
18 Triumf	39,020	34,176	87.6
19 Christian Children's Fund	38,021	3,261	8.6
20 Foster Parents Plan of Canada	37,628	3,591	9.5
21 National Arts Centre	37,319	22,015	59.0
22 Victorian Order of Nurses, Hamilton–Wentworth	37,075	36,009	97.2
23 Children's Aid Society, Ottawa	37,050	36,009	97.2
24 Canadian Cancer Society, National Office	36,794	NIL	0
25 United Jewish Appeal of Metro Toronto	36,701	NIL	0

[1] The Canada Council spent nearly $90 million on "gifts to qualified donees"—i.e., artists and writers—which it should have shown as "spent on charitable projects." Thus, the "% of revenue spent on charity" is actually 75.8.

[2] World Vision shows management and fundraising activities as charitable spending, on the argument that "Expenditures to raise funds and to administer charitable activities are an integral and necessary part of carrying on such activities." In fact, World Vision spent $11,173,708 on fund raising in its most recent year and $7,480,931 on administration. Charitable spending should be shown as $75,630,000 and the percentage as 79.0.

				% of
	Spent on		Spent on	Revenue
	Fund	Management,	Charitable	Spent on
Spending	Raising	Administration	Projects	Charity

All dollar figures $'000

Spending	Spent on Fund Raising	Management, Administration	Spent on Charitable Projects	% of Revenue Spent on Charity
17,155	1,160	1,857	11,398	26.8
40,510	40.8	3,642	38,826	90.3
41,070	*not shown; salaries paid = $26,490*			
38,359	2,244	1,738	34,106	89.7
37,513	2,794	3,476	31,242	83.0
36,382	NIL	3,723	25,885	69.4
44,959	.45	7,976	36,482	98.4
37,273	*not shown; salaries of $9,551 shown*		37,273	100.6[4]
37,224	1,069	432	2,421	6.6[5]
37,915	2,244	1,100	34,570	94.2

[3] For reasons known only to itself, the Ontario Arts Council doesn't count the money it spends to support artists as charitable spending, but instead calls it "gifts for qualified donees," which is the category for donations to other charities. If these are calculated as charitable expenditures, the dismal figure of 3.3 per cent of receipts spent on the actual objects for which the body was founded becomes 75.1 per cent.

[4] Children's Aid of Ottawa managed to spend more than 100 per cent on charitable activities by (1) going into the red and (2) counting all wages, administration, and fund raising as charitable.

[5] The Canadian Cancer Society's National Office gave $32,920,099 to associated charities, so this figure is actually 96%.

Table 2 TWELVE HEALTH CHARITIES

Name	Revenue	Received from Government	% from Government
	All dollar figures $'000		
Alzheimer Society	3,493	113	3.2
Arthritis Society	9,606	249	2.6
Canadian Cancer Society, National Office	36,794	NIL	NIL
Canadian Diabetes Assn.	26,959	1,577	5.8
Canadian Hearing Society	15,413	6,324	41.0
Canadian Liver Foundation	7,226	NIL	NIL
CNIB	6,498	1,992	30.6
Heart & Stroke Foundation	10,545	45	0.4
Kidney Foundation	13,545	45	0.3
Muscular Dystrophy Assoc.	10,140	83	0.8
Multiple Sclerosis Society	9,870	44	0.45
Ontario Society for Crippled Children	28,841	23,577	81.7
War Amputations of Canada	28,540	30	1.0

Table 2 (continued)

Spending	Spent on Fund Raising	Management, Administration	Spent on Charitable Projects	% of Revenue Spent on Charity
3,493	633	325	2,689	76.9
8,048	NIL*	372	7,675	79.9
37,224	1,069	432	2,421**	6.6**
25,188	5,396	4,811	12,073	44.8
15,434	327	1,488	13,619	88.3
8,558	2,302	1,496	4,755	65.8
6,644	328	657	4,401	66.2
10,594	618	1,022	6,708	63.6
13,524	3,876	1,718	6,639	49.0
9,581	4,201	371	2,858	28.9
10,579	3,294	851	6,387	60.3
29,155	not shown	not shown	29,155	101.0 †
25,967	NIL‡	223	25,745	90.1

* The Arthritis Society shows no fundraising costs, but somebody certainly spends money on fund raising for them.

** The Canadian Cancer Society's National Office gave $32,920,099 to associated charities, so this figure should actually read 96%.

† Another medical miracle.

‡ The War Amputations of Canada sends us all those licence tags, but the cost of its campaigns is not recorded.

Note that most of these medical charities spend a very large proportion of their revenue on raising revenue. One exception, the Canadian Hearing Society, gets almost half its funding from the government; the other is the War Amps, a vigorous fund-raiser with a volunteer army.

Table 3 FIFTEEN CULTURAL CHARITIES

Name	Revenue	Received from Government	% from Government
All dollar figures $'000			
Canada Council	118,491	99,335	83.8
Canadian Museum of Civilization	23,425	21,453	91.6
Canadian Opera Co.	15,265	4,965	32.5
Metro Toronto Zoo	18,975	9,466	50.4
Montreal Symphony	13,438	4,978	37.0
Musée des Beaux-Arts	29,782	22,783	76.5
National Arts Centre	37,319	22,015	59.0
National Ballet	17,566	5,863	33.4
Ontario Arts Council	49,262	43,084	87.4
Royal Ontario Museum	32,967	21,647	65.7
Royal Winnipeg Ballet	8,703	2,627	30.2
Shaw Festival	12,535	1,317	10.5
Stratford Festival	21,716	2,563	11.8
Toronto Symphony	14,781	4,067	27.5
TVO	83,949	70,178	83.6

Table 3 (continued)

Spending	Spent in Canada	Spent Outside Canada	Spent on Charitable Projects	% of Revenue Spent on Charity
112,505	not shown	not shown	not shown	not shown[*]
22,906	8,526	not shown	8,526	36.4
14,341	not shown	not shown	12,377	81.8
18,975	not shown	not shown	not shown	?
13,863	9,728	2,040	11,769	87.5
25,838	21,550	not shown	21,390	71.8
36,862	not shown	not shown	25,885	69.4
16,503	15,109	1,393	14,991	85.3
44,177	1,625	not shown	1,625	3.3[**]
41,536	not shown	not shown	26,786	81.2 [†]
8,531	not shown	not shown	7,157	82.2
12,428	not shown	not shown	10,043	80.1
23,359	not shown	not shown	21,882	100.8 [‡]
15,612	not shown	not shown	not shown	?
83,683	64,403	1,267	65,680	78.2

[*] See note 1 on page 234.

[**] See note 3 on page 235.

[†] The Royal Ontario Museum spent more than it took in, and that helped it look better here; general administration and management costs were $10,187,864, not so good.

[‡] The Stratford Shakespearean Festival shows $878,162 paid in fundraising costs, including $232,611 to fundraising agents. It manages to show this remarkable efficiency by (1) spending more than it took in and (2) showing "renumeration paid to employees" as "charitable programs." Fair enough, I think; most of this was paid to actors and actresses.

Table 4 **TWELVE CHARITIES WITH MAJOR SPENDING ABROAD**

Name	Revenue	Received from Government	% from Government
All dollar figures $'000			
Amnesty International	3,334	NIL	NIL
Canadian Foodgrains Bank	23,422	17,871	76.3
CARE Canada	75,330	18,525	24.6
Christian Children's Fund	38,012	3,261	8.6
CUSO	23,918	19,624	82.0
Foster Parents Plan of Canada	37,628	3,591	9.5
Oxfam Canada	11,157	4,855	43.5
Save the Children Canada	7,846	2,787	37.2
UNICEF Canada	21,577	4,763	22.0
Watch Tower Society	22,199	NIL	NIL
Worldwide Church of God	15,743	NIL	NIL
World University Service of Canada	21,234	12,732	59.9

Table 4 (continued)				

Spending	Spent in Canada	Spent Outside Canada	Spent on Charitable Projects	% of Revenue Spent on Charity
4,058	1,812	1,059	2,872	86.1
23,249	NIL	22,316	22,316	95.3
not shown	not shown	not shown	not shown	?
38,359	1,446	32,660	34,106	89.7
24,637	5,558	14,822	20,380	84.9
37,513	NIL	31,242	31,242	83.0
10,818	1,248	7,487	8,774	78.6
7,011	310	4,617	4,927	65.8
23,076	317	17,370	17,687	81.9
16,388	10,384	3,651	14,174	63.8
15,054	11,782	1,457	13,239	59.6
20,959	13,317	6,097	19,414	91.4

Table 5 SOME OTHERS WORTH LOOKING AT

Name	Revenue	Received from Government	% from Government
All dollar figures $'000			
Aga Khan Foundation	18,457	7,084	38.8
Babbar Khalsa Society	2.6	NIL	NIL
Canadian Centre for Philanthropy	2,248	64.9	2.9
C. D. Howe Institute	1,811	NIL	NIL
Ducks Unlimited	11,400	1,069	9.4
Fraser Institute	18,329	NIL	NIL
Kids Help Foundation	3,333	NIL	NIL
Missing Children Society	1,126	NIL	NIL
National Anti-Poverty Organization	596	298	50.0
Pacific National Exhibition	32,553	71.8	0.2

				% of
		Spent	Spent on	Revenue
	Spent in	Outside	Charitable	Spent on
Spending	Canada	Canada	Projects	Charity
15,495	4,105	8,321	12,427	67.3
1.1	N.A.	N.A.	0.9	39.6
1,890	1,840	NIL	1,840	81.8
1,583	not shown	not shown	1,369	75.6
10,584	not shown	not shown	not shown	?
16,862	13,430	NIL	13,430	73.7
3,981	1,405	NIL	1,405	42.1
1,157	not shown	not shown	463	41.1
568	213	NIL	213	37.5
31,922	73	NIL	73	0.2*

* The Pacific National Exhibition, like a number of other organizations, seems confused about what is a "charitable" expense, which explains this dismal figure. It has listed as "management and general administration" costs an amount of $31,837,955—almost its entire spending. It counts as "charitable" only the cost of supporting 4-H activities, though why cows shown by kids are more charitable than those shown by adults is not clear. If, in fact, putting on an exhibition is a charity, the PNE ought to be able to charge everything except "remuneration paid to employees carrying out any other activities," an amount of $17,003,406 for staff wages. This would make charitable spending $14,834,549 and the percentage of total income spent on charitable programs 45.5.

The T3010
Revenue Canada Form

This particular T3010 Revenue Canada form was filled out by World Vision Canada for the year ending September 30, 1994. As a charitable organization, World Vision Canada is required to devote all of its resources to its own charitable activities in order to maintain its status as a registered charity under the Income Tax Act. Expenditures to raise funds and to administer charitable activities are an integral and necessary part of carrying on such activities. If such expenditures were not regarded as a devotion of a charity's resources to charitable activities, no charity could qualify as a charitable organization. Accordingly, expenditures to raise funds and to administer the charitable activities of a charity are amounts expended on charitable activities for the purposes of paragraph 149.1(2)(B) of the Income Tax Act. Thus, the amount shown in Line 114 ("Total amount spent on charitable programs carried on by your charity") includes such amounts.

Revenue Canada Taxation

2135123

Registered Charity Inform
Public Information Return

Please complete and mail this copy together with confidential schedules and financial statements

T3010 Rev. 90

Mailing Copy

A IDENTIFICATION

Registration Number

0202796-47   C   YEAR END: 30/09/94

26156

WORLD VISION CANADA-VISION MONDIALE
CANADA
C/O CONTROLLER
6630 TURNER VALLEY RD
MISSISSAUGA
L5N 2S4   ON

If the
the necessary corrections below. If organization's name is incorrect, print

Return for Fiscal Period Ended	3 0 | 0 9 | 9 4
	Day Month Year

Is this the first return your charity has filed? ☐ Yes ☒ No

If "NO", has the fiscal period changed from that shown on the last return? ☐ Yes ☒ No

Does your charity meet ALL the exemption criteria set out in the Guide? ☐ Yes ☒ No

Is this the final return to be filed by this charity? If so, please attach an explanation ☐ Yes ☒ No

DESIGNATION OF CHARITY:
Is your charity
a Public Foundation   A ☐
a Private Foundation   B ☐
or a Charitable Organization? C ☒

C/O Name or Position	
Postal Address	
City	
Province	Postal Code

B CALCULATION OF RECEIPTS AND DISBURSEMENTS FOR THE FISCAL PERIOD

Receipts from Gifts

Total gifts received for which your charity has issued "official receipts" for income tax purposes .... **100** 76,908,851 |00

Please give details about the amounts on line 100 as follows:
- Gifts from foreign sources .... **900** 256837 |00
- Gifts of capital received by way of bequest or inheritance .... **901** 1582326 |00
- Gifts received subject to a trust or direction by the donor that they be held not less than 10 years ..... **902** |
- Total gifts received from other registered charities .... **101** 590304 |00
- Gifts from line 101 which have been designated as "specified gifts" .... **903** |

Total gifts received for which "official receipts" have not been and will not be issued (gifts from other charities on line 101 and grants on line 103 are not to be included) .... **102** 3,120,245 |00

- Gifts from line 102 which are from foreign sources .... **904** 8615 |00

Receipts from Other Sources

Federal, provincial or municipal grants and payments received .... **103** 14,867,766 |00
Investment and property income .... **104** 8,762 |00
Net realized capital gains (losses) **105**
Income (loss) from any "related business" ...... Gross **905** | Net **106** |
Memberships, subscriptions, fees received .... **107** |
Other Income (please specify) .... **108** 176,802 |00

Total Receipts (add lines 100 to 108 inclusive) .... **109** 95,672,730 |00 ▷95,672,730 |00

Please do not use this area	701	702	703	704

AGE 2

Disbursements

Total fund-raising costs .... 11,173,708 → **110** _____ | See Appendix E

• Total fees from line 110 paid to fund-raising agents .... **906** _____ ← 109,021

Management and general administration costs _____ 7,480,931 → **111** _____

Total amount spent on political activities .... **112** _____

Total amount of gifts to "qualified donees" (complete "Summary of Gifts to
Qualified Donees" on page 4) **113** 377,000 00

Please give details about the amount on line 113 as follows:

• Gifts designated as "specified gifts" .... **907** _____ 0 00

• Gifts to "associated charities" **908** 278,500.00

Total amount spent on charitable programs carried on by your charity **114** 94,283,676 00

Note: Do not include amounts representing disbursements made during the
fiscal period for the purpose of property accumulated — see relevant
schedule and line 115 below

Please give details about the amount on line 114 as follows:

• In Canada **909** 25,177,944 00

• Outside Canada **910** 69,105,732 00

Amount accumulated with the permission of the Minister of National Revenue
during the fiscal period .... **115** _____

Other disbursements (please specify) .... **116** _____

Total Disbursements (add lines 110 to 116 inclusive) .... **117** 94,769,697 00 ▷ 94,769,697 00

C STATEMENT OF ASSETS AND LIABILITIES

Assets

Cash on hand and in bank **118** 8,051,233 00

Amounts receivable from founders, officers, directors, members, or
organizations related to them .... **119** _____

Amounts receivable from others (not included on line 119) **120** 278,925 00

Investments other than rental property **121** 1,161,879 00

Rental Property .... **122** _____

Other fixed assets (e.g. land and buildings, etc.) **123** 6,009,083 00

Inventory .... **124** _____

Other assets (please specify) **125** 202,870 00

Total Assets (add lines 118 to 125 inclusive) .... **126** 15,703,990 00 ▷ 15,703,990 00

Liabilities

Contributions, gifts and grants payable **127** 840,675 00

Amounts payable to founders, officers, directors, members, or organizations
related to such persons .... **128** _____

Amounts payable to others (not included on lines 127, 128 and 130) **129** 4,498,663 00

Mortgages, notes payable .... **130** _____

Total Liabilities (add lines 127 to 130 inclusive) .... **131** 5,339,338 00 ▷ 5,339,338 00

D REMUNERATION

Total remuneration paid to employees carrying out charitable activities **132** 8,388,751 00

Total remuneration paid to employees carrying out any other activities .... **133** _____

Total remuneration paid to all employees (add lines 132 and 133) .... **134** 8,388,751 00 ▷ 8,388,751 00

Total remuneration (including benefits of any kind) paid to employees who were
executive officers, directors or trustees of the charity .... **135** _____

Number of individuals whose remuneration appears on line 135 .... **136** _____

E VOLUNTARY INFORMATION (Your co-operation in completing lines 137 to 143 would be appreciated)

Voluntary Work

Approximate total number of hours contributed
by all volunteers on all activities .... **137** _____

Percentage of volunteer hours devoted to:

Fundraising activities .... **138** _____ %

Charitable activities .... **139** _____ %

"Related business" activities .... **140** _____ %

Donations

Approximate percentage of donations received from:

Individuals .... **141** _____ %

Corporations .... **142** _____ %

Other Sources .... **143** _____ %

APPENDIX II

Staple all required schedules, statements and any other necessary documentation to the top of this page   **PAGE 3**

F   INFORMATION DESCRIBING CHARITY'S PURPOSE(S) AND ACTIVITIES

To be completed by all registered charities.   Note: If you do not have enough space, please attach a separate sheet and
                                                            label it "Attachment to form T3010"

— Purpose(s) —

Give a brief statement of the primary purpose(s) of your charity.

REFER TO APPENDIX A

— Activities in Canada —

Briefly describe the charitable programs which your charity carried on in Canada during the fiscal period. Please specify the location for
each activity.

REFER TO APPENDIX A

— Activities Outside Canada —

Briefly describe the charitable programs which your charity carried on outside Canada during the fiscal period. Please specify the location
for each activity.

REFER TO APPENDIX A

Were the activities outside Canada carried on
(a) by the employees of your charity itself?   ☐ Yes ☒ No
    If "Yes", print the total amount of salaries (including benefits of any kind) paid to them.   1. _____
    Print any other amounts provided to them for the purpose of carrying out these activities
    (e.g. for equipment, supplies, etc.)   2. _____
(b) through an appointed agent(s) or authorized representative(s) of your charity?   ☐ Yes ☒ No
    If "Yes", print the total amount of the fees paid for their services including, in the case
    of an individual, amounts provided for personal living expenses.   3. _____
    any other amounts provided to them for the purpose of carrying out these activities   4. _____
(c) in joint venture with a foreign charity or charities?   ☒ Yes ☐ No
    If "Yes", print the total amount your charity spent on projects of this nature.   5. 69,105,732 |00
(d) by other means (please specify)   6. _____
Total amount spent on charitable programs outside Canada (add lines 1 to 6 inclusive)
Note: This amount should be equal to the amount printed on line 910 on page 2.   7. 69,105,732 |00

Briefly describe the extent to which your charity directs, supervises and controls the application of its funds
by agents, representatives or foreign charities acting in joint ventures.

Refer to Financial Statement Notes

248

The T3010 Revenue Canada Form

G SUMMARY OF GIFTS TO "QUALIFIED DONEES"

To be completed by all registered charities that have reported gifts to "qualified donees" on line 113

Note: If you do not have enough space to list all the donees, please attach a separate sheet, using the headings below, and label it "Attachment to form T3010"

Name of Donee	Registration Number of Donee if a Charity	Location	Amount (Omit Cents)	Specified Gift (√)	Associated Charity (√)
SEE ATTACHMENT					

H IDENTIFICATION OF EXECUTIVE OFFICERS

To be completed by all registered charities

Please list below the name, address, telephone number and occupation of each current directing officer of the charity including, in the case of a parish or congregation, the name of the priest, minister or religious leader in charge.

Note: If you do not have enough space to list all the officers, please attach a separate sheet, using the headings below and label it "Attachment to form T3010".

Name	Position with Charity	Address	Telephone Number	Occupation
REFER TO APPENDIX B				

RETURN COMPLETION

Please provide the name, address, telephone number and occupation of the individual who completed this return.

Name: Mr. Gary Leonard   Occupation: Controller

Address: 6630 Turner Valley Road

Mississauga, Ont.   L5N 2S4

Telephone Number: (905) 831-3033

CERTIFICATION

To be signed only by a current executive officer of the charity.

I GARY LEONARD of MISSISSAUGA, ONTARIO

Name of officer whose signature appears below (please print)   Address

HEREBY CERTIFY that the information given in this return and in all schedules and statements attached is true, correct and complete in every respect.

Signature of Authorized Officer	Position or Office within the organizational structure of the charity
	CONTROLLER

Charity's Telephone Number
1 — 9 0 5 — 8 2 1 — 3 0 3 3

Date
Day 2 1   Month 0 3   Year 9 5

Form authorized and prescribed by order of the Minister of National Revenue.

Index